# VOLUME EDITORS

**KRISTIE MILLER** is a research fellow in philosophy at the University of Sydney, Australia. She is the author of *Issues in Theoretical Diversity: Persistence, Composition and Time* (2006) as well as numerous journal articles on related topics.

**MARLENE CLARK** is an Associate Professor of English at the City College Center for Worker Education, City University of New York. Her composition textbook, *Juxtapositions: Ideas for College Writers* (2005), is in its third edition.

# SERIES EDITOR

**FRITZ ALLHOFF** is an Assistant Professor in the Philosophy Department at Western Michigan University, as well as a Senior Research Fellow at the Australian National University's Centre for Applied Philosophy and Public Ethics. In addition to editing the *Philosophy for Everyone* series, Allhoff is the volume editor or co-editor for several titles, including *Wine & Philosophy* (Wiley-Blackwell, 2007), *Whiskey & Philosophy* (with Marcus P. Adams, Wiley, 2009), and *Food & Philosophy* (with Dave Monroe, Wiley-Blackwell, 2007).

# PHILOSOPHY FOR EVERYONE

Series editor: Fritz Allhoff

Not so much a subject matter, philosophy is a way of thinking. Thinking not just about the Big Questions, but about little ones too. This series invites everyone to ponder things they care about, big or small, significant, serious … or just curious.

Edited by Kristie Miller and Marlene Clark

# DATING
## PHILOSOPHY FOR EVERYONE
### Flirting with Big Ideas

Foreword by Joshua Wolf Shenk

**WILEY-BLACKWELL**

A John Wiley & Sons, Ltd., Publication

This edition first published 2010
© 2010 Blackwell Publishing Ltd except for editorial material and organization
© 2010 Kristie Miller and Marlene Clark

Blackwell Publishing was acquired by John Wiley & Sons in February 2007. Blackwell's publishing program has been merged with Wiley's global Scientific, Technical, and Medical business to form Wiley-Blackwell.

*Registered Office*
John Wiley & Sons Ltd, The Atrium, Southern Gate, Chichester, West Sussex, PO19 8SQ, United Kingdom

*Editorial Offices*
350 Main Street, Malden, MA 02148-5020, USA
9600 Garsington Road, Oxford, OX4 2DQ, UK
The Atrium, Southern Gate, Chichester, West Sussex, PO19 8SQ, UK

For details of our global editorial offices, for customer services, and for information about how to apply for permission to reuse the copyright material in this book please see our website at www.wiley.com/wiley-blackwell.

The right of Kristie Miller and Marlene Clark to be identified as the authors of the editorial material in this work has been asserted in accordance with the UK Copyright, Designs and Patents Act 1988.

Wiley also publishes its books in a variety of electronic formats. Some content that appears in print may not be available in electronic books.

Designations used by companies to distinguish their products are often claimed as trademarks. All brand names and product names used in this book are trade names, service marks, trademarks or registered trademarks of their respective owners. The publisher is not associated with any product or vendor mentioned in this book. This publication is designed to provide accurate and authoritative information in regard to the subject matter covered. It is sold on the understanding that the publisher is not engaged in rendering professional services. If professional advice or other expert assistance is required, the services of a competent professional should be sought.

*Library of Congress Cataloging-in-Publication Data*

Dating – philosophy for everyone: flirting with big ideas / edited by Kristie Miller and Marlene Clark.
    p.   cm. — (Philosophy for everyone)
  title: Dating – philosophy for everyone
  Includes bibliographical references.
  ISBN 978-1-4443-3022-9 (pbk.: alk. paper)  1. Dating (Social customs)
2. Mate selection.  I. Miller, Kristie Lyn.  II. Clark, Marlene.  III. Title: Dating – Philosophy for Everyone.
  HQ801.D336 2010
  646.7'709051—dc22

                                                                    2010004708

A catalogue record for this book is available from the British Library.

Set in 10/12.5pt Plantin by SPi Publisher Services, Pondicherry, India
Printed in Singapore

1   2010

# CONTENTS

Notes on Contributors     233

# FOREWORD

Some years ago, I got my stomach in a twist about an Israeli-born actress (I'll call her Rachael). We were set up on a blind date in New York, and, when I saw her, I couldn't believe my luck. She had dark, curly hair, long legs, and a summer shirt that gave her hips plenty of room to breathe. Her smile warmed me like a heat lamp. I came upon her sitting on the stoop of the restaurant where we'd planned to meet. As she uncurled herself to greet me, I wondered if she would stretch beyond three dimensions. I barely had voice enough to suggest we go inside, and I hoped my legs wouldn't buckle on the way.

The restaurant was an intimate, narrow room. With the delicate smells and the soft light, the edges of the outside world dissolved. I felt myself fumbling at first in conversation, but she seemed to find my awkwardness charming. She laughed at my jokes, and her eyes went wide at my ruminations on how to find meaning in a life full of so much suffering.

I loved what she had to say, too. As we found our rhythm, I felt comfortable, assured even. The more I settled back into my chair, the more she leaned over the table towards me. But then, the more I felt her presence, the more I longed for her – and the more I found myself teetering on the edge. When she asked for a bite of my food, her lips closed around my fork, and she let her teeth slide faintly along its metal edge. It was one of the most erotic moments of my life – and one of the most precarious.

On one level, dating consists of a series of practical problems: How can we meet good people? How can we keep them interested? But as the ritual that underlies our desire to connect with other people, dating also opens a window into the most basic existential dilemma of social creatures. The desire to connect is the desire to jointly create a mutual reality that transcends our separate selves – and even, in ecstatic moments, obliterate them. But our only prayer at making these connections comes in holding onto our discrete identities.

My only chance of realizing my desire for Rachael depended on deftly containing it.

And that only got harder. After dinner, she came back to my place and immediately made herself at home. She put an album on my stereo – Morcheeba's "Big Calm," which would make a rock melt. At some point in the night – I think it was right before she put a spoonful of ice cream on her breast for me to lick off – she told me she wouldn't be my girl-friend. After we settled into bed for the night, she told me she wouldn't have sex with me. In the morning, we went to the Russian baths, a cav-ernous, primordial cellar of steam heat in New York's East Village. In the wet air, her eyes looked as deep as some fairy-tale well.

I waited as long as I could before I called her again.

In between, I talked about her incessantly. I didn't just want to figure out the perfect next moves. I wanted to know: What did it all *mean*?

If you're holding this book in your hand, you want to figure out what it all means, too. This volume will bring new light to some of your most familiar conversations – and also provoke new and surprising ones. How do we approach intimacy in a virtual space? What do brain science and psychology teach us about the real mental dynamics behind the "mad-ness" of love? How do the ancient teachings connect to modern bar scenes?

On one level, it may seem odd to bring the weight of philosophical inquiry to the casual topic of dating. Actually, there's no place where philosophy matters more. Camus said the most important philosophical question was suicide. Perhaps, but once you've decided to live, the ques-tion quickly becomes how to best relate to other people.

Oddly, these questions have long been neglected. For most of the last hundred years, we've considered "self" as the basic unit. René Descartes set the stage in 1641 when he declared that each self "inhabits its own subjective realm" with a mental life that "has an integrity prior to and independent of its interaction with other people." Though Descartes had his challengers this became a core assumption of the Enlightenment, as did Thomas Hobbes' notion that the natural state of man was "solitary" (as well as "poor, nasty, brutish, and short"). Following this line, the indi-vidual emerged as the fundamental focus for students of psychology, polit-ical theory, even linguistics. We talk of self-expression, self-realization.

But can we consider the self in isolation?

Increasingly, science is answering this question with a resounding No. The new field of social neuroscience shows how social connection bolsters psychological and physiological health, and how loneliness makes us wither – leading to everything from depression to obesity and heart disease.

Groundbreaking research into the way we form relationships as small children also shows how our reactions to other people operate beneath a level of ordinary detection. To see how infants respond to their mothers, it turns out, we need to film them and play it back frame by frame. We don't take in a social stimulus and then form a response. The two twist and leap together like figure skaters intimately entwined in their routine. From these roots of connections in our infancy comes our greatest adult desire. As much as we want contentment, "happiness," and so on, what really drives us is the pursuit of "ecstasy." The word comes from the Greek *ekstasis*, which means "standing outside oneself."

At first, when Rachael told me she wouldn't be my girlfriend, I thought she was bluffing. Maybe she was. Maybe she meant that she could only give herself to someone who didn't need her. Maybe she needed someone strong enough for her to bounce up against. Or maybe she just wanted, on some deep level, to replicate her relationship with her father, an explosive man who doted on her but never let her forget her faults.

It's not that she didn't like me. She did. Actually, in many ways, she saw the best in me, my smarts, my intuition, my impatience with bullshit. I took her seriously, and, like many beautiful people, she seemed always to fear she couldn't be seen as more than an object. But she decided that staying in this serious position meant withholding her affection. And that made me insane. On the first date, the potential to merge seemed limitless, and, fueled by that fantasy, I could stay rocked back on my heels. But the more it became clear that she wouldn't give herself to me, the more I rolled onto the balls of my feet, forever losing my balance.

One night, I got a message from her, and as I planned to call her back, I asked a friend if he would give me some kind of mantra to keep my head clear.

He told me to think: "I was complete before I met you. I'll be complete long after you're gone." I thought this was brilliant. It was precisely the frame I needed to stay strong. But, of course, it wasn't true. If I really felt complete without her, I wouldn't have wanted to talk to her. This is a paradox I've never been able to work out, nor do I expect I will.

Let's turn it over to the philosophers.

JOSHUA WOLF SHENK

# ACKNOWLEDGMENTS

The editors of this volume have never met or, for that matter, even spoken to one another on the telephone. To complicate matters even more, the entire time this book was in progress, one was (for the most part) in Sydney, Australia, while the other was (again, for the most part) in Brooklyn, New York. And so we must first thank each other for the great patience and flexibility extended to one another as we "worked together" on this book so distant from one another in space and time. The situation made for many late nights and early mornings, and a few groggy laughs, but we trust the quality of the book remained unharmed.

For that quality, we owe a great deal to our contributors, also far flung across the United States, Australia, and indeed the world. We communicated with all of them exclusively through email, and we greatly appreciate their prompt responses to our seemingly endless editorial nitpicking. The contributors represent a range of disciplines, though each shares a philosophical bent with the "true" philosophers of the group. Their essays, while often very different in subject matter and approach, share a seriously light-hearted attitude toward a topic over which people agonize and about which, in response to a need to quell the agony, numerous "experts" offer advice. That daters of all stripes can learn something from the often humorously profound insights of our contributors is without doubt true in this case.

We would also like to thank our publisher, Wiley-Blackwell, and especially our editorial contact there, Tiffany Mok. Most importantly, perhaps, we thank the *Philosophy for Everyone* series editor, Fritz Allhoff. How he keeps up with the email from all his editors is beyond us. Even more amazing, he answers almost immediately, even at ungodly hours and on holidays. His unstinting attention to detail has made us better editors and we thank him for his patience and generosity.

Last but not least, we thank our readers. We hope you enjoy reading this book as much as we enjoyed pulling it together. If you date, we hope there's some wisdom here to help you date with greater awareness. If you don't date, maybe this book will change your mind – but if it doesn't, we do have one contributor who clams he got married without ever going on a single date!

Kristie Miller, Sydney
Marlene Clark, Brooklyn, New York

# FLIRTING WITH BIG IDEAS

## An Introduction to *Dating – Philosophy for Everyone*

*The friendship between man and woman seems to be inherent in us by nature. For man is by nature more inclined to live in couples than to live as a social and political being, inasmuch as the household is earlier and more indispensable than the state, and to the extent that procreation is a bond more universal to all living things. In the case of other animals, the association goes no further than this. But human beings live together not merely for procreation, but also to secure the needs of life. There is division of labor from the very beginning and different functions for man and woman. Thus they satisfy one another's needs by contributing each his own to the common store. For that reason, this kind of friendship brings both usefulness and pleasantness with it, and if the partners are good, it may even be based on virtue and excellence. For each partner has his own peculiar excellence and they can find joy in that fact.*

Aristotle, *Nichomachean Ethics*, 1162a17–27

While dating in its current cultural guise is very different from anything Aristotle ever encountered, our chosen epigraph shows that philosophers have pondered the nature of the human drive to seek out intimate romantic relationships for as long as they have thought about anything. As Aristotle notes, the human drive to live in couples is stronger than even the very strong need to live as a social and political being. And not just for procreation. Aristotle, like most of today's theorists, believed that human fulfillment rests largely in the ability to form close and loving relationships with others. This book is a collection of essays that looks afresh at the complicated issues surrounding creating, fostering, engaging in, and evaluating our romantic relationships. Authors come from divergent backgrounds, including those of philosophy, psychology, political science, theology, cognitive science, mathematics, and computer science, to ask and answer both age-old questions and pressing new ones about the world of romance and dating.

If we think of dating as a sort of "game" we all play, a game with social rules that is, at least sometimes, pleasant in itself, but which is also designed to foster certain sorts of outcomes, we can ask ourselves important questions about the nature of that game. What are the rules of the game? Can the rules be broken and, if so, when and why? What is the aim of the game and how do we judge whether a particular round of the dating game is going to lead to the winning the game, i.e., the outcome we want? How does technology bear on the way the game is played? Does it change the game itself, the rules of the game, or just the particular way the game is manifested? When we think of the project of forming intimate romantic relationships in this abstract way we attain enough distance from our subject matter to think seriously about the various ethical, practical, and psychological issues we all face in the exciting but scary process of discovering and forging connections with others. This book explores the delicate balance of dealing well with others while making careful and often strategic evaluation of other persons and our relationships with those persons.

The book has three key aims. The first is to bring a modern perspective to age-old questions about the ethics involved in romantic relationships. The pace of social change is frightening, and though the question of how to deal well, and ethically, with our fellow human beings is not a new one, the circumstances in which we each find ourselves change radically as society changes. Behaviors and practices that were once taboo are now acceptable. So it is important to bring the careful analytic skills of philosophers and their brethren to questions about how, in our current culture, we should approach romantic relationships. To that end, this book considers how we ought to think about and treat prospective romantic partners.

The second aim of the book is to use new research in philosophy and the empirical and social sciences to help us better understand what is going on in the process of mate selection. In the last fifty years or so research in evolutionary psychology and biology, for instance, has flourished, and with it, the field of philosophy of biology has bourgeoned. Like all living things, human beings have evolved through natural selection. How it is that organisms select mates is a crucial research interest of evolutionary biologists. Yet, until recently, little of this research has informed our understanding of our own psychologies. The book aims to remedy this by introducing a number of essays that explore the ways in which our evolutionary history and our evolved psychological mechanisms influence our decisions and behaviors within the dating arena.

The other new research that the book introduces comes not from the empirical sciences, but from mathematics and economics and philosophy. An odd combination of disciplines, one might think, to help shed any light on romantic relationships. But not so. While we can learn a lot from evolutionary psychologists about why we have the preferences we do, and we can learn a lot from ethicists about how to interact in a principled and virtuous manner with prospective partners, dating is also a process that involves making decisions. Whom should I date, for how long, and at what point should I either move on or get serious? Dating is goal directed. Fortunately, philosophers, mathematicians, and economists have been developing accounts of how to make decisions when we are faced with lots of options. Decision theory and game theory are relatively new research areas in philosophy, and both aim to tell us how to choose between various options given that we have certain desires, goals, or preferences. The book introduces some of this new research and applies it to the domain of dating.

The third aim of the book is to bring all of this research to bear on new questions about the nature of dating and intimate relationships that have only recently emerged in the light of new technologies. With the advent of the Internet, the prospects not just of finding a date online, but also of cyberdating, now present themselves. We can now meet others in an online world in which we might present ourselves in an entirely different light than we present ourselves in the real world. What sorts of ethical implications are raised by this technology? Is cyberdating really dating and can cyberdating involve cheating? What sorts of duties do I owe someone whom I only meet in a game? Can genuine relationships grow out of, or exist entirely within, the online game? As we spend more and more time attached to our computers, should we be embracing technology as a way of finding like-minded people whom we might otherwise never connect with, or should we be worried that genuine relationships are not to be found in the cyberworld, and that our obsession with the computer is ruining our chances of finding true happiness? These are important questions that the book also takes up.

We hope that the very different essays in this book, offering as they do very different perspectives on the dating world, will not only entertain, but also propel readers to think about romantic relationships in general, specifically, the reader's own role in his or her own relationships. Critical examination of our own motives, preferences, and decision-making processes is something we should all engage in from time to time, and we hope that the reader will find these essays both stimulating and helpful in this regard. With that in mind we thank readers for joining each of the writers on this journey and hope that it is both exciting and enjoyable.

In the second part of this introduction, we offer a more in-depth look at each unit and the essays contained within. A quick perusal of the table of contents informs the reader of our semi-chronological approach to dating: we begin with the vicissitudes of flirtation, and end the volume with essays about choosing a mate. As is the case with the dating life itself, a number of surprising and, we hope, fruitful and entertaining detours mark the path from the first flirtatious moment of eye contact to the squishy comfort of settling in with a mate of choice.

Our first unit focuses on the complex issue of the terms upon which we found a dating relationship. It asks, for instance, what is flirting, and how do we move from flirting with someone to dating someone? Do attitudes about flirting vary depending upon the attitude of one's peers? What exactly is a date anyway – we all think we know one when we see it, but is that really true? Are there essential features that make a social interaction a date, rather than something else entirely, and if so, how do we all manage to figure out what those features are, and how do we know whether someone is a prospective date or a disinterested party? If we do manage to get a first date with a partner with potential, in what ways do we move the relationship along?

And so, "Getting Started: From Flirtation to Dating" begins with Carrie Jenkins' groundbreaking essay on flirting. Her aim is to construct a useful account of flirtation that will enable each of us to consider our own and others' behavior and determine whether some set of acts constitutes flirtation or not. In particular, Jenkins is keen to offer an account of when a person counts as flirting, rather than the related question of when the behaviors of that person are flirtatious, since she thinks that one can be flirtatious without flirting. For Jenkins, the crucial distinction is whether or not in engaging in flirtatious behavior one has certain intentions. According to Jenkins, only if one has particular sorts of intentions does one count as flirting.

In sharp contrast, Emily Langan looks at flirting from a seldom-seen vantage – that of conservative Christian men. To fully understand their viewpoint, Langan went straight to the source, interviewing young male daters who described themselves as "conservative," asking some probing questions and incorporating parts of the resulting transcripts of these conversations in her thoughtful exploration of the topic. The candid responses from these men add another, analytical dimension to something most of us think of only as light-hearted fun.

Then, Jennifer A. Samp and Andrew I Cohen argue that traditional representations of dating and intimate relationships are hopelessly misleading. They suggest that we are mistaken to suppose that unbridled and unconditioned passion or unconditional devotion is the defining feature of a healthy relationship. Instead, they suggest that dating is a process of social exchange in which each party constantly evaluates the features of the other party in an attempt to determine whether to maintain the relationship. While longstanding relationships might require considerable negative evaluation in order for it to be reasonable for us to decide to terminate them, no relationship fails to be subjected to evaluation in terms of the extent to which the needs of the parties are being met. This evaluative process is, they claim, entirely proper, and it is to our detriment to represent intimate relationships as being unconditional in any sense.

As with Jenkins, John Rowan and Patricia Hallen's final essay of this unit focuses on the communicative intentions of those involved in the romantic interaction. They use the appealing metaphor of an elevator ride to present their account of how we negotiate and communicate with one another to come to a mutual understanding about where a relationship is headed. They suggest that just as an elevator moves between floors, likewise relationships transition between phases. They stress the importance to those in the dating process of understanding these transitions and communicating to one's dating partner which "level" one is on.

The essays in our second unit, "No-No's: Dating Taboos," focus on what sorts of behaviors we ought *not* to engage in within the dating sphere. Dating "experts" abound, each elaborating the one, sure-fire plan to attract dates galore. But what of more unorthodox approaches, those that may yield insight, if not results, at odds with conventional wisdom? This unit explores a number of just such thoughts.

Here, for example, Mary Beth Yount playfully asks whether dating is like being mentally ill in certain ways. She suggests that although daters and those in the early phases of romantic love are clearly not, in any good sense, mentally ill, there are surprisingly many features of the behaviors and psychological profiles of daters that are very like those of people suffering from psychological problems. She also argues that it helps to understand the nature of romantic love, in all its permutations, under the premise that if one understands the nature of the "illness," one is less likely to be driven "crazy" by it.

Next, in a surprising turn, Kristie Miller asks whether there are any behaviors *at all* that ought to be taboo when it comes to dating. As she puts it, is it okay to date my sister or a gorilla? Tantalizingly, she answers in the affirmative. This essay focuses not on the ethical "ought" but on the prudential "ought." It asks what each of us ought to do, if we are primarily interested in getting what we most want. The suggestion is that there are no sets of behaviors that we should presuppose are prudentially bad for us: nothing is taboo.

Anne Barnhill, on the other hand, is interested in the ethical "ought." Her essay considers the extent to which, in the process of dating, one can violate the boundaries of another individual in order to facilitate a relationship. As Barnhill frames the question: When is serenading a prospective but unwilling party harassment and boundary violation, and when it is perfectly acceptable and how can we tell the difference? To gain some insight, she sets out a range of criteria designed to tell us when we are being pushy, rude, and manipulative, and when we are violating a boundary in an acceptable manner.

Then, in the final essay of this unit, Kyla Reid and Tinashe Dune take issue with the dating commandments set forward in books like *The Rules* that have recently become so popular. They argue that the sorts of rules espoused in these guides will not lead to a happy dating life or to finding a good partner. Indeed, they argue that this rules-based approach promotes a psychology in women slanting them towards obeying the "rules," behavior which is, in important respects, much like that of prostitutes and professional girlfriends. This, they argue, is no way to cultivate a real relationship.

Unit three, "Rolling Right Along: Dating Like a Pro," focuses on how we *ought* to date, rather than on how we ought not to date. Though the ways in which dating taboos often can be turned on their head to good effect are made evident in the previous unit, this unit returns to topics more in keeping with received ideas about dating – not that the authors move lock-step with what many accept as "conventional wisdom" in the dating area. On the contrary, at least two of the essays in this unit argue forcefully – though often humorously – that time-held assumptions about such conventions as the "fix-up" and dating as the one sure route to mating just don't hold water. These essays point to what Nabokov might have called the "signposts and tombstones" dotting the dating landscape glimpsed while rolling right along the dating route.

Accordingly, the first essay here, by Joshua S. Heter, is a manifesto against matchmaking in favor of what Heter argues are more natural ways of bringing people together in a romantic setting. Heter believes the artificiality of a fix-up presages the death knell of any potential relationship attempted under such circumstances; rather, he follows Aristotle in holding that each of us has a natural function, and that living according to that function makes us happy and fulfilled. For men especially, part of that function is to actively seek out a life partner in a masterful manner. Since matchmaking usurps this mastery it is antithetical to individual flourishing and not therefore a good way to find a romantic partner.

Likewise, Richard Hamilton's essay also focuses on an Aristotelean account of ethics and flourishing. Hamilton offers a critique of some of the recent books aimed at offering men a guide to attracting women by using a set of tricks or devices. He suggests that if we are at all worried about these books, it must be because we think that there is some small grain of truth in there somewhere: we suspect that some of these tricks might just work. Hamilton's claim is that the various tricks offered by these books are really just ways of trying to make a man appear to be a jerk rather than a nice guy, where for Hamilton, being a certain kind of jerk is being authentic and fulfilling one's human function, while being a nice guy is not. No surprise then, argues Hamilton, that women are attracted to jerks and not nice guys. By Hamilton's lights, successful daters should focus on being the right kind of jerk, and avoid being the wrong sort of nice guy!

There follows another essay in a counterintuitive mode much like Joshua Heter's manifesto against matchmaking, Andrew Terjesen's "I've Never Been on a Date (yet Somehow I got Married!)," which delves more deeply into the question of just what it is that constitutes a date. After all, the sorts of typical behaviors associated with dating can just as well be associated with interactions that are not dates. So how do we know when we're on a date and how does one manage to marry without dating? Terjesen's answer is that we mind-read: we use, albeit often unconsciously, a complex theory about others' intentions and mental states based on reasoning we engage in from our own behaviors and mental states. This is a complex process, which explains both why having dinner with someone is not in itself sufficient for an event to count as a date, but also why people can sometimes be confused as to the intentions of the other party, and thus confused as to whether they really are on a date or not. True dating involves a sort of meeting of the minds that might sometimes fail to occur. That's why dating can be a fraught enterprise.

Finally, we end this unit with Christopher Brown and David Tien's appeal to the Western insights of the philosopher Immanuel Kant, combined with the Eastern insights of Zhuangzi, to offer the reader a nuanced account of how we each ought to behave when on a date. In the process of dating we all present a particular image of ourselves to the person we are with, and sometimes that image is less than completely truthful. Brown and Tien explore the ethical implications of the ways in which we present ourselves on dates. They argue that rather than constantly attempting to put one's best foot forward, the work of Zhuangzi and other meditative philosophers shows that one is best served by entering a state of "flow" when on a date. This allows us to be both relaxed and authentic, and in this sense to present ourselves in the best way possible.

Our cyberdating unit, "Another World: Cyber-Rendezvous," explores the relatively new phenomenon of cyberdating: both finding a mate through online "meeting" at Internet dating sites and dating a "person" online in online worlds such as *Second Life*. No doubt, sites such as Match.com, eHarmony, and JDate have changed the dating landscape forever. With the bonds of close family and friends weakened by the mobility of early twenty-first century society, endless work demands taking up most of people's lives, and an ever-more atomized culture keeping people single for longer periods of their lives, many now say that surfing Internet dating sites in the wee hours of the morning is the only way to "meet" potential dates. Yet others substitute cyberdating games for dating "in real life" or augment existing real-life relationships with a cyber romance or marriage in an alternate world, say the world of *Second Life*.

And so, Bo Brinkman's essay "Dating and Play in Virtual Worlds" investigates just such a second world and the ethics of cyberdating in that world. Brinkman argues that although the various virtual worlds in which such encounters take place are games, they are the kinds of games that facilitate genuine interactions. Since it is their nature as games that tends to undermine the idea that interactions within the game are in some good sense real, Brinkman pays careful attention to the nature of games and their ontological status. In his view, our real world is full of important games with very serious implications. The cyberworld is no less real because it is a game. So, he argues, cyberdating can count as genuine dating, and cyberdating when you already have a partner can count as cheating.

Dan Silber's cyberworld, on the other hand, is much more down to earth. In his essay, he recounts "meeting" his wife online – and soon after, in person – and explores the issues of authenticity attached to such meetings. In a number of creative approaches to his topic, Silber revisits Derrida's speech/writing dichotomy and its implications for "meeting" a potential mate via a written profile posted on the Internet, as well as notions of existential "authenticity," including Martin Buber's poetical I-Thou philosophy. His essay is an enlightening blend of personal experience mixed with more contemporary philosophical approaches to interpersonal relationships.

Flirtation has morphed into dating, questions about whether an encounter actually *is* a date have been answered (in the affirmative), issues concerning motivation, the prudential and ethical aspects of "oughts," and authenticity have been dealt with in turn – time to think about "The Talk" on the way to the final destination: selecting a mate. The essays in this last unit, "From Date to Mate: 'Natural' Selection?" focus on how each of us ought to behave in order to increase our chances of finding a good mate. These essays appeal to new research both in evolutionary psychology and philosophy of biology, as well as in decision theory.

No surprise then that the first essay in this last unit, Hichem Naar and Alberto Masala's "Evolutionary Psychology and Seduction Strategies: Should Science Teach Men How to Attract Women?" offers the reader insight into the latest scientific understanding of how organisms attract a mate. It uses that information to argue that it is ethically permissible to alter one's behavior in ways that make one appear to be more attractive to the opposite sex. That is, they argue that it is permissible to engage in the sorts of tricks and deceptions that seduction coaches teach, because deception and manipulation are part and parcel of ordinary dating, and that is just what you would expect when you understand mate selection from an evolutionary perspective.

There follows, in a novel twist, Mark Colyvan's "Mating, Dating, and Mathematics: It's All in the Game," an essay approaching the problem of mate selection as one of mathematics and decision-making. Given that each of us has a number of prospective mates to choose from, Colyvan wonders what sort of "search algorithm" should we employ in order to make sure that we don't search for too long, on the one hand, and on the other hand that we don't settle for unsatisfactory outcomes too quickly. Colyvan's essay is an attempt to offer answers to those questions through the mathematical modeling of game theory.

And finally to close this unit and our book, Marlene Clark appeals to developments in the philosophy of decision theory and psychology to suggest that a sense of overwhelming choice often inhibits any choice at all; to put it in other words, environments offering a seemingly limitless pool of choices can turn even those inclined to settle upon a very good choice into one for whom only the "absolute best" will do. Consequently, the relentless focus on the endless, most likely fruitless search for that elusive "absolute best" can blind us to satisfying alternatives right under the proverbial nose. A light-hearted look at the examples of the dating lives of the women in *Sex and the City* helps to illustrate the point.

We hope that daters everywhere – past, present, and yes, sometimes once again, future – will enjoy this book as much as we enjoyed putting it together. Maybe after reading some or all of these essays you will think differently about relationships; maybe these essays will help you get to a mental place where you can be "philosophical" – in every sense of the word – about your dating life.

# PART 1

# GETTING STARTED

From Flirting to Dating

CARRIE S. JENKINS[1]

CHAPTER I

# THE PHILOSOPHY OF FLIRTING

What is it to flirt? Do you have to intend to flirt with someone in order to count as doing so? Can such things as dressing a certain way count as flirting? Can one flirt with an AI character? With one's own long-term partner? With an idea?

The question of whether or not an act of flirtation has taken place is often highly significant in our practical decision-making. For example, one may want to know whether or not one's partner has been flirting with other people in order to decide whether to continue the relationship. Or one may want to know whether two of one's friends have been flirting with each other in order to decide whether to give them some time alone. To facilitate such decisions, it would be helpful to have a secure grasp on what flirting actually amounts to. And there are many other uses to which such a grasp could be put. If, say, one stands accused that one's own behavior of the previous evening constituted an act of flirtation, one is equipped to respond to the accusation if one can point to some necessary condition on acts of flirtation which was not met in this case.

Dictionary definitions of flirting seem to be somewhat deficient, suggesting that one cannot flirt when one has serious designs on the person being flirted with. The *Oxford English Dictionary*, for instance, suggests one only counts as flirting if one lacks "serious intentions" and is "playing" at courtship, "without any intention of responding to the feelings awakened." This seems to me to be false. A committed relationship could well begin with a flirtation between two people who have perfectly serious intentions towards each other. The definition also suggests that anyone playing at courtship will count as flirting, but this looks wrong too: clearly, kids can play at weddings without flirting with each other.

Can we improve upon the proffered definitions? If we draw a few potentially important distinctions, I believe we can.

The first distinction is between flirting and behaving flirtatiously, where the latter is to be understood as behaving in ways that would, according to accepted social standards, normally constitute acts of flirtation. One can behave flirtatiously without flirting. There could be a person who, quite accidentally, acts in a way very similar to the way most people act when they are flirting, but does this entirely without realizing, at any (even subconscious) level, that this behavior is at all the sort of thing likely to excite or maintain anyone's admiration or sexual interest.

Suppose, for instance, that Joe has a habit of maintaining eye contact for just a few seconds longer than is usual, but this is due to the fact that his attention wanders very easily, with the result that he stares at whatever he is looking at for a few seconds before coming back online. Some of his behavior could plausibly be described as flirtatious, but he is not flirting. Similarly, an English woman visiting Italy who touches her earlobes a lot in the presence of a particular person, without realizing the cultural significance of this action, would be behaving flirtatiously in that context, but doing so without flirting.

I am also tempted to think that one can flirt without behaving flirtatiously. Provided the right background is in place, one could flirt in a very non-standard way. With someone one knew very well, for instance, humming a section of a Puccini aria or scratching one's forearm might constitute an act of flirtation, although it would not normally do so, and hence does not count as flirtatious behavior.

The second distinction, or rather group of distinctions, is between flirting and various other actions (which, distinctions notwithstanding, may on some occasions *constitute* acts of flirtation). These are: making explicit *suggestions* of a romantic or sexual nature ("We could go to the party as a couple"), making explicit *declarations* of feelings of that nature ("I'm really attracted to you"), and making explicit *requests* for interactions of that nature ("Will you go on a date with me?"). Flirting, I would suggest, is not in general the same thing as making such suggestions, declarations, or requests. One can flirt without doing any of these things, and I think that all of them can be done without flirting.

Let me now turn to the question of what has to be true of someone in order for that person to count as flirting. I propose, controversially I expect, that one cannot flirt without *in some sense intending to do so*. That is to say, flirting is always intentional, although in quite a weak sense to be explained in a moment. Flirtatious behavior where there is no underlying intention of the required kind is, by my lights, *mere* flirtatious behavior, and does not constitute flirting.

The sense in which I want to claim that flirting is always intentional is weak in that I intend this claim to be consistent with its being possible to flirt without *realizing* one is doing so, and consistent with its even being possible to flirt without possessing the concept of flirtation, or related concepts. These consistency facts are due to its being possible to possess the relevant kind of intention without being reflectively aware that one possesses it and/or without being aware that it constitutes an intention to flirt. Possession of this kind of intention is pretty cognitively undemanding, and it is therefore available to the conceptually unsophisticated.

The question is: What *does* one intend to do when one intends to flirt? To encourage or inspire attraction, perhaps? But one can flirt without that aim. It may already be common knowledge that the flirtee is attracted to you, or you might know that this is a hopeless case, such that the flirtee will not be attracted to you however much you flirt.

Perhaps the intention is to raise one's own attraction to the flirtee to salience for the flirtee? But this is not a necessary condition on flirting either: one needn't *be* attracted to the flirtee in order to flirt with him or her. It is also insufficient: there are ways of raising to salience one's own attraction without flirting (e.g., by making a straight-up declaration to that effect).

Another suggestion is that the intention is to raise the possibility of flirter-flirtee romance and/or sexual contact to salience. But again, it may be common knowledge that there is no such possibility. This does not prevent flirtation from taking place. Maybe the intention is to raise the *question* of flirter-flirtee romance/sex to salience. But it can also happen that flirting occurs when this question is already salient.

A better shot is that the required intention is the intention to do things that, in the kind of situation the flirter is in, *either* will raise flirter-flirtee romance/sex to salience between flirter and flirtee *or* would do so if it weren't already salient. However, one can object to this proposal by considering the case of "killer-flirts" (with apologies to Saul Kripke's notion of "killer yellow"). When a killer-flirt flirts with someone, both flirter and flirtee immediately die. So nothing would be raised to salience between them were the killer-flirt to flirt. According to the current proposal, no killer-flirt can start flirting in a situation where flirter-flirtee romance/sex is already salient. For we would need to appeal to the second option mentioned in the proposal to cover this case, but that clause is not true for killer-flirts. So despite appearances, killer-flirts are not that dangerous after all; just make sure that when you meet them, you keep mentioning how attractive they are.

Maybe the intention required in order to flirt is the intention to act in ways that are *disposed* to raise flirter-flirtee romance and/or sexual contact to salience for the flirtee. (Philosophers are pretty widely agreed that something's being disposed to do X under conditions C is not the same as being such that it *would* do X were it in conditions C.) There is still an obvious objection to this as it stands, however, which is that there are many actions which are so disposed, yet are not such that intending to perform them would amount to intending to flirt. For instance, serious and sincere requests for romantic involvement are disposed to raise romance to salience, but do not in general plausibly count as acts of flirtation.

What matters, I suggest, for distinguishing flirtations from these other actions is the fact that in any genuine flirtation there should be an element of *playfulness*. Flirtation is, of its essence, playful. But, *contra* the dictionary definitions, this type of play need not be *mere* play. One can be playful in the required sense despite having perfectly serious intentions. This solves the problem of committed flirts, mentioned above. Also, I believe that not all play counts for these purposes. Flirtation involves a kind of *knowing* playfulness (which addresses the problem of kids playing at weddings). A third point to note here is that the play need not be enjoyable: you can force yourself to flirt, just as you can force yourself to play bridge or Monopoly.

So far, I have not considered whether the possibility of flirting depends in part on whom (if anyone) one is flirting with. At the extreme, we can ask whether it is possible to flirt without flirting with anyone at all. Or, less radically, we can ask whether it is possible to flirt without flirting with anyone *in particular*. The latter question may appear to be answerable in the positive. Suppose, for instance, that one leaves the house one morning with the intention of acting in ways disposed to raise the issue of romance/sex to salience, in the right (knowing, playful) kind of way, with whomever one meets. Will one end up flirting with everyone one meets? Perhaps. But this might plausibly be said to be in virtue of the fact that person-specific intentions of a similar nature are formed at each meeting, rather than in virtue of the general intention.

Is it ever possible to flirt without having a specific flirtee in mind? I am inclined to think there must be some specification of a flirtee or group of flirtees, but I am not sure that a single flirtee need be singled out. It doesn't sound too bad to say that a performer can flirt with a live theatre audience without his forming any specific intentions about each member of the audience. However, he would at best be flirting with his audience considered collectively and not distributively; it would sound wrong for an individual member of the audience to claim that the performer in question had been flirting with *him*, just because he had been flirting with the audience.

Note that in saying that a flirter must have certain intentions which single out her flirtee(s), I do not mean that there must really *be* some person or persons with whom she intends to flirt, but that she must *intend* to flirt with some person or persons. Hence, I am leaving room for the possibility of flirting with a purely imaginary person. Someone might count as flirting by dint of believing there to be a person present and having the right kind of intentions towards the imagined person. In that sense, it is possible to flirt without flirting with anyone at all.

One final question worth considering is whether it is possible to flirt with non-people. I think it is, at least if one mistakes them for people, because what matters are the flirter's intentions. If the flirter believes the flirtee to be a person, (s)he can have all the required flirtatious intentions towards the flirtee. But what if one *knows* that the target is not a person? Well, according to recent research, "people frequently insult and flirt with computer characters placed in Internet chatrooms to entertain or provide information" despite knowing that they are talking to AI characters (or "chatbots") rather than real human beings.[2]

It may be thought that this talk of "flirting" with chatbots is metaphorical, or at best derivative from the primary notion of flirtation, which requires the intention to flirt with another person. But I doubt whether this is necessarily correct. I suspect that what is important is the intention to flirt with something that can *respond* in some significant way. If one thinks of the chatbot as capable of thinking and feeling, and hence of responding in the required way, then one may count as flirting with it. If one does not, however, then one may still be behaving flirtatiously (perhaps even *pretending* to flirt), but one won't be flirting.

For similar reasons, I take it that talk of flirtation with ideas, theories, pursuits, and so on is (at least almost always) purely metaphorical, since these things are not generally taken to be capable of responding in the relevant way.

In short, I think we can fix on the following as a set of necessary and sufficient conditions on flirting. First, the flirter should act with the intention to do things which are disposed to raise flirter-flirtee romance and/or sex to salience for the flirtee, in a knowing yet playful manner. Second, he or she should believe that the flirtee can respond in some significant way. No doubt there is room for reasonable disagreement about this proposal. But I am confident that it is an improvement on the existing dictionary definitions, and hopeful that the foregoing discussion will open avenues for further philosophical reflection in an under-explored field.

## NOTES

1  This essay was first published in *The Philosopher's Magazine* 36 (October 2006): 37–40. Reprinted with permission.
2  Reported by Tony Tysome in the *Times Higher Education Supplement*, March 17, 2006.

CHAPTER 2

# GOOD GIRLS DON'T, BUT BOYS DON'T EITHER

## Toward a Conservative Position on Male Flirting

 In the 2005 movie *Hitch*, Alex "Hitch" Hitchens (portrayed by Will Smith) offers his clients this advice: "Basic principles – no matter what, no matter when, no matter who, any man has a chance to sweep any woman off her feet; he just needs the right broom."[1] For Hitch, a man's ability to flirt successfully is just such a tool which, when utilized appropriately, is the ticket to a promising relationship. Hitch's advice is flawed in at least two ways: it assumes that, if given the opportunity, a man would use any tool at his disposal and having the right equipment all but guarantees success. Inarguably, some men are shameless and would gleefully follow Hitch's words of wisdom, doing anything they deem effective in their romantic pursuits. But this is unlikely the case for more conservative men, an often-overlooked group who are bound more by morals than libidos. For these men, a different ethic is likely to drive their choices and behaviors when it comes to romance. This essay is an attempt to explore uncharted waters and to argue for a position on male flirting contextualized in an ideologically conservative mindset.

## Flirting and Courtship

Undeniably, flirting is part of the initial courtship dance, an often-confusing tango of mixed messages, unclear intents, and ambiguous interactions. Researchers have identified five typical stages of courtship, a process of moving from unknown strangers to an intimately connected pair.[2] In the beginning, the attention-getting phase, ambivalence dominates, with almost childlike tendencies toward both approach and avoidance cues. During this initial stage where potential mates are identified, behaviors are generally intentionally ambiguous and indirect, such as a tentative smile or a fleeting glance. The task is to make one's self stand out among eligible others. While the risk of being ignored or rejected remains, the ambiguity and indirect nature of the interaction allows for a certain degree of "plausible deniability" which mitigates the emotional risks involved. When couples move to the recognition stage, their interest and availability are more readily apparent. Sustained eye contact and positioning the body more directly towards the other person signal interest and a willingness to interact. Having perceived a green light and assuming a favorable response, the pair moves to the interaction phase with more pronounced behaviors and highly animated exchanges. Also called the positioning stage, the couple becomes occupied with each other and, at least temporarily, is off-limits to others. Both verbal and non-verbal channels are utilized; conversation and behavior both grow increasingly more intimate. Anthropologist David Givens claims that humans are the only animal who can talk and court at the same time.[3] After the highly kinetic interaction phase, the pace slows down during the sexual arousal or invitation stage. Increasingly more intimate and provocative behaviors suggest partners are highly attracted to each other; implicit and explicit overtures invite further contact. Actions ranging from hand-holding and brushing hair from the partner's face to touching the other's legs are used in suggestive ways. To both the partners and to the external world, their status as a couple is clearly communicated. During the final stage of courtship, the resolution phase, sexual interaction occurs with some couples moving directly to intercourse while other pairs increase their intimacy over time. With their bond secure, partners often pull back from overtly solicitous behaviors and typical courtship behaviors cease after resolution, much to the dismay of some new couples. Yet, speaking from an evolutionary perspective, what else would one expect? Once couple-hood is achieved, flirting seems redundant.

Though flirting is certainly a component of courtship, the two terms are not interchangeable. The five stages of courtship, or even the lesser quasi-courtship (the first four stages, without the intention of sex), suggest an expressed desire for a romantic relationship. Clearly, people flirt to achieve this end goal. From his research, David Henningsen concluded that people flirt predominantly to intensify a relationship or for sexually motivated reasons.[4] All flirting, however, cannot be contextualized as relationally driven behavior. Henningsen also found that people flirt for fun, to boost their own self-esteem, or to achieve some instrumental goal. In other words, flirting may signal "I'm into you" but it also may suggest "I'm amusing myself," "I need to feel better about myself," or "I'm trying to get something for myself." Put much more bluntly, it's about me, not about you or us. Just as the motivations for flirting are complicated, so too are the interpretations of a flirtatious gesture or comment.

Flirting, like most other forms of human behavior, requires interpretation and the potential for miscommunication causes many a flirt to alter their actions. The desire to avoid misleading potential suitors ranks high among the concerns of more ideologically conservative people. To avoid being chased by more sexually aggressive admirers, chaste women and men likely minimize their invitations. The issue is further magnified when it moves beyond a semantic matter: Walking a tightrope between being perceived as a prude or a tease, what is fair game and what's out of bounds when it comes to flirting appropriateness? Come-hither glances might be seen as too suggestive and even fleeting touches too provocative. Can one flirt, sending messages about attraction and availability, without sexual intent? This query is raised for ideologically conservative people of either gender. The concern is not only with how their flirting gestures are *perceived*, but, at a more fundamental level, the appropriateness and acceptability of any and all forms of flirting. This virgin-vixen, madonna-whore tension is not a new paradox for women; it is a timeless battle of wanting to be seen as desirable yet respectable. Yet, despite age-old roots, it is nonetheless a contemporary struggle as well. Put in current vernacular, "How can I let him know I'm into him without saying I'm easy?"

## Conservative Ideology

We know how a "good girl" is supposed to act, but how is a conservative *boy* to behave? Arguably, there might be a parallel struggle for conservative men where the most widely used seduction strategies fall outside of acceptable parameters. While flirting can range from ambiguous and indirect to overt and sexualized,[5] men of moderation must consider their motivations, actions, and reactions in much the same way as conservative women do. Both men and women watch the other sex's behavior for clues as to which title is the best fit: *Love Happens* or *He's Just Not That Into You*. In the past, flirting might have been seen as a way to help a woman fall in love with you, all the while assuming if a man would start using his "tools" and stop behaving like *a tool*, he would find success. This piece of cultural wisdom seems in chorus with a commonly held position: men are the aggressors in relationships and women the restrainers. Prudence and restraint in dating interactions is "women's work." Men are encouraged to hit the gas pedal ("more, more, more"), while women are to man the brakes ("Whoa there, Tiger!"). In the bestselling book *The Rules*, authors Ellen Fein and Sherri Schneider go one step further, advising female readers to never call a man: "Trust in the natural order of things, namely that man pursues woman."[6] Observational research seems to suggest, however, that many women either disregard *The Rules* or choose to break them.

In her study of female flirting behaviors, psychologist Monica Moore observed 52 different flirting techniques ranging from routine behaviors such as darting glances and smiles to the more overtly flirtatious hair flip or exaggerated laugh.[7] Women have a lot of tools at their ready disposal and, especially in the early stages of an interaction, seem to be utilizing them. Women of the twenty-first century are less likely than their predecessors to wait for love to happen; they are more apt to take matters into their own hands and take the initiative. In follow-up studies, Moore and other researchers have consistently found that, contrary to expectations, women can and do flirt. Though culturally defined gender roles concerning "pursuer" and "pursuee" might suggest otherwise, even the casual spectator on any given Saturday night has likely observed women in action. This change in roles, from women as target to women as initiator, has dramatic impacts on the interpretation of flirting behavior. The same behaviors, when executed by a woman, are consistently evaluated as more alluring, more sensual, and more inviting than when performed by a male counterpart.[8] Perhaps it is logical, therefore, that the bulk of scholarly attention concerning the ethicality or propriety of flirting is directed at women's actions and intentions. But the imbalance of the scholarly and layperson's focus on the actions of women has overshadowed the decisions facing more traditionally minded men. It is possible that for some men a culturally scripted role as aggressive pursuer is ill-fitted at best.

## Power Dynamics and Relationships

As with any social structure, dating and courtship have embedded power dynamics. From one vantage point, the commonly ascribed gender roles seem to award women a measure of social power. By controlling if and how a relationship develops, the person with more selectivity and power of restriction exercises greater influence. Givens argues that this controlling influence belongs to women who exert greater influence in early courtship when their signals of availability can make or break an interaction.[9] If misinterpreted, a man has little chance at success, and if missed entirely a man may not be afforded another opportunity. From an evolutionary perspective, women's selectivity would dominate in the early stages of courtship. In order to insure the propagation of his lineage it is in a man's best interest to be less discriminating.

This position, however, may appear somewhat dated and harkens back to an earlier era in dating. Sociologists Mary Riege Laner and Nicole Ventrone suggest that a power shift occurred in courtship in the early part of the twentieth century.[10] When courtship occurred largely in the home, women (and their families) controlled the interaction, but as dating moved into the public sphere and economic factors arose, the pendulum shifted in favor of men. These traditional principles about date initiation still prevail: men assume a dominant, planning role (e.g., select the location, pay the bill, provide transportation) while women's roles are reactive in nature (e.g., wait for date to arrive, be polite, primp). At least where date initiation is concerned, young men and women may claim egalitarian beliefs but hold very traditionalist assumptions. Under these circumstances, the power remains in favor of men.

Further empowerment is given to men who hold to a conservative or Christian ideology. One logical deduction is that, as the divinely appointed head of a household, a man is also encouraged to take the reins initially to establish a relationship. In the proverbial driver's seat, men are not reactive but proactive. They are not merely the targets for flirting women, but are also the flirts. This perspective stands in contrast to more mainstream courtship roles where men are seemingly at the mercy of women's behaviors. Given a new measure of influence, how might their ideology alter the choices of these men in regard to flirting? In other words, how do they answer the question, "How does a good boy behave?"

## Exploring the Views of Conservative Men

Based on the data from 75 young men in focus group discussions, this essay explores the meanings and values placed on flirting by those who would consider themselves ideologically conservative. Each focus group, which consisted of 6–10 men, was led by a trained moderator with the assistance of two observers.[11] As the bulk of scholarly attention has focused exclusively on the flirting behaviors of women, much of the design employed here was exploratory in nature, with questions ranging from direct inquiries about flirting practices (e.g., "What is your favorite technique?") to more abstract queries about the nature of flirting (e.g., "How do you know when you've been successful?"). The transcripts were then coded for common themes across groups using Glaser and Strauss's constant comparative method.[12] What emerged from these coded memos were three consistent themes – themes widely shared among the participants – and three themes of contradictions – themes that involved the participants struggling between opposing views about flirting.

Since the participants share an ideological position and, in the case of most participants, a deep-seated Christian faith, the consistency in viewpoint might be expected. These commonly held attitudes further suggest that ideas about flirting and indeed courtship in general are likely acquired from teachings in widely read books, mutually attended events, or shared religious organizations. As a result of being exposed to similar messages, some uniformity in ideas emerged. Across groups, conversations focused on three central considerations about flirting: motives, timing, and responsiveness.

Not surprisingly, for ideologically conservative men, a person's motive for flirting is an important consideration. First and foremost, flirting isn't about sex. Breaking from what they see as more progressive or secular beliefs, collectively these men saw themselves as distinct based on a non-sexualized characterization of flirting. This theme was widely evident across the groups:[13]

| | |
|---|---|
| *Michael*: | Flirting is not done with the intention to have sex with a girl. That's the primary way in which it's different for us. |
| *Charles*: | Because we all know this isn't about sex, we're all kind of [pause] guarded....You can't flirt with the intention of getting married. That's too big a step, you know, it's more of a process than that. So if you're not flirting to get married or to have sex, you know what I mean, I wonder if it's why so many guys are guarded in a kind of way. |
| *Gabe*: | Heck yeah there's a Christian way to flirt. |
| *Don*: | If you really like her, if you like the girl and are not just trying to like … |
| *Dave*: | … get into her pants. |
| *Mitchell*: | You do it, just more conservatively, less physical, less sexual. |
| *Frank*: | There might be other differences but I think the conservative way is we flirt to get the first date you know or to get them to go out with us but most people flirt yeah – |
| *Isaac*: | – they flirt to get some … |
| *Matt*: | … some nookie. |

As Henningsen's research highlights, people flirt for various motives.[14] From a conservative position, however, some of those intentions are considered out of bounds. For these men, all behavior, including flirting, should have a clear and appropriate desired outcome. In other words, true courtship is not encouraged; quasi-courtship, which lacks a sexual end goal, is okay. There is also an explicit value in being sincere or honest. Misrepresenting either oneself or one's desires is discouraged:

| | |
|---|---|
| *Charles*: | I feel like you need to be honest, you need to check your motives … like if I was really flirting with a girl in a way that would make her interested in me when I have no interest in her at all I just would never even say that was right. You have to be aware of your intentions, not that you have to be guilt-ridden all the time or be really serious but aware. |
| *Adam*: | When it comes to flirting, it can be a really healthy way to build relationships with people. And above all, like I said, I think being honest about who you are and what your intentions are is really like the key to having it be a good and growing experience. I mean, you're not trying to be someone you're not when you're flirting, and you're not trying to get someone else to think that you're like someone you're not.... You're just being honest about what you are doing or what you're trying to find out. |

In contrast to a more mainstream ideal, where rules about flirting might be summed up as "anything goes," these men conceptualized flirting as a more candid undertaking. Communication scholars Jeffrey Hall and Michael Cody claim there are five styles of flirting: *traditional* (following culturally ascribed gender roles), *physical* (direct and sexualized), *sincere* (aimed at creating an emotional connection), *playful* (light-hearted without relationally minded intent), and *inhibited* (cautious, rule-governed approach).[15] Based on espoused values, conservative men tend toward either a sincere or inhibited flirting style and, as they are likely not entirely homogeneous in perspective, it seems highly plausible that some are more willing to engage in what they deem appropriate flirting (embracing a sincere approach) while others would see very limited application (an inhibited style). Overall, the intent of the flirter seemed to dominate the perceptions of the flirtee. In other words, they attributed responsibility to themselves to behave appropriately and though they discussed the potential for miscommunication, even within the arena of flirting, the highest value was placed on honestly portraying oneself.

## Timing and Reciprocity

A second unifying theme was the timing of flirting within the greater context of the relationship. In other words, if relationship development is seen as a sequence of verbal and non-verbal actions, where does flirting enter in? For most, flirting was not the initial form of contact, though it was important early on as an attempt to establish a connection and at some level a prerequisite to moving into some sort of relationship with a woman:

> *Steve*: I'd say it's a good means to getting girls to go out with you or whatever. I think it's almost essential. You're trying to start a relationship from scratch.
> *Gabe*: You can't just hop right into a deep conversation when you're getting to know a girl 'cause you kinda have to break down walls.
> *Don*: Doesn't it always start with flirting?
> *Dave*: I don't know that it ever starts without flirting. I can't think of a time where you're not slightly flirting with anyone. If you want to get to know her, you just naturally flirt.
> *Steve*: Do you think Adam and Eve flirted or did they just get right to it?

From this conversation it is clear that flirting is viewed as a natural part of the getting-to-know-you process of early courtship. In fact, the place of flirting is so solidified that its absence is so unlikely as to be unthinkable. In the earliest stages of relationship development, flirting is used as a way of getting past awkwardness or uncertainty and moving into more comfortable, and in some cases deeper, conversation. However, although it is utilized early in the relationship development process, flirting may not be the initial step taken by these men, as voiced by this more cautious position:

*Tim*:   I think here [at this school] you have to develop a bit of a relationship first, a foundation before you flirt openly with a girl because very few girls will just flirt right out of the gate. You have to usually get to know them, have some sort of basic "I've hung out with you once" or something in your relationship before you can jump in and flirt with them.

*Matt*:   Except during Orientation week.

Here, the nature of flirting requires a different sort of timing. Flirting is only viable once you have a previously established, even if rather superficial, connection. Flirting is not the way into a connection but something done with someone you've already been in contact with. In both cases, flirting might be contextualized as part of the interaction phase of courtship; it is used after he's gained the woman's attention and determined that she seems willing to move to the next level. Much the same way, some men expressed a function of flirting later in a relationship:

*Grant*:   I think it is much comparable to relationships where you have to wait for the right time for certain types of flirting to occur in a relationship once you're already within the relationship, of course.... So I think there are certain stages in a relationship that's very appropriate to introduce, say, the next level of flirting, if you will, but to enter that prematurely can be very detrimental to a relationship because then that oftentimes will become then the center of the relationship.... But if you get to a point within the relationship that those flirting needs occur then, and they don't, you almost start stifling it and you'll just kinda get boxed in more.

Again, the timing of certain flirting behaviors is critical to the advancement of the relationship. But rather than jumpstart a budding relationship, flirting can push an existing relationship to the next step, yet it must be done with moderation. Aggressive flirting too early can squelch a relationship on an otherwise positive trajectory, yet an overly cautious approach, which excludes flirting, also appears problematic. Each example highlights that timing is critical when it comes to flirting.

A third point of overlap is the dyadic nature of flirting: it has to be a two-way street. These men do not buy into images of a man aggressively pursuing a seemingly disinterested woman. Instead, though they still saw themselves as the pursuer, it was only deemed "worth it" or reasonable if signs of life existed:

> *Danny*: I think the object of flirting is to get them to flirt back, doing something, hoping to get them to interact with you in order to pursue the interaction further.
>
> *Mitchell*: I think it's a safe way to test the waters, I guess, and take it from a platonic relationship into something possible. But then if she doesn't respond, it might still be a friendship. You don't have to have an RDT [Relationship Defining Talk] and be like, "Hey, what's up?" If she doesn't respond, you just back off.

Evidently, response from the target is a requirement, a position that may be in contrast with more liberal ideologies where metaphors of "hunting one's prey" abound. In those cases how she responds seems almost inconsequential, whereas from the conservative position flirting seems more choreographed and dance-like. Indeed, the lack of synchrony is taken as a warning signal:

> *Gabe*: You know it's working when she flirts back.
>
> *Steve*: When you got them on the chain.
>
> *Dave*: Yeah, when she flirts back, that means she likes it, she's into it. When she's picking up on your signals. When she's interested and you can feel that they are reciprocated, then you're on your way. Otherwise, run. It's a lost cause.

For one participant, flirting is not ambiguous: it's easy to tell when it's not working and you should abruptly change direction:

> *Frank*: It's pretty easy to get the message if the girl's not flirting back. If you're getting feedback, it's pretty easy to tell. If a girl doesn't like what you're throwing out man, if she's not feeling it, get out.

But the exact nature of reciprocity seems somewhat in question. For some men, there was a clear desire to be matched in terms of flirting intensity and apparent interest level. Other men, however, were willing to take more subtle indicators of interest:

Greg:    It's not necessarily the results but the knowledge that she wants more. That's a flirting victory –

Jack:    – You have to have made some kind of forward progress that's all.

Darren:  I don't think it has to be much of a response, just positive interaction.

Chad:    I'd say flirting works when she smiles back and says "Hey" and remembers your name next time she sees you.

Cooper:  Maybe she'll kind of ignore other people in deference to you when you're there, that's pretty big.

Trey:    That's huge.

Grant:   And you know you've had a failure when you're the one being ignored.

Much like the call and response speaking style of preachers to their congregations, conservative men evaluate success and make judgments of continuation or cessation based on the response of their targets. This interactive approach towards flirting might appear gentler, less assertive than a "no holds barred" style. Clearly, from their words, responses are not required to be grand gestures but do necessitate clear evidence of interest. It doesn't seem a great stretch to suggest that underlying the need for a response is a hesitation and uncertainty that may suggest these men also tend to be somewhat risk-averse, at least where relations with the opposite sex are concerned. Flirting is only deemed valuable (and continued) when risk is low, when one is achieving a desirable response. In more risky situations, with either an ill-responding or ambivalent woman, flirting is seen as too costly, a poor investment of one's energy.

Taken together, control undergirds all three of these common themes, yet each appears more democratic in nature. While the men ascribed value to being clear with one's own motives and intentions, this clarity is only achieved if rightly understood by one's partner. Likewise, the timing and appropriateness of flirting within courtship is mutually determined. When using flirting to advance a relationship, partners need to make similar assessments; too soon or too late for either party would be disastrous. Finally, as clearly evident from their views on reciprocity, flirting is like a good tennis match: it's best when both sides play. And, just as in tennis, without a willing partner, it's not worth the effort.

## Themes of Contradiction

While maintaining a consistent core set of beliefs, three themes of contrasting views also emerged, giving evidence of some diversity of opinion. In each case, both ends of a continuum were represented, oftentimes within a given group or discussion. There was marked contradiction about the advisability of flirting: Is it healthy and harmless or precarious and harmful? The appropriate tone of flirting was also under debate, with some men arguing that flirting is a superficial way to get to know someone while others favored a more serious nature. Finally, there were some discrepancies as to the right approach towards flirting and which style is best, overt or covert tactics.

Some participants saw flirting as a very natural and organic part of getting to know someone. Appropriately contextualized and executed, some men expressed little hesitation about the value of flirting. When construed as a healthy form of interaction it was quickly endorsed as a positive, even essential behavior:

> *Dan*: I don't think there's anything immoral or unholy about flirting. So there's nothing wrong with Christians flirting. Christians should flirt – it's healthy social interaction, aside from pinching girls' butts or something like that. The type of flirting we're talking about is mainly healthy interaction so yeah, I think there's a Christian way of flirting that's fine.
>
> *Jason*: Is it harmful? You got me. Is it biblical? As I see it, procreation is so therefore flirting is.

Indeed, for these men, flirting is not out of character with one's beliefs but perfectly aligned as a way of getting closer to a woman. Not scandalous or problematic, flirting is actually a helpful way of pursing a relationship, something seen as an ordinary and natural drive:

> *Caleb*: Yeah, it's more like a part of our daily lives than we think it is. I think we flirt all the time, in most interactions with the opposite sex whether it's like a little or a lot.
>
> *Dave*: I think it's already been said but I think it's a natural thing, done by every person because we're always on the lookout for a future mate 'cause that's how we were created, that's how we are designed. It's a totally natural thing, just let it be.

In contrast to these consenting opinions other men raised great concerns about the possible risks and harms of flirting. Rather than a natural, even God-appointed form of interaction, flirting was characterized as fraught with problems stemming from misrepresentation, misunderstandings, and damage to the other person. As would be expected of anything considered dangerous or potentially harmful, it was not endorsed:

*Mark*:   I'm going to say that it's dangerous not so much in that you can get burned but sometimes when you get in the habit of flirting with people, you send like the wrong message out that you're interested, and then that just leads to awkward turtle time and you get the reputation for it.

*Doug*:   Yeah, it can be misleading because you can easily lead someone on by flirting with them.

*Ryan*:   I think it's a dangerous thing if you have no intention of following through.

For some, flirting was not universally harmful, but it has the potential to turn problematic:

*Adam*:   I mean it's fun to flirt with just people who are friends and fun to flirt with the intention of actually being a girlfriend but there are always points where it goes too far and it can bring a lot of pain and a lot of hurt and a lot of trouble when done inappropriately.

With these sentiments the men might be voicing an internal contradiction: flirting seems to be natural and everyone does it, but my church or pastor or parent says it's bad. In a book widely read by the participants, Joshua Harris asserts that any form of romantic relationship before one is ready to marry is wrong, that intimacy without lifelong commitment can be devastating, and that women *and* men should practice the highest standards of purity so as not to cause damage to the other person.[16] These ideals are largely incongruous with mainstream culture and the participants' discrepancies may be a result of these mixed messages. While movies, television, and more liberal minded peers claim that to flirt is to be human, books such as Harris's and the perennial Christian classic, Elizabeth Elliot's *Passion and Purity*, make the opposing position seem the more acceptable option.[17]

Similarly, participants struggled with the tone of flirting. If an action is deemed shallow or superficial, it likewise seems trivial or of little consequence. For some, flirting clearly falls into this category and is hardly worthy of serious consideration:

Danny: Flirting is usually pretty harmless, it's like surface level.

Ken: Yeah, I'd say there's only so much substance to it. You don't have to have a goal, really. You just want to get to know these people better.

One participant voiced his position more metaphorically:

Charles: I don't know, when I see two people flirting, I think of two butterflies [laughs]. I was gonna throw it out there. I think of two butterflies dancing around not getting much done.

Jason: I kind of think of superficiality too.

As with the tension between healthy and harmful, in much the same way that some participants trivialized the role of flirting, others magnified its consequences beyond the here and now. For these men, flirting is a more serious enterprise based on long-term repercussions. From a conservative ideology, the goal of dating is (at some point) marriage and anything potentially related to finding one's life partner is of more significance:

Matt: I think there's a whole other aspect of dating and flirting that comes up because you, you joke about the whole marriage thing all the time, but I mean there's actually like a serious thing. I mean, the people that we meet might end up being our spouses some day so there's even a little extra effort that goes into it.

Dameon: All right, I would say flirt with a purpose. Like don't, as much fun as it absolutely can be, don't flirt for flirting sake.... Don't flirt just because it's fun and you get that rush. Flirt with like, intentions or means in mind, like don't just waste it. Flirt with someone you actually want to get to know.

At the heart of this contradiction seems to be an uncertainty over the precise nature of flirting. As one participant claimed, "It's all part of a game, baby." But whether the game is a folly to pass the time or a serious, strategic enterprise seems to be in question. Though some people might quickly dismiss all flirting as innocent fun, these men seemed far less certain to make those claims. Caution was more the rule of the day, as summarized by one participant:

Cooper: I'd say be wise in who you flirt with because it's not easily taken as just a game. It's something that's serious. You're dealing with people and oftentimes, you can hurt people pretty easily by just playing.

One final source of tension was the appropriate approach towards flirting. If one chooses to flirt – and based on their conversations this is not a foregone conclusion – is it better to be brazen or bashful? Undeniably, there are few hard and fast rules when it comes to flirting, with much left to personal style or preference. Men wrestled with the tension of wanting to be noticed and attract attention while alternately seeing the value of flying below the radar, being more smooth in one's approach. For some, flirting was an act of showmanship:

*Jacob*:   Flirting is using verbal or physical language to make yourself more identified.
*Gabe*:   Yeah, more noticed than your competition.
*Caleb*:   Going out of your way to make yourself known –
*Gabe*:   – like peacocks open feathers
*Steve*:   – it's upping your value
*Tim*:   – separating yourself
*Dan*:   The goal is to do something that separates you from all the other guys.

From this lively exchange it's clear that for some men flirting is a way to be on display, both to a potential partner and to others competing for her attention. In this case the shamelessness of one's flirting is an attribute, a position strongly supported by an evolutionary perspective. Survival of the species does not go to the timid but to the brave, and in a world where competition for a mate is real, every advantage counts. As one participant noted:

*Ryan*:   You try to offer something unique.

Not everyone shared this flair for the outlandish. For some men, strategies of concealment seemed more effective or appropriate. A commanding presence accompanied by crass dialogue were frowned upon as they tended to be viewed as objectifying women and at odds with a more traditionally conservative mindset, as mentioned by these men:

*Garrett*:   I think there is a lot less of the overt thing happening [with us]. You know a guy is a lot less likely to walk up to a girl and say something about her chest. That would be standard for some, but not gonna happen here.
*Tim*:   The difference is the guys, they don't want to be that way. There's just a lot more respect for women. It will be cleaner, subtler.

Here, overt connotes crude, but, as is clear from the two examples, overtness may take many forms. A distinction may help explain the contradiction: be bold about yourself but coy with her. When it is discouraged, the participants were referencing overtly flirty or outrageous words addressed to a woman. In contrast, when obvious flirting is endorsed, the men were speaking more of their own actions or projected image. Once again, one measure of what's valued is relative risk. Certainly, bold self-presentation has the potential to be ill-received and when one's attempts to be distinct are received as ordinary, it likely stings. Comparatively, however, those risks are less harsh than "in-your-face" rejection – a possibility when one approaches a woman too bluntly – or unreturned emotions, when one makes one's affections obvious. In two different groups a common theme emerged: subtle flirting is best to hide your real feelings:

> *Trey*: I guess if it's real attraction I don't want to make it obvious that I'm flirting. Yeah, I'll go over the top if it's not real. If I'm just messing around or I was put up to it by some of the guys.
>
> *Isaac*: I think a guy would use the excuse that it's friendship level because they don't want anyone to know that they really do have a crush on the girl.
>
> *Frank*: That's so true.
>
> *Isaac*: So they'll say it's a friendship when really they do have a crush on her, they just don't want other people to know.

While one might be emboldened by less serious affection, it seems to be more common to downplay genuine interest. Drawing once again on research regarding flirting styles, a more overt approach to flirting is likely more in keeping with a playful flirting style that values capturing a target's attention without an expressed desire for a relationship than with either a sincere or inhibited style, both of which have more long-term objectives.[18]

## Conclusion

While applied ethics is often concerned with such noble endeavors as the bioethics of stem cell research or stewardship of the environment, flirting may be as fertile a ground and no less noble an enterprise for moral decision-making. The actions of both women and men are often driven by their beliefs. In the case of flirting, those attitudes have significant sway. Conservative men cling to purity in motive, valuing sincerity and honesty. Only under these conditions is flirting advisable and deemed appropriate. They carefully weigh the timing, stressing the relationship-advancing potential of flirting. Finally, they see their actions in relation to the other person and emphasize the reciprocal nature of the exchange. Not to be misunderstood as being entirely in unison, there are points of divergence even among those with a shared ideology. Tensions arise related to the harmfulness of flirting, the overall tone of flirting, and the obviousness with which one should flirt. While not reaching a firm conclusion, their struggle with these issues clearly refutes a modern view that only women worry about relationships. In this moment of truth, what does it mean to be risqué yet respectable, bewitching without being devilish, and enticing but not tempting? Clearly, there's plenty of work here to be shared between the sexes.

## NOTES

1  *Hitch,* directed by Andy Tennant (Los Angeles: Columbia Pictures, 2005). "m"
2  Albert E. Scheflen, "Quasi-Courtship Behavior in Psychotherapy," *Psychiatry Interpersonal and Biological Processes* 28 (1965): 245–57; Michael R. Cunningham and Anita P. Barbee, "Prelude to a Kiss: Nonverbal Flirting, Opening Gambits, and Other Communication Dynamics in the Initiation of Romantic Relationships,"in S. Sprecher, A. Wenzel, and J. Harvey (eds.) *Handbook of Relationship Initiation* (New York: Psychology Press, 2008), pp. 97–120.
3  David B. Givens, "The Nonverbal Basis of Attraction: Flirtation, Courtship, and Seduction," *Psychiatry* 41 (1978): 346–59.
4  David D. Henningsen, "Flirting with Meaning: An Examination of Miscommunication in Flirting Interactions," *Sex Roles* 50, 7/8 (2004): 481–9.
5  Matthew F. Abrahams, "Perceiving Flirtatious Communication: An Exploration of the Perceptual Dimensions Underlying Judgments of Flirtatiousness," *Journal of Sex Research* 31, 4 (1994): 283–92.
6  Ellen Fein and Sherri Schneider, *The Rules: Time-Tested Secrets for Capturing the Heart of Mr. Right* (New York: Grand Central Publishing, 1996).
7  Monica Moore, "Nonverbal Courtship Patterns in Women: Context and Consequences," *Ethology and Sociobiology* 6 (1985): 237–47.
8  Abrahams, "Perceiving Flirtatious Communication."
9  Givens, "The Nonverbal Basis of Attraction."
10  Mary Riege Laner and Nicole A. Ventrone, "Egalitarian Daters/Traditionalist Dates,"*Journal of Family Issues* 19 (1998): 468–77; Mary Riege Laner and Nicole A. Ventrone, "Dating Scripts Revisited,"*Journal of Family Issues* 21, 4 (2000): 488–500.

11 The description provided is a very brief overview of the methodology. Further details regarding the demographics and procedures can be obtained from the author.

12 Barney G. Glaser and Anselm L. Strauss, *The Discovery of Grounded Theory: Strategies for Qualitative Research* (New York: Aldine, 1967).

13 The names have been changed for all participants.

14 Henningsen, "Flirting with Meaning."

15 Jeffrey Hall and Michael Cody, "Individual Differences in the Communication of Romantic Interest: Development of the Flirting Styles Questionnaire," *Conference Papers – International Communication Association* (2008): 1–56.

16 Joshua Harris, *I Kissed Dating Goodbye* (Sisters, OR: Multnomah Books, 1997).

17 Elisabeth Elliot, *Passion and Purity: Learning to Bring Your Love Life under Christ's Control* (Grand Rapids: Baker Books, 1984).

18 Hall and Cody, "Individual Differences."

CHAPTER 3

# LOVE FOR SALE

Dating as a Calculated Exchange

 The notion of dating is often tied to romantic hopes of a lifelong partnership and often romanticized as a moment of "magic," as described in popular movies such as *The Notebook* or in self-help manuals about how to find "the love you have been looking for." In these and other examples the process of dating is assumed to be defined by a level of intense intimacy and attachment, unbridled passion, and an experience that it was all "meant to be." Dating relationships are often assumed to be reflective of the "ultimate friendship" in that the participants accept one another wholly and unconditionally.

While we agree that romance is a form of deep friendship, we reject the idea that it must be unconditioned. Unconditional attachment is rarely realized and, we argue, neither prudent nor morally supportable. We also reject the idea that romantic pairings are, or ought to be, founded on notions of "love at first sight," or that "it was just meant to be." Rather, guided by social scientifically supported research and animated by recent work in ethics, we argue that human beings' behavior is explainable and rightly guided by rational self-interest. To do so, we begin with an exploration of some historical accounts about how and why people date, then examine research on how people decide to initiate relationships, and then turn to how they react to moments when such relationships are not going well. We then argue that considerations about dating relationships are analogous to those of complete friendships, and then round out the essay with an argument against the notion of unconditional love.

## Why Do We Date? A Brief History of Dating

A review of the cultural anthropology of dating illustrates that human beings pair off carefully and with an eye on their interests. Before the twentieth century, individuals partnered in order to fill a variety of political, social, and economic ends, such as the merger of properties and families and the attainment of social position.[1] Dating during this period was referred to as "courtship" and often involved a male visiting with a female in her home, at a church social, or a local dance. The results of such visits were controlled by the woman's parents, who ultimately determined when dating turned to marriage by determining when land would be turned over to the couple or when the male would be allowed to work for his new family. Courtship was thus not primarily an institution to gratify the romantic aspirations of the young couple, but rather was intended to determine whether a man could support his wife. If "love" were a factor, people expected it to blossom after marriage. But love was not tied to passion or romance; it embodied an openness, sincerity, and connection that would stand the test of time.[2]

The loosening of kinship ties and the migration to new homesteads soon weakened parental influences on courtship. By the twentieth century, the rise in urban environments brought dating out of the home and into unchaperoned spaces. But, then as now, dating cost money. Economic considerations had always shaped the structure of dating norms, but in the modern era the male's role was to pay for dates.[3] This served an important "signaling" function: it showed how a male could direct and provide for a couple's shared life. The male's ability to pay for fancy dinners, flowers, chocolate, and all things decadent figured in the woman's conception of romance. But by the 1970s the counterculture imperative of defying traditional expectations resulted in a dominant cultural norm founded on men and women as equals. In turn, sex increasingly became an important part of some dating relationships. Changes in sexual norms, however, also brought the acceptability of sexual relations that were *not* an indicator of dating or romance, as seen in cases when couples have sex as a "hookup" or in cases of "friends with benefits."[4] Further, a growing

🐾    JENNIFER A. SAMP AND ANDREW I. COHEN

awareness of the implications of unprotected sex and the rise of AIDS seemed to dampen the ideal of uninhibited sexual passion.[5]

## Calculated Relationship Initiation and Maintenance

Leading theories concerning relationship formation largely conclude that the decision to initiate a dating relationship is not based on fate. It is instead a function of how individuals assess several considerations. One consideration is attraction to another. Judgments of attractiveness are often a product of three considerations: (1) *physical*, whereby individuals assess whether romantic prospects are physically appealing; (2) *social*, in that prospective partners are assessed by the degree to which they could open up or provide an enhanced world of interaction and activity; and (3) *instrumental*, whereby individuals are assessed as to whether a prospective partner will help accomplish a task or assignment. While attraction may result from all or a combination of these three needs, physical appearance is a dominant predictor of attraction in the early stages of a potential relationship. Across gender and sexuality, body symmetry and body proportionality are considered to be attractive and associated with other positive qualities, including intelligence, success, and competence.[6] We do not maintain that this research shows human beings unfailingly do whatever is in fact in their rational self-interest. But it does show that *human beings act for reasons* – even if they misunderstand what those reasons are or how significant they are. So, for instance, human beings may overestimate the significance of physical attractiveness and consequently pass over potentially fruitful relationships with partners who might not make it to *GQ* or *Cosmo* covers, or they might stay in dysfunctional relationships with persons who could easily grace such magazine covers. But their attachments are not *unconditioned*.

The degree to which each of the factors described above contributes to decisions related to relationships is rooted in the motives and goals that people have for forming relationships. Considerable research supports the notion that the salience of particular attributes is different for individuals seeking short-term versus long-term engagements. Those with short-term motives place greater emphasis on qualities such as physical attractiveness and sex appeal. Those who have long-term goals are more likely to emphasize the importance of commitment, dependability, emotional stability, and the capacity to love. Other motives may not be tied to goals associated with forming short- or long-term relationships, such as forming a relationship to promote personal growth or to enlarge one's social network.[7]

A motive-based explanation for forming and staying in relationships is reflected in exchange theory, which assumes that individuals follow a "pleasure principle" whereby they seek and pair with partners with whom interaction promises to be rewarding rather than costly.[8] Rewards are associated with positive experiences that one gets from a relationship that he or she could not get otherwise, such as lending a sympathetic ear, sharing a favorite activity, or having monogamous sex. Costs are the "negatives" experienced as part of being in a relationship with another, such as having to spend time with a partner's family members who are not enjoyable, the implicit prohibition against spending time with friends who are not "couple friends," or maintaining sexual exclusivity. Interdependence theory[9] builds on principles of social exchange and adds the important caveat that relationships are interdependent. Thus, interdependence theory explains why relationships are assumed to be maintained when rewards exceed the costs, yet adds an explanation as to why individuals stay in relationships that appear to be "costly" to outsiders. In particular, the theory stipulates that individuals make two sorts of judgments: (1) *comparison level*, which is a person's expectations for a given relationship, and (2) *comparison level of alternatives*, which refers to the value of rewards that could be obtained in a different relationship or in being alone. Most ideal relationships will fall into the category of those where an individual's comparison level is exceeded and their comparison level of alternatives is low. Thus, such an individual would see his or her dating relationship as ideal and unparalleled by other opportunities. Many relationships, however, are far from this ideal. Many relationships stay together even when an individual's comparison level is low, in particular when it is perceived that better alternatives to the relationship (including being alone) do not exist (that is, when comparison level of alternatives is also low).

## All "Perfect" Dating Relationships Stumble, but Not in the Same Way

In any intimate relationship, daters encounter challenges. Jealousy, deception, and infidelity are among the more forceful challenges in close relationships, but even mundane disagreements or misunderstandings highlight that the process of carrying on a romantic relationship is not automatic.

JENNIFER A. SAMP AND ANDREW I. COHEN

Inevitably, even the best-intentioned individual leads a partner to believe that he or she has violated a norm. Considerable research suggests that successful relationships overcome challenges, great or small, by communicating and negotiating about perceived transgressions. This process of discussion, response, and mutual adjustment entails a willingness to consider the importance of the relationship in light of anticipated future payoffs and the cost of overcoming current challenges. This is not to say that individuals always frame relationship maintenance in such terms, or that they always respond correctly to the reasons relevant to their case, but only to indicate that social science supports the idea that people have to *work* to sustain their relationships, and that they are at least disposed to consider alternatives should the transgression seem sufficiently severe. For example, research suggests that for "perpetrators" the most explicit and relationally maintaining option is to seek a partner's forgiveness and to ask the "victim" to reframe the situation as a constructive opportunity for the relationship to be strengthened or redefined.[10] Individuals sometimes pursue other strategic options, however, including apologizing for wrongdoing, justifying or excusing behavior as due to some external or emotional circumstance, or even refusing to acknowledge that the behavior is a problem at all.[11] At a different extreme, individuals may instead decide to focus on their own self-sufficiency and personal autonomy.[12] Thus, people do not always act as if the relationship is "meant to be" in the face of troubles.

Given this brief review of social science research on the less rosy moments of dating, we suggest that two important claims emerge. First, *unconditional love is not part of dating.* People who consider prospective romantic partners are typically not animated by a belief in unconditional love. Whether they acknowledge it or not, they have standards. Dating consumes resources. It consumes emotional and financial resources, and it comes with what economists call "opportunity costs." Spending time with a romantic prospect means you're not spending time reading alone, playing video games alone, or spending time with other friends. Is it worth the sacrifice? People make their best guesses. If someone does not measure up, she or he is not pursued. The choices people make before relationships begin and in their early stages can be understood as complex functions of various considerations. Some social scientists build their careers constructing such functions and measuring people's behavior. People constantly evaluate their prospective and developing relationships in terms of their expectations and the reality of the relationship, but obviously, once a relationship is more established and more committed, the stakes begin to change.

Second, *there is no unconditional love in committed relationships.* Just as when dating, a relationship brings rewards but entails costs. Couples in committed intimate relationships give and receive without much thought to amounts – in the short term. But challenges invariably arise. There are no committed relationships without occasional conflict. Of course, people handle conflict in many ways. The choices people make when there is some conflict in committed relationships can be studied and measured, and can be expressed as complex functions of many considerations. Some social scientists earn their keep studying these, too. But they have always found that romantic partners are at least prepared to consider whether their relationship is worth sustaining. They have not found unequivocally that romantic partners are typically animated by (or that their behavior can be explained by) any notion of unconditional love.

While we are suspicious that there is such a thing as unconditional love, we are not prepared to assert that there cannot be such a thing. We doubt there is; we suspect that the lovers are ignoring the ways in which their love is conditioned by considerations they choose not to acknowledge. Their love arises and is sustained by various considerations, and their love can be defeated. Experience confirms this. Passion often wanes, and if commitment is not strong enough, attentions wander to potentially better prospects. But we are prepared to admit there might be a love that resists any changes in circumstance. Some lovers or prospective lovers might take that as an ideal worth emulating. So suppose all the social science research has not persuaded you that people act on what they take to be reasons (and so, would act differently if the reasons changed). In keeping with that idea, we next move beyond social science to argue that the notion of unconditional love is gravely misguided and ethically unsupportable.

## Dating as a Particular Genre of Friendship

A romantic relationship is a type of friendship, in that it is a voluntary relationship founded and sustained on reciprocated good will and mutual caring.[13] The parties care about each other. They take pleasure in each other's company. They wish the other well. They take delight in the other's successes and share in the other's failures.

Among other things, a friendship is a relationship for the mutual exchange of values. Now, a friendship is not like a business relationship, where the parties are very careful to tabulate costs and benefits and demand a *quid pro quo*. Unlike such relationships, friendships feature exchanges of goods that often have no market value. And unlike such relationships, friendships can and sometimes must be a forum for asymmetric exchanges: sometimes we support friends by giving more than we receive. All friends enjoy spending time with each other and have good will. But as far back as Aristotle, philosophers have distinguished among various types of friendship. First, there are *instrumental* friendships of utility or pleasure. Such friends' mutual commitment is not especially strong. They care for each other as a function of what the other can provide. These friendships can be valuable and rewarding, but what makes the friend valuable in such cases is something incidental to the friend as a person. The poker buddy, the pleasant neighbor good for local gossip, the "friend with benefits," the witty maintenance crewmember at the apartment building – we might treat such persons with good will and enjoy their company. We may even call them friends. But the friendship would only be a function of how well the person fulfills other goals we have. We are not committed to the other person for who she is, but for what she provides us. Other persons could just as readily provide what we get from her. If circumstances change, we would readily withdraw our affections and commitment without any great disruption to our self-image or view of the world.

By contrast, in "complete friendships" persons care for one another for who they are, and are committed to them as ends in themselves. In complete friendships the friends do not merely take an interest in each other's affairs as a means of achieving pleasure or utility.[14] No doubt, good friends are sources of pleasure and utility. But in complete friendships one wishes a friend well and promotes his or her wellbeing not merely as a means to some end, but as an end in itself. One takes an interest in the friend for whom he or she is and not for what he or she can provide. One wishes the friend well for her own sake. In complete friendships one takes the friend's wellbeing as part of one's own. This is part of what explains Aristotle's remark that the friend is "another yourself";[15] friends amplify what you care about; they provide what you cannot get on your own; and they are a forum for cultivating virtue and achieving the rewards of companionship and mutual caring. And so, as Aristotle points out, friendship of the complete sort is among the greatest goods in the good life.[16]

Aristotle and other philosophers maintain that such complete friendships are rare, but they are essential to any complete life. A life featuring all the goods except such complete friendships would be judged seriously impoverished and not worth living. All the longevity, health, toys, fame, money, and sex are ultimately worthless unless they are part of a life featuring complete friends (and, ideally, when they are shared with complete friends). This is not to say that longevity, health, toys, fame, money, and sex are worthless. They might also be a part of the good life. But no life, rich or poor, has the chance of being a decent life unless it features complete friends.

We offer the account of friendship because we agree with the consensus among philosophers writing on the topic: a certain sort of complete friendship is key to any good life. We also believe that the best romantic relationships are those in which the lovers are complete friends. Complete friends, though, are not, and must not be, unconditionally devoted to each other.

To be clear: romantic prospects and partners in the early stages of a romance might very well attend to each other as a means of promoting utility and pleasure. But their choices are calculated to make good impressions, cultivate intimacy, and generate the sort of spontaneous other-regard characteristic of the mature complete friendships found in lasting and committed romantic attachments. You take care to look good and seem interesting early in the relationship because you want the relationship to escalate. You pay attention to your partner's interests in order to show that you can care about his or her welfare. You "put on your best face," literally and figuratively, in order to encourage and perpetuate your partner's further interest. Basically, we "practice" commitment in order to explore whether we wish to invest in a relationship. We explore whether we wish to bring the relationship to the point where we are automatically disposed to advance the partner's good for his or her own sake.

Complete friends treat one another with a respect and spontaneous affection that is mutually enriching. We want friends like that in our lives and we want to be such friends. This is the highest and most rewarding form of romantic attachment: we treat our lovers as ends in themselves whose interests we regard as worth promoting as ends in themselves. Our lovers are "other selves" in that we include their welfare in assessments of our own. What is good for your lover, other things being equal, is good for you. Lovers who are complete friends genuinely think that way. Their wellbeing is part of what constitutes one's own wellbeing.[17]

This is but a sketch of a wider theory of romantic love. In a wider theory we would discuss several other key themes, such as what justifies romantic love, the ways in which love uniquely figures in the good life as a special form of friendship, and how and whether love is a moral phenomenon. That is not our task here. Here our task is only to argue that unconditional love is misguided. It is to this to which we now turn.

## Against Unconditional Love

Consider the ideal romance as a sort of complete friendship. If we can show that even a complete friendship is properly conditioned, then we will have opened the door to show that the same is likely true of a committed romantic relationship. Good friends are there for each other because they care, not because they hope to register a debt that they can call in later. Good friends have a shared history of a shared life, and they do not second-guess their friends. This is not to say that they must or would stop short of offering a friend advice or constructive criticism. But their attachment to their friend is not dispensable the way a bottle of shampoo might be. They stick by their friends in good times and bad because that is what friends do. They do not regard their attachment as a burden; it is part of how they understand their own wellbeing.

A romance featuring a complete friendship would typically be above accusation, suspicion, or the tabulating of accounts. But even in a complete friendship (and, we believe, in the most rewarding of intimate romances), friends' mutual commitment is and must be conditioned. Otherwise their attachment is not to each other as persons and is not a part of a good life.

Persons in a deep romance may sometimes describe their love in poetic terms as absolute, eternal, and unconditional. An unconditioned attachment is one that knows no bounds. Among the bounds it does not and could not know are considerations that could defeat it. If nothing, in principle, could defeat the love, then the love is not a response to the person's inherent value as a dynamic being. The love is not an expression of one's highest values. It seems to be an attachment without reason and without regard to reason. We have names for such devotions. They are neuroses.

But let us do more than assign a derogatory label. Consider again the notion of a boundless "love." A commitment that knows no bounds is unfailing. But if it were genuinely unfailing, the discovery that one's lover is secretly a child molester who murders his/her victims would not undermine the attachment. If it would not, then the least we can say is that such an attachment is morally deeply problematic and potentially profoundly self-destructive. Now, of course, in our most tender and intimate moments we do not promise undying love conditional on non-performance of child molestation or spouse battery. And the fact that we are open to reconsider the attachment on discovery or development of deeply worrisome behaviors does not make the love any cheaper. One can still love a person as an end in his/herself, treat the advance of his/her welfare as part of one's own, and delight in one's lover's gains and share in one's lover's losses with all the authenticity and emotional depth and spontaneity characteristic of "true love." That commitment, conviction, and attachment are not undermined by the fact that one is disposed to end the relationship or reconsider its terms on discovery of some unsavory character traits.

But, of course, it is one thing to discover a lover is a child molester; it is another to discover that one's lover snores, leaves off the toothpaste cap, or has a different (or what you think is "crazy") view of where to set the thermostat. When two lovers are complete friends, their love does not change in any substantial way for insubstantial circumstances. Indeed, the best loves are those that evolve with the lovers: just as we are each dynamic persons who develop over time, so too our committed loving relationships evolve with us to cement our commitment through changes.[18] This suggests that even in the best of romantic friendships, partners are prepared to reconsider the terms of the relationship at certain points. This is not to suggest, however, that romantic friends must be vigilant to discover whether their partners are secretly child molesters. Without any good reason to think otherwise, the good friend is spontaneously involved in his/her friend's life and supports his/her projects without second-guessing the friend. But should some disturbing traits emerge, a concern with integrity and moral decency should have one reconsidering a relationship.

More broadly, any friendship or dating relationship – especially including complete ones – is a forum for the exchange of certain values. Sometimes relationships change in a way that makes it no longer appropriate to remain as a couple. This is the fodder for the unfortunate tales of divorce and other broken relationships. But that we are sometimes rightly disposed to end a relationship should it no longer seem fruitful to continue does not necessarily show that we are in it for the wrong reasons or that we regard a lover in the wrong way.

Sometimes persons in such relationships will be exposed to real risks, not just from being hurt by the objects of their affections, but by being vulnerable to the loss of their loved ones. But this risk is typically remote, and the gains from true love are enough to discount the chance of loss, either by being automatically disposed to "take a bullet" for one's lover, or by suffering the anguish of losing a loved one to disease or tragic accident. That one is disposed to withdraw one's affections should a relationship deteriorate, or should one's lover turn out to be a raving lunatic, does not cheapen one's love. It makes it a proper response to the actual value one's lover represents, and to the value of having one's lover in one's own life.

## Conclusion

The majority of Americans still believe that marriage affords them the best opportunity to enjoy a good life, and they continue to express the desire to marry.[19] Dating is one road to this ideal paring. We have discussed some of the social science theory that illustrates how individuals cultivate, nurture, and sustain their relationships according to assessments (conscious or not) of the significance of many considerations. We have cast love as a sort of complete friendship. There are great rewards and some risks to any intimate relationship. Lovers who are complete friends may speak in certain poetic terms about their boundless commitment. They speak and think in such terms because it makes sense to do so. But lovers who share a complete friendship, we argue, rightly sustain the relationship provided no horrific defeating conditions emerge. True love knows bounds. If it didn't, it would not be part of a good life.

## NOTES

1   Stephanie Coontz, *Marriage: A History* (New York: Viking, 2004).
2   Ellen K. Rothman, *Hands and Hearts: A History of Courtship in America* (New York: Basic Books, 1984).
3   Beth L. Bailey, *From Front Porch to Backseat: Courtship in Twentieth Century America* (Baltimore: Johns Hopkins University Press, 1988).
4   Mikayla Hughes, Kelly Morrison, and Kelly Asada, "What's Love Got to Do with It? Exploring the Impact of Maintenance Rules, Love Attitudes, and Network Support on Friends with Benefits Relationships," *Western Journal of Communication* 69 (2005): 49–66.
5   Susan Sprecher and Pamela C. Regan, "College Virgins: How Men and Women Perceive Their Sexual Status," *Journal of Sex Research* 33 (1996): 3–15.

6    J. H. Langlois, L. Kalakanis, A. J. Rubenstein, A. Larson, M. Hallam, and
     M. Smoot, "Maxims or Myths of Beauty? A Meta-analytic and Theoretical
     Review," *Psychological Bulletin* 126 (2000): 390–423.
7    Glenn D. Reeder, "Perceptions of Goals and Motives in Romantic
     Relationships," in Susan Sprecher, Amy Wenzel, and John Harvey (eds.)
     *Handbook of Relationship Initiation* (New York: Psychology Press, 2008),
     pp. 499, 516–18.
8    John W. Thibaut and Harold H. Kelley, *The Social Psychology of Groups*
     (New York: Wiley, 1959).
9    Harold H. Kelley, John G. Holmes, Norbert L. Kerr, Harry T. Reis, Caryl
     E. Rusbult, and Paul A. Van Lange, *An Atlas of Interpersonal Situations*
     (New York: Cambridge University Press, 2003).
10   Vincent R. Waldron and Douglas L. Kelley, "Forgiving Communication as a
     Response to Relational Transgressions," *Journal of Social and Personal
     Relationships* 22 (2005): 723–42.
11   Bernard Weiner, Sandra Graham, Orli Peter, and Mary Zmuidinas, "Public
     Confession and Forgiveness," *Journal of Personality* 59 (1991): 281–312.
12   Jennifer A. Samp and Denise H. Solomon, "Communicative Responses to
     Problematic Events II: The Influence of Five Facets of Goals on Message
     Features," *Communication Research* 26 (1999): 66–95.
13   Andrew I. Cohen, "Examining the Bonds and Bounds of Friendship,"
     *Dialogue* 42 (2003): 321–44.
14   See Aristotle's discussion of complete friends in *Nichomachean Ethics*,
     Books VIII and IX. (This is widely anthologized and appears in many edi-
     tions of Aristotle's works.)
15   *Nichomachean Ethics* IX.9, 1169b6.
16   *Nichomachean Ethics* IX.9.
17   Lester Hunt, "Flourishing Egoism," *Social Philosophy and Policy* 16 (1999):
     72–95; reprinted in Russ Shafer- Landau (ed.) *Ethical Theory* (Oxford:
     Blackwell, 2007), p. 202.
18   Amelie O. Rorty, "The Historicity of Psychological Attitudes: Love Is Not
     Love which Alters Not When It Alteration Finds," in Neera Badhwar (ed.)
     *Friendship: A Philosophical Reader* (Ithaca: Cornell University Press, 1993),
     pp. 73–88.
19   William G. Axinn and Arland A. Thornton, "The Transformation in the
     Meaning of Marriage," in Linda J. Waite (ed.) *The Ties That Bind:
     Perspectives on Marriage and Cohabitation* (New York: Aldine de Gruyter,
     2000), pp. 147–65.

# CHAPTER 4

# THE DATING ELEVATOR

Pushing the Right Buttons and Moving from Floor to Floor

Imagine two individuals, Ann and Bob, who are the sole occupants of an elevator.[1] One (it matters not which) has asked the other to embark on this elevator ride, and the two have consensually entered the cabin and are now engaged in mostly superficial discussion. Once inside, Ann pushes the button that will take them to the second floor, and on the way she tells Bob a bit about her family. He responds by asking the polite follow-up questions one would expect, then shares some information about his family and (introducing a new topic) tells her how his father motivated him to become an accountant. Upon doing so, he pushes the button for the third floor. Ann hesitates, concerned about the prospect of being in an elevator with an accountant, but for now she does nothing. More discussion takes place, hobbies and interests this time. It is Bob again who pushes the button for the fourth floor. When they get there, Ann is troubled. As Bob begins talking about more personal information, informing her of a medical condition and the therapy he is undergoing, he starts to push the button for the sixth floor in an apparent effort to bypass the fifth floor altogether. Her level of discomfort is now substantial; she stops him and pushes the button instead for the first floor where the jaunt began. During the short ride down, she rehearses the lines Bob has heard before. There is an apology, a claim to have enjoyed the ride, a declaration that Bob should not blame himself because it she who is to blame – she just isn't over her "fear of heights"

yet and isn't ready to go any further with anyone. Once back on the first floor, she waves, tells him she hopes to see him occasionally in the lobby, and walks out quickly when the doors open. Bob, meanwhile, lingers a bit before departing, contemplating what went wrong and what could have been. Perhaps he should wait a while before calling for another elevator – but then he sees Charlotte across the way, thinks otherwise, and heads off in her direction.

Philosophers have long been interested in aspects of human relationships. In ancient Greece, Aristotle wrote of friendship and social interaction with others as generally being an essential part of the good life – the type of life appropriate for human beings. Most philosophers concur. These are, after all, aspects of humanity itself; they are part and parcel of who we are. Although the history of philosophy is littered with disagreements about just what constitutes human nature, there is substantial agreement that it is highly social. Observation reveals that with few exceptions, we seem to desire and even require the company of other people. Most of us choose to live in communities with others. We value friendships and family, and there exists the persistent desire to find that special someone, that significant other with whom we can share our innermost selves.

It should not be surprising, therefore, that philosophers would have something to say about the topic of dating and that a book such as this would make its way into the public arena. Of course, since it can rightly be said that philosophers have something to say about, well, almost everything, perhaps the point should be put more strongly: given the longstanding interest in the topic of dating, social theory, and human nature, it should not be overly surprising that philosophers might have something *interesting, helpful*, and, in general, *worthwhile* to say about this topic.

The specific issue we address in this essay is the ongoing change that exists in every dating relationship. This change is represented by the metaphor of an elevator. The philosopher Heraclitus observed 2,500 years ago the prevalence and significance of change and is known for the idea that everything changes but change itself. He meant this to apply to reality and offered the claim in response to the observation that objects in nature (e.g., trees, streams, people) are constantly changing in that they are moving, aging, and/or transitioning from one stage to another. As Plato later pointed out, however, reality consists of more than just such physical objects; the purely conceptual can be just as real (or even more real, according to Plato) as physical matter. As human beings, we are subjects of various emotional and psychological realities, as well as other non-physical realities that we construct in our interactions with each other. The dynamics inherent in the dating process is one example of the interaction between these realities. A dating relationship is very real and is undergoing constant change.

In the next section of this essay we will review our definition of "dating," including what it is and what it is not. This step of defining key terms is central to philosophy and is needed here in order to demonstrate the parallel between the phenomenon of dating and the elevator ride of the sort in which Ann and Bob engaged. In our third section we provide more detail about this parallel, and in our fourth we review some strategies that make sense in light of this elevator idea of dating. Our fifth section includes some ethical considerations along the lines of virtuous behavior and individual moral character.

## What Dating Is

It may seem strange to theorize about something that appears to be rather natural and straightforward. We meet others; we decide we like them and would like to get to know them better; and we date those people. True, this is easier said than done. If dating were really so simple it would not be the case that so many struggle with it.

Philosophers are prone to thinking about, and constructing theories of, even those aspects of our lives (such as dating) that initially seem straightforward. This is not to suggest that we in the field of philosophy regularly engage in *over*analysis. (Do we? Perhaps this question itself should be analyzed?) Indeed, upon reflection the phenomenon of dating should seem much less straightforward than we often suppose. The issues involved are practical, psychological, and ethical, and they require significant reflection and self-assessment. In this way the issue of dating is, from a philosopher's perspective, ripe for careful scrutiny, for it is often the case that issues in need of the most examination are the ones that initially appear beyond the scope of philosophical concern.

The definition of dating that we offer here will not fit all instances commonly accepted as such. This should not count against the definition we offer, however. One of the tasks in our field is to consider all facets of a term's meaning, to contemplate what is acceptable (or not), what is consistent (or not), and what is actually or potentially problematic with the meanings. Based upon the findings we then offer revisions to the definitions and proceed to further discussions which incorporate those definitions. Without having clear definitions in hand the ensuing analysis would be sloppy and prone to misinterpretation.

So without further ado we present the operational definition of dating, which is *the process of exploring, investigating, and gauging the possibility of eventually reaching "commitment" with another person.*

Several aspects of this definition should be emphasized. First, the meaning of "commitment" here is the point at which the individuals in the relationship make the decision to marry or otherwise make permanent their status as partners, where "permanence" is not an absolute. There can be levels of commitment and these levels depend on the circumstances of the arrangement and just how "permanent" that arrangement is. Absolute permanence is a fiction. In line with the elevator image, society's emphasis on the institution of marriage might make this particular arrangement the "penthouse" whereas a mutual decision to live together but not marry might be represented by something slightly less grandiose, a floor or two below. A mutual decision to maintain the status quo at any point should be interpreted as a decision to exit the elevator together at the floor agreed upon, wherever that may be.

The second point to be noted is that the aim of exploring the possibility of commitment need not be a conscious exercise; there need not be a formal "intention" along these lines. It could, and in many cases probably is, simply the execution of an innate process that occurs without a lot of thought for the future. After all, dating is, at root, a function of human nature, in that we seek out significant others for various reasons and purposes, such as companionship, intimacy, and reproduction. "Dating" simply appears to be our society's method of carrying out the innate process.[2] As such, the concept of a "date" is a societal construction, but that just means it is the way in which we as civilized, autonomous, responsible individuals have institutionalized that which is natural. So, the 20-something-year-old at a bar, the teenagers who (using the language of long ago) "go steady" for a while, and the 30-something-year-old who subscribes to an online dating service are all trying to find one who is compatible, whether or not this is the conscious aim.

A third point is that dating itself, and the question of whether any two people are "dating," may be a matter of degree. Although we will work with the definition presented above, we acknowledge that there is no hard and fast algorithm for determining when a relationship becomes a "dating" relationship. Some relationships clearly do fall within the realm of dating and some clearly do not. For other relationships, it will just be unclear, at least temporarily. Rose and Gregory, the characters portrayed by Barbra Streisand and Jeff Bridges in the movie *The Mirror Has Two Faces*, were very good friends. It was a dating relationship from his perspective because he was assessing compatibility for commitment; it was not a dating relationship from her perspective because there was no physical intimacy. Imagine her shock when he proposed to her and indicated the marriage would work because it would be free of physical intimacy.

The point is that sometimes we just don't know whether we are actually dating (generally) or even whether we are on a date (in a specific instance). Communication between the two individuals who may or may not be dating is likely important here, but that communication can be very difficult. After all, opening the lines of communication also opens the possibility of rejection or failure, so there is a natural tendency to be cautious.

In general, there is likely a positive statistical correlation between age and dating, in that those who are older tend to be more aware of the elevator, more focused on the destination (be it penthouse or other), and less apt to date simply for fun with no sense of any degree of commitment.

This leads into a fourth point, which is that dating "for fun" may or may not count as "dating" in our sense. Dating should be fun – not enjoying the company of one's date suggests that a return to the first floor is in order – but "dating" as we define it does not allow for fun to be *the* aim. Individuals who are "sex buddies" are not involved in a dating relationship. They do not conceive of themselves as being in an elevator on a possible trip to the penthouse (even if this accurately describes a rendezvous of theirs). More accurately, the analogy would be that of two people wandering the lobby who occasionally duck into the janitor's closet or a dark corner and have themselves some fun before sneaking back into the crowds in the lobby. Other examples of uncertain status might include work colleagues who go to dinner; individuals who are friends spending significant time together; 16-year-olds who attend a school dance together; and many other situations. As indicated above, whether or not any or all of these couples is on a date greatly depends on communication between the individuals.

There are two final points to be made here concerning items which are not included in the definition and are thus not deemed relevant to "dating" as such. The first is gender. The two-person image we describe rules out relationships among three or more people from counting as dating; however, the two people involved need not be of opposite sex. The other item lacking in our definition is that of sex or physical intimacy in general. It is not uncommon for a "level" of relationships to be judged largely by the level of sexual involvement. We believe this is a mistake in the context of our definition of dating. There are different types of intimacy and sharing, and while the sharing which is physical intimacy is likely of some importance,[3] in the long run it is no more important than the sharing of deeply held beliefs, emotions, dreams, and thoughts of other kinds.

## The Elevator Image

To reiterate, the aim in providing the elevator as an apt metaphor for dating is to highlight the inherent inclination toward change that is part of dating relationships. The two individuals in the relationship control it to the extent that they push the buttons and send the car on its way, either up or down. There are other factors affecting the movement of the car/relationship that are more difficult to control, including momentum and gravity, for instance. We assume that the basic image is clear enough, and we leave to the reader the freedom to insert into the following discussion any additional details that might make this metaphor more conducive to his or her own personal experience.

In pushing buttons and calling for the relationship to be taken to a higher floor, dating individuals are looking for more intimacy, the aim (conscious or not) being to find out more information that will aid them in deciding how far to go in the relationship and, ultimately, whether to take it all the way to "commitment." There is almost constant movement. Indeed, the point of being in an elevator, or a dating relationship, is to change levels. If an elevator car stalls, something is not right; if a relationship stalls and is not moving at all, the sense of awkwardness is palpable.

At any given stage of a dating relationship a decision is needed about where to go with it. The obvious option is to continue up – to continue spending more time together and learning about each other. Perhaps early on the discussion is about the basics: jobs, interests, hobbies, and the like. Should both parties be comfortable with each other and wish to continue, the discussion might tend toward matters of a more personal nature. These can include topics such as personal insecurities and families, and future plans and dreams. At higher levels, the discussion may be

JOHN ROWAN AND PATRICIA HALLEN

more personal still and include, for instance, past relationships with others (how they began, why they failed, what the feelings were at various stages) and the place of a successful long-term relationship in one's life plans. At what point does the discussion in the elevator become explicitly about the relationship itself? Sharing internal feelings about the person with whom you are riding carries risk and can of course be quite scary! Finding an answer to this question is extraordinarily difficult because of the numerous variables to consider, and the appropriate strategy will depend on the specifics of the particular relationship developing.

There is any number of considerations to bear in mind when dating. What is the velocity of the elevator? Sometimes a floor or two may be skipped, as when both parties feel wonderful about the relationship and communication is successful, thereby allowing for agreement to proceed upwards more swiftly. There are even rare instances in life where a single date is sufficient for the parties to know that they desire commitment.[4] What about the nature of the communication between the individuals? The philosopher David Hume (1711–76) wrote that natural justice among people was usually not a matter of explicit but implicit communication. He utilized the image of two people in a canoe who are both aware of a general destination but end up at a specific destination through observing the other person – the direction in which she paddles, the speed, the style, and so forth. This basic idea that much can be learned through observation and implicit communication can be applied to many contexts of human relationships, including dating. "Decisions" to move to a higher level may be communicated explicitly but they may also be implicit understandings between the individuals.

Other than pushing the buttons to go up, there are other options when in the dating elevator. First, one may decide to go down a floor – to slow down the relationship. This is often taken as a harbinger of the end, so if the intent really is to continue the relationship but at a lower level of commitment, the communication of this intent must be very clear. Second, one may decide to push the "hold" button and keep the elevator car where it is, with no upward or downward movement. Here, too, such an action is usually interpreted as a sign of an imminent trip back down, and as noted previously, two people together in an elevator that is not moving creates an awkward and even tense situation for both. This is especially true when the "hold" button is pushed between floors, as the suddenness of this action is jarring and usually accompanied by a demand for immediate information: "Before we go any further with this, I need to know exactly [where you were last night / what you mean by saying you someday want a 'traditional' marriage/why you would support such backwards legislation/why you didn't tell your mother that I was divorced/ (insert favorite line here)]." Third, one may push the "alarm" and call for immediate assistance: "Get me out of here!"

Gravity is a factor in dating regardless of direction. When going up, the ascent on the elevator must overcome natural gravitational forces. When the elevator is holding steady, the downward pull of gravity must be exactly countered so as to keep the elevator steady, and as noted above this is difficult and generates a strong sense of awkwardness. When going down a floor, gravity can be difficult if not impossible to manage and may well result in a full trip all the way down. In many cases the descent stops only when the first floor is reached. At the end of a relationship the trip down will be short and uneventful when the ride has been brief. For those rides that have been more extensive and have involved significant heights of commitment, the descent is more precarious. It may be smooth but it may be quite turbulent, perhaps even to the point of bringing on nausea; it may be slow but more likely will be fast, thus risking a crash and burn that can result in significant (emotional) injury and scarring, perhaps to the point of making it psychologically difficult to enter the elevator again in the near future.[5]

## Strategies

What it means to "move up," then, is difficult to put into words though not overly difficult to understand. It involves an increase in the level of commitment, the sense of obligation, the sense of how important the relationship is, the increased willingness to take on each other's feelings and commitments, and the increased willingness to make oneself vulnerable by relying on the other person. With this in mind, we present some basic strategies recommended for a maximally enjoyable elevator experience.

First, be yourself. If, to repeat our definition, dating is the process of exploring, investigating, and gauging the possibility of eventually reaching "commitment" with another person, then what is the point of presenting to your potential partner a mere facade? Sometimes our desire to be in a successful relationship is so strong that we end up compromising who we are, either because there are aspects of ourselves we don't want the other person to see or because we want to alter our true selves to better suit the other person and/or the relationship. The problem is that this approach is likely not sustainable over a long period of time. The image to bear in mind is a lifetime in an elevator (or perhaps the penthouse) with this person. That's a long time to spend with someone and a lot of energy invested in not being yourself. Psychologically, maintaining a pretense over such a long period of time is not feasible, and practically, it isn't something that will make either party happy. It's better to find out earlier on if personalities, interests, and styles are not conducive to a long-term relationship (i.e., a long time together on an elevator).[6]

Second, the same thinking above can be applied in the other direction: allow the other person to be himself or herself. Trying to change one's potential partner is an endeavor fraught with hazards. The subsequent strategy is to avoid riding all the way to the penthouse (commitment) with someone not adequately suited for you. Here again, a desire to be in love and make a relationship work is the culprit. That desire can induce a willingness to unwisely bend the criteria for what one considers a successful relationship and generates a sense that the other person can be changed. The hazard is a false sense of optimism for what the future might hold. It amounts to "settling" for a partner and a relationship that will include certain undesirable aspects. No relationship is perfect, of course, but most people know this and establish their own particular reasonable criteria for success; it is these criteria, already with reasonable imperfections built in, that are sometimes bent further in the name of making a relationship work.

A pragmatic approach is appropriate as a description of this second strategy. Philosophical pragmatism, which bears certain similarities to the more common everyday usage of the term, focuses on the importance of usefulness. Although scholars of pragmatism often apply the concept of usefulness to deep questions of truth and knowledge, they also apply it to questions of how we ought to live.[7] The application of pragmatist philosophy to the dating elevator suggests that if we should act in the way that is most useful to the achievement of our goals, and if our goal in dating is primarily to explore, investigate, and gauge the possibility of eventually reaching commitment with another person, then the appropriate course of action is to be ourselves and allow the person we are dating to be himself or herself. Failing to do this is failing to engage in an accurate assessment, which defeats the very purpose of the relationship.

Moving on to the third strategy, it is better for the elevator to go slowly rather than quickly, all things considered. In one way this is commonsensical, but in the midst of a relationship with all of its excitement and its potential to skew rational thinking, making a conscious effort to revisit this strategy regularly is important. The end of a relationship, which is almost always difficult, is more likely to come about when things progress too quickly. One party may panic and press the button for the first floor or even the alarm button. Even if there is sudden reconsideration of one's position rather than outright panic, there will be motivation to press the button for a lower floor, which more often than not generates a sense of awkwardness and doubt about the relationship which signals its end. Proceeding slowly, with due caution, will minimize the likelihood of this backtracking.

Fourth, maintain an "awareness" of the movement of the elevator in terms of its velocity and location. At times, the company one keeps in an elevator can be so engaging and captivating that one loses track of the floor one is on. In order to avoid the panic or reconsideration noted above, be aware of what your dating partner is doing! Some partners are sneaky and strive to push buttons discreetly in an attempt to elevate a relationship to a more serious level before the other person realizes what is happening. Sometimes the focus is so heavily on the conversation that one doesn't even realize when she herself unconsciously reaches out and pushes the button for a higher floor. "Oh goodness, I did move us along, didn't I!" The suggestion is not that the direction/movement of the relationship should always be at the forefront of one's mind. That would certainly have a negative effect on the conversation and general interaction! "OK, where is this going? Are we more 'serious' than we were last time I asked, an hour ago?" Rather, the suggestion is that it not be forgotten amid everything else!

Fifth, communicate! At times it will be appropriate and helpful for the individuals to talk about the relationship itself. Doing so has a way of putting the daters more at ease, while not doing so has a way of creating tension and uncertainty; much like the elephant in the room that no one is acknowledging, spending time with someone in an elevator will feel strange without some occasional acknowledgment of that fact: "Hey, we're in an elevator!" A dating relationship without the same sort of occasional acknowledgment will be similarly problematic.

Sixth, bear in mind the importance of friendship and its role in successful dating. There is a fair amount of research suggesting that the best relationship partners are those who enjoy a deep sense of friendship.[8] Each takes on a psychological commitment toward the other person's goals, wishes, and desires. Indeed, with true friends this is something that cannot be helped. Frank finds himself wanting Elise to be happy. He wants her to enjoy her traditional Tuesday evening out with her friends because it makes her happy; he wants her to participate in the chorus which rehearses on Friday evenings because it makes her happy; he wants to occasionally make dinner for her at his place, even though she never reciprocates (because she doesn't like cooking), because it makes her happy. In short, her happiness generates his happiness because he is fully committed to her goals and in essence adopts them as his own. This is a core aspect of true friendship. By contrast, Harry does not like it that Geraldine has a standing weekly dinner outing with her friends or that she never returns the favor of sending him cute cards through the mail. Driven by insecurity or an excessive sense of "fairness," he (unlike Frank) is unable or unwilling to commit to deep friendship and thus makes it a habit of regularly stopping the elevator and asking for explanations.

Sometimes there is talk (in both scholarly circles and in the population generally) of balancing friendship and (romantic) dating against each other, as if they were mutually exclusive and cannot occupy the same moments in time. We reject this. The strategy of clear communication is especially beneficial in this context; occasional discussion in the elevator of romantic feelings for each other can occur even while the basic aspects of friendship are taking place. Indeed, they can reinforce each other. Irene says to Jason, "I really like you and want you to go away with your friends for the weekend if that will make you happy. If it will help, I'll feed your cat while you're gone. I'll miss you, because I love spending time with you, but maybe we can get together for a date next week after you return." Such an approach reinforces and strengthens the friendship while at the same time emphasizing romantic feelings and the desire to date and be together. The two do not compete; they are mutually reinforcing, not mutually exclusive. Of course, the motivation for action is crucial. One who makes offers to help his friend/dating partner but requires compensation or payback is not acting in accordance with the deep sense of friendship we are describing. If Irene and Jason are real friends, then he will not expect payback, but ideally he would not have to worry because Irene, being a true friend, will find herself wanting to do things for Jason anyway.[9]

The seventh and final strategy we will offer here stems from the fact that everyone, at some point, feels the need to end a relationship. So have an "exit strategy"! Waiting too long to develop a way out usually makes for even more discomfort during the ride down than is usually the case. Like a fire escape plan, you may never need it, but you don't want to be caught in a situation where one wasn't developed. The specific plan will likely vary depending on the specifics of the particular relationship. Relying on friends or family can be quite useful.

Though not a specific strategy for dating, it is also recommended to bear in mind throughout the elevator ride that if it does end and you both return to the lobby, word will spread about the experience, each of you conveying it from your own perspective. This realization may affect some of the ways you choose to interact with your date.

## Elevator Ethics

Ethics is the branch of philosophy pertaining to right conduct. Usually the emphasis is on the treatment of others, though it is also appropriate to consider your own interests as well. There are different theories (approaches) to ethics, among them some with an emphasis on the consequences of action, some with an emphasis on the motivation of action, and some with an emphasis on good moral character. We will utilize the last of these, specifically virtue ethics and its idea of good moral character as being virtuous.

A virtue, Aristotle wrote, is a habit that lies in the golden mean, which is the point of appropriate balance between the two extremes of deficiency and excess. One acts well (ethically) when one acts in accordance within the mean, the right distance from deficiency and excess. Honesty, for example, is a virtue. One can fail to act virtuously by not being honest enough (deficiency), but one can also be too honest (excess). One who tells others every single thing that is on his mind (à la Jim Carey in the movie *Liar Liar*) will say things that are inappropriate and rude and thus not be viewed as virtuous. So the idea is that acting ethically means being a good person, and a good person is one who strives for and is generally successful in acting virtuously – acting in the golden mean. One who does so acts ethically in that she treats others well and also treats herself well in that she acts in ways that give her the best chance of achieving her goals. This virtue-based approach to ethics is therefore particularly useful in the context of dating, since it speaks to one's own aims in dating and also to the appropriate ways of treating one's dating partner.

The example above, honesty, is one of the central virtues that should be practiced in dating.[10] It can be said that we owe it to our dating partners to be honest, and that is almost certainly true, but we also owe it to ourselves and to the relationship. Without honesty, there is little or no chance of the relationship working out well. Again, the virtue of honesty requires that one be neither deficient nor excessive. The vice of deficiency is what we think of most often in the context of not being honest. Lies are told ("I'm not seeing anyone else," "I love you," "I've never had a sexually transmitted disease") and vague or misleading statements are given ("I haven't had too many boyfriends in my life"). Being in the golden mean of honesty probably requires avoiding lies and seriously misleading statements. When it comes to being excessively honest, one must consider how much information to share. Volunteering to one's date that the dress she is wearing makes her look slutty or overweight, for instance, would likely count as an excess of honesty. In the movie *Look Who's Talking*, Mollie, the character played by Kirstie Ally, goes on a series of dates in search of a good father figure for her young son. On a first date with a certain man, her date discusses with her problems he is having with his bowel movements, and does so during dinner. In addition to sharing information that is appropriate (if ever) only at a higher level, he is failing to act virtuously by being excessively honest. (Given the dinner setting, he is also probably failing to act in accordance with a virtue of tactfulness!)

Another very important virtue in the context of dating is that of courage. In order to engage in successful dating, one must be willing and able to make oneself vulnerable to criticism and rejection. This is not an easy thing to do, and the unwillingness to put oneself "out there" leads to the problems cited in the previous section about compromising who one is. Overcoming self-doubt and being yourself, your true "self," takes courage. One who acts with deficiency in this way treats oneself poorly by putting oneself in an ultimately regrettable position, and it also treats one's dating partner poorly by misleading her into thinking she is different from the way she really is. On the other hand, an excess of courage, what Aristotle called foolhardiness, is likely to result in unwanted consequences. Having too much courage could motivate one to attempt a kiss (or much more) at inappropriate places, times, or levels of the dating elevator. It could also lead one to be overly honest.[11] Again, the guiding principle with courage, as with all the virtues, is that of balance.

When it comes to loyalty, the appropriate point of balance is likely to change as the elevator climbs higher. In general, it makes sense that more loyalty to one's dating partner is appropriate as the relationship grows more serious. Still, there will always be the possibility of an excess – of being loyal to a fault.

The basic idea – that the virtues should represent balanced ways of acting – is likely clear. Other virtues that may be relevant to the context of dating include gratitude (being sufficiently grateful without acting over the top), patience (accepting certain faults – within limits!), and trustworthiness. There are other virtues that may be less applicable to dating specifically though still important for good character generally; these might include, for instance, industriousness or beneficence. Overall, it is the core idea of balance that should be emphasized. Losing one's balance in an elevator can have some very unfortunate results.

## Concluding Remarks

The image of the elevator can be helpful. It is not a perfect metaphor for dating, but there is more than enough to make for an apt comparison. Bearing in mind this image of dating as pushing buttons and moving from floor to floor, the central idea we will emphasize in the conclusion is balance as discussed in the previous section. Balance applies to what we want, or even need, in a relationship partner: no relationship is perfect, and while striving for that unrealistic goal will result in failure, one's standards for success should not be unduly compromised. Balance applies to the strategy of communication: a successful relationship will likely involve the right amount of communication about the relationship itself, neither too little nor too much. Balance applies to the velocity of the elevator in its upward climb: although the recommendation is to go slowly, going *too* slowly can cause a relationship to stall out. Balance applies to the sixth strategy, friendship: one should be a friend to the person one is dating and thus adopt the other's goals and wishes as one's own, and while this should be done without a motive of reciprocation, it is wise to keep in mind the possibility for being exploited. And there are any number of other aspects of dating to which balance is applicable.

Finally, balance applies to the fourth strategy, awareness of the elevator's movement. Dating should be fun, but be aware of the ongoing changes and make sure to push the right buttons to get you where you want to go!

## NOTES

1   In using names beginning with A and B, we are already utilizing a philosophical method whereby names themselves are not relevant. Instead, the persons involved can be represented simply by letters (although having names consistent with those letters makes it more fun and more interesting!).

2 Beginning in the second half of the twentieth century, feminist philosophers, as a response to a longstanding emphasis on individualism (dating back to the Enlightenment), began reminding us of the importance of the social aspect of human nature. At the same time, there are some feminists who maintain that the specific institution of dating in its current form is oppressive to women in various ways.

3 Without giving anything away, this importance is suggested by the way the storyline in *The Mirror Has Two Faces* progresses.

4 We maintain that while this is possible, it is extremely rare. More likely is the explanation put forth by the contemporary philosopher Simon Blackburn, that what we sometimes call "love at first sight" is something else, often lust or something along those lines. See Simon Blackburn, *Lust* (New York: Oxford, 2004).

5 Human emotion is certainly the core contributor to the difficulties that accompany the end of a relationship. Sometimes, however, this apparently "negative" emotion that usually coincides with a breakup is, ultimately, a positive contribution to one's longer-term happiness. Emotions are obviously complex, and oversimplification should be avoided. For a clear and accessible discussion of emotion by a contemporary philosopher, see Robert Nozick, *The Examined Life* (New York: Simon and Schuster, 1989).

6 Remember that if the aim is not long term – if it is a relationship in which both individuals are clear about their aims being purely short term – then it is not really "dating," since it is not consistent with the definition we provided.

7 Philosophical pragmatism has American roots in the scholars John Dewey, Charles Peirce, and William James, whose work became popular in the early part of the twentieth century. One of the more famous contemporary philosophers was Richard Rorty (1931–2007).

8 See, for example, John M. Gottman and Nan Silver, *The Seven Principles for Making Marriage Work* (New York: Random House, 1999). Although the focus is marriage, the principles are just as well suited for general relationships. Indeed, much of the advice is applicable to important decisions at the beginning of dating relationships or even decisions about whether to date a particular person in the first place.

9 Aristotle conceived of friendship largely in terms of intimacy, and since intimacy is a key component of successful dating, there is certainly a connection to be made between friendship and dating. For specifics, see Aristotle's *Nicomachean Ethics*, Book VIII, Chapter 4.

10 Philosophers talk about "practicing" a virtue because of the great difficulty in achieving the habit, which is the golden mean. Knowledge of the mean's location is not innate, according to Aristotle and most philosophers. Rather, it is learned through experience.

11 The suggestion here of a connection between courage and honesty speaks to a deeper level of virtue ethics, one where the appropriate overall balance

among the various virtues is considered. An adjustment in the practice of one virtue may affect other virtues, or there may be conflicts in which one must choose one virtue over another. The ancient Greeks referred to justice as the supreme virtue because justice was about the harmonious relationships among all the virtues – what is sometimes referred to as the "unity of the virtues."

PART II

# NO-NO'S
Dating Taboos

CHAPTER 5

# "CRAZY IN LOVE"

## The Nature of Romantic Love

 Oftentimes people who are "in love" are on such an emotional rollercoaster that they feel as if they are losing their minds. They might have dramatic and unpredictable mood swings with excessive happiness or sadness, increased or decreased energy and sex drive, the need for more or less sleep, and other serious shifts in their mood, energy, thinking, and behavior – shifts that are not unlike those characteristic of bipolar disorder (commonly called "manic depression"). At other times lovers may feel confusion, an inability to make decisions, a sense of living in a fantasy world, nervousness, anger, and a sudden indifference to the opinions of others – symptoms not unlike those of paranoid schizophrenia. Rest assured, however, that these emotions can be normal during the "falling-in-love" stage of one's life: we even see evidence of these wild feelings in classical times. Ancient Greek philosophy helps us to understand the different qualities of love, while recent biopsychological studies of the brain cast light on physiological reasons for the cross-cultural "craziness" that is romantic love.

## The "Symptoms" of Love

Believe it or not, lovesickness was a serious diagnosis for nearly two thousand years. (Many of our current diagnostic tools, such as the ICD-10 or the DSM-IV, are less than a hundred years old.) According to the classical model of the four humours, if love becomes too fiery, vital fluids will evaporate; the result is a cold state, "love melancholy." Until that model collapsed in the eighteenth century, the mental health field (such as it was) acknowledged passionate love as a "sickness."[1]

Even earlier, the Greeks believed romantic love was a form of madness that they called *mania theiai* ("madness from the gods"). Gods such as the deities Eros or Cupid afflicted lovers by shooting arrows or darts into them. The well-known poem "If Love's a Sweet Passion," from Henry Purcell's *The Fairy Queen* (1692), nicely expresses this "love dilemma":

> If Love's a Sweet Passion, why does it torment?
> If a Bitter, oh tell me whence comes my content?
> Since I suffer with pleasure, why should I complain
> Or grieve at my Fate, when I know 'tis in vain?
> Yet so pleasing the Pain is, so soft is the Dart,
> That at once it both wounds me, and tickles my Heart.[2]

While we no longer classify love as a mental illness, sometimes love can involve, as Frank Tallis says, "obsession, irrational idealization, emotional instability or emotional dependency."[3] While these symptoms *can* be found in the insane, they are more commonly found in lovers – who may feel they are going insane. If you are experiencing some of these "symptoms," rest assured that you are not alone, and know that there are reasonable explanations for your feelings.

## What is Love?

What is the nature of romantic love? In English we use "love" to express many things. At one end of the spectrum is the simple declaration that we really enjoy something ("I love chocolate!"). At the other end of the spectrum is the deep connectedness and emotional intimacy that we convey when we say "I love you." What are the differences between romantic love and other types of love? Greek philosophy and literature distinguished four kinds of love: *eros, philia, storge,* and *agape.* We will examine each in turn.

*Eros* is at the root of our contemporary notion, "erotic." As you can imagine, this is an exciting form of love to talk about (and engage in!).

It refers to a passionate desire or longing for something or someone, usually a sexual desire. I say "usually" because *eros* has been given different explanations at different times in history. For Plato, the desire of *eros* should be for eternal things, like knowledge. If the longing is based on the appreciation of physical beauty, it should become something greater than the physical beauty of one person: it should become the appreciation of transcendental beauty, the true beauty that exists in the world of Forms or Ideas. For Plato and later Platonists, the physical love of a person should be redirected to the Ideal beauty of which physical beauty is a mere reflection. Physical love is not a proper form of love *per se*. (Think here of the term "Platonic love," love which does not involve a sexual relationship.)

Most often *eros* has been used to focus especially on sexual or other all-consuming longings. C. S. Lewis used the term to describe the sense of being in love that is really more like blind devotion, the type of love at the root of many of the tragedies in literature. The passionate longing of *eros* is energizing, yet can be very painful – especially if the feeling is not reciprocated.

*Philia* is often translated "friendship," but for the Greeks it also involved loyalty to family and nation. The motive of this friendship and loyalty can be either the lover's best interest or it can issue as a result of the attributes of the beloved compelling the lover's love (such as when you are moved by the consistent kindness of a person). Aristotle's *Nicomachean Ethics* (350 BCE) describes the qualities of people with good character, those who, in his view, will thus have the best friendships and be loved. People with no virtues can have friendships based on utility (for business transactions), and they may have a friendship based on pleasure (perhaps they both enjoy fishing), but they will not be capable of a deep friendship, one that enjoys the other's good character and one in which each truly cares for the other.

Another type of love recognized in ancient Greece is *storge* (pronounced STORE-gay), which is natural affection that grows through familiarity, like that felt between a parent and child. It occurs naturally and does not necessarily come as a result of those qualities that make one loveable. Think here of a parent's love for the rebellious teenager who fights the parent at every turn: *storge* transcends such a situation because it develops naturally.

*Agape* (a-GAH-pay) describes the ultimate love – love that is unconditional and self-sacrificing. It is often used in the Christian Bible to describe God's gift of himself to humans and the love that humans give one other when they emulate God. This form of love is thought to be the purest form of love possible, far exceeding the other types of affection. C. S. Lewis identifies this form of love with the virtue of charity and says that we should strive to love everyone with this unconditional love.

A romantic relationship can have elements of all of these forms of love. In Greek philosophy and literature romance often has physical and emotional desire (*eros*), a deep and lasting friendship (*philia*), and self-giving love (*agape*). A relationship limited only to *eros* would involve simply appreciating the person as an object – not as a human with dignity and personality. On the other hand, a romantic relationship that lacked emotional and physical desire might be lacking in the passion that can both express and increase love. *Philia* adds a further dimension to a romantic relationship that can help a couple feel connected and weather the trials of life. Lastly, *agape* can reach the deepest levels of a relationship: as the partners constantly keep the good of the other in mind, they continually nurture each other and avoid self-destructive (and relationship-destroying) patterns.

## The Biology of Romantic Love

In their overview of scholarship on love, Helen Fisher, Arthur Aron, and Lucy Brown conclude that human romantic love stems from a brain system common to mammals that allows for mate selection and thus the reproduction of the species. In fact, the traits exhibited by humans in romantic love are the same as those characteristic of mammalian courtship attraction, including "increased energy, focused attention, obsessive following, affiliative gestures, possessive mate guarding, goal-oriented behaviors and motivation to win a preferred mating partner."[4] Moreover, since romantic love centers around "mate *preference*," the authors hypothesize that this love in humans is a developed form of the neural mechanism that lower mammals use in mate selection.

In a previous study the same authors used functional magnetic resonance imaging (fMRI) to watch the brain activity of 17 people who classified themselves as "in love." They discovered that looking at an image of the person's beloved (versus images of acquaintances) activated the parts of the brain (i.e., in the right ventral tegmental area and the right caudate nucleus) that are associated with "reward and motivation func-tions," increasing the production of dopamine and other "feel-good" chemicals.[5] This experience is cross-cultural, and sometimes even cross-species.[6]

Couples who had been in love eight to seventeen months showed the same activity in the reward and motivation areas of the brain as those in love for one to seven months; but they also had increased activation in other areas, including those that have been associated with attachment activity in other mammals. The authors speculate that this might serve the purpose of increasing the stability of the relationship and motivating "parenting behaviors."[7]

This and similar brain imagery research suggest that human romantic love is a primary drive, designed, in part, to result in mating. It is, how-ever, different than the human sex drive, which activates different areas of the brain. In fact, the authors tell us, the drive to fall in love is "evi-dently stronger than the sex drive."[8]

The human sex drive is associated with androgens (the primary and best known of which is testosterone) in humans and primates. Humans with higher circulating testosterone levels are more sexually active. This is true also of women, whose testosterone level (and often sexual desire) rises around the time of ovulation. Though androgens are central to the sex drive, other factors, of course, play a role; cultural and religious beliefs, for example, often influence when and how often the sex drive is expressed.

The brain networks activated by the sex drive are different than those for romantic love. The sex drive and romantic love, the authors suggest, are separate but related systems "designed to orchestrate different aspects of the reproductive process."[9] The sex drive enables people to begin courtship with a range of prospective partners, while romantic love "motivates them to focus their mating energy on specific individuals, thereby conserving time and metabolic energy."[10]

The brain networks for the sex drive and romantic love do interact. For example, increased production of dopamine can result in an increase of testosterone; so the stimulation of the brain that correlates with the feeling of "falling in love" also elevates androgens, sexual arousal, and sexual performance.[11] These two systems, which respectively allow humans to sample a large range of partners and then to find a preferred partner, lead to "partner attachment," which allows humans to form a lasting bond with the preferred partner.[12]

## Rejection in Love

What happens biopsychologically when love goes awry and a lover is rejected? Fisher, Aron, and Brown did fMRI studies of 15 people who classified themselves as still in love though they had recently been rejected by their beloveds. Their preliminary findings indicate an increase of activity in "neural regions associated with risk-taking for big gains or losses, physical pain, obsessive/compulsive behaviors, ruminating on the intentions and actions of the rejecter, evaluating options, and emotion regulation."[13] These results may help explain some of the incidences of stalking, suicide, homicide, depression, and so forth that sometimes occur when a relationship is terminated.

Interestingly enough, the results of Fisher et al. differ from those of a preceding study, one done by five other scholars. In this study, "Regional Brain Activity in Women Grieving a Romantic Relationship Breakup," the impacts on brain areas were very different, and while the subjects in the Fisher study reported anger and hope that they would regain that relationship, in the second study the subjects reported more acceptance of the separation coupled with despair. In fact, participants in this "grieving" study experienced grief that involved "depressive-type symptoms lasting from days to several months," increasing their risk for clinical depression.[14] These various results do not seem to me to be mutually exclusive. It could be that the participants of the two different studies were at different stages in their grief over the rejection and subsequent loss of the relationship. Also, the Fisher study specifically looked at "rejected" lovers (and advertised for such when recruiting subjects), while the second study simply had participants who were ruminating upon the ending of the relationship and could not get it out of their minds. It could be that some of those women ended the relationship themselves but still struggled with grief over the loss of the relationship. Another difference between the studies is that the Fisher study included both men and women, while the grieving study only included women, but whether, or how, gender is significant in these scenarios has yet to be seriously explored.[15]

In the loss of a love relationship there are two main emotional stages that a person goes through. First, there is "protest," when the spurned lovers obsessively attempt to reunite with their rejecters. Biologically, the protestor's heart rate and body temperature increase, along with levels of catecholamines in the brain (chemicals similar to adrenaline that raise a person's level of alertness and activity), and cortisol, a stress hormone.[16] Protest

72    🐾🐾    MARY BETH YOUNT

often begins with what Fisher has termed "frustration attraction," which is her attempt to convey the fact that when love is frustrated, it increases. This happens because when dopamine is produced at the base of the brain (as it is when one is first separated from a source of attachment), it is "pumped up to the caudate nucleus and other brain regions where it generates the motivation to win designated rewards" such as reunification with the beloved. When, however, the reward takes a while to be produced, the brain continues producing and conducting the dopamine, thus resulting in higher than usual brain levels of this stimulant – increasing both goal-directed behavior as well as anxiety and fear.[17] Once the person realizes that this reward is unattainable, frustrated attraction then turns into "abandonment rage": this destructive anger obliterates the already tattered remains of the relationship (which eventually frees the spurned lover from the relationship after subsequent stages have been passed through).

After protest comes resignation. In this stage the despair is correlated with a disruption of many bodily rhythms: the heart rate lowers with irregular, serrated beats; sleep becomes lighter, with less REM (dreaming) sleep and frequent nighttime awakenings; circadian rhythms shift; and even the efficacy of the immune system decreases.[18] Often, the sense of hopelessness in people undergoing this is overwhelming, and nothing seems to be able to lift their spirits. Fisher explains the chemical reaction that correlates with this: as the person realizes that the reward (the relationship with the other partner) is not going to come, "the dopamine-making cells in the midbrain (that became so active during the protest phase) now *decrease* their activity. And diminishing levels of dopamine are associated with lethargy, despondency, and depression."[19]

It is clear that human romantic love, while it involves complex social factors, activates specific cross-cultural (and even cross-species, in many instances) dynamic brain systems that contribute to mate choice, a crucial aspect of reproduction. The difference between human mate selection and that of other species is that we feel more. Our brains are bigger, more complex, and have larger regions for specific activities.[20] Because of this, we are not only able to recall more and plan ahead, we also able to associate feelings with events in a different way. Our amygdala is more than twice the size of that of apes, and the role this area of the brain plays is central to generating emotions such as fear, rage, aversion, pleasure, and aggression. Even more importantly, the human caudate nucleus is twice as big as that of the great apes, and this allows us a more focused attention and a greater motivation to win rewards – intensifying the urge to find and bond with a mate.[21]

Because of the positive biochemical rewards for being in love, it can be addictive – in fact, many of the same areas of the brain become activated in love as during the use of cocaine or opioids.[22] How can rejected lovers break the accompanying cycle of tolerance, withdrawal, and relapse? Cut off all contact with the lover, remove all evidence of him/her, stay busy, and do things that are new and exciting (thereby elevating the dopamine levels in the brain).[23]

## Conclusion

Dating can be confusing. People often wonder if what they are feeling is normal, since some symptoms of love – violent mood swings, obsessive thinking, emotional dependence, and the like – can be overwhelming and even scary.

As Greek philosophy demonstrates, the multiple aspects of romantic relationships have been recognized throughout history. The Greeks usefully distinguished four types of love: physical and emotional desire (*eros*); natural, familiar affection (*storge*); friendship (*philos*); and self-giving love (*agape*). Though romantic love is predominantly associated with *eros*, all four types of love can be factors in a romantic relationship.

In addition, recent biopsychological research helps to explain the purposes and trajectories of love. Many scholars point out that the purpose of the romantic drive is to bring about mate attraction, selection, and attachment, thereby allowing for the perpetuation of the species. Understanding chemical reactions in the brain during love can help us understand how these processes happen – along with the attendant symptoms of falling in love and rejection during love.

So the next time someone refers to someone else as "crazy in love," assure the speaker that there is no need to refer to mental disorder. To be in love is to be head over heels, but in a most delightful way.

## NOTES

1   Frank Tallis, "The Year of Relationships: Crazy for You," *The Psychologist* 18, 2 (February 2005): 72.
2   Henry Purcell, *The Fairy Queen in Full Score* (London: Novello, 1903), p. xv.
3   Tallis, "The Year of Relationships."

4   Helen E. Fisher, Arthur Aron, and Lucy L. Brown, "Romantic Love: A Mammalian Brain System for Mate Choice," *Philosophical Transactions of the Royal Society B (Biological Sciences)* 361 (2006): 2173–86.

5   Helen E. Fisher, Arthur Aron, and Lucy L. Brown, "Romantic Love: An fMRI Study of a Neural Mechanism for Mate Choice," *Journal of Comparative Neurology* 493 (2005): 58–62.

6   William R. Jankowiak and Edward F. Fischer, "A Cross-Cultural Perspective on Romantic Love," *Ethnology* 31, 2 (1992): 149–55.

7   Fisher, Aron, and Brown, "Romantic Love: An fMRI Study."

8   Ibid., p. 60.

9   Fisher, Aron, and Brown, "Romantic Love," p. 2177.

10  Ibid.

11  Ibid.

12  Ibid., p. 2178.

13  Ibid., p. 2180.

14  Arif Najib, Jeffrey P. Lorberbaum, Samet Kose, Daryl E. Bohning, and Mark S. George, "Regional Brain Activity in Women Grieving a Romantic Relationship Breakup," *American Journal of Psychiatry* 161 (2004): 2245–56.

15  Although, for those who are interested, Helen Fisher did look at this briefly in her book *Why We Love: The Nature and Chemistry of Romantic Love* (New York: Henry Holt, 2004).

16  Thomas Lewis, Fari Amini, and Richard Lannon, *A General Theory of Love* (New York: Vintage, 2000), p. 77.

17  Fisher, *Why We Love*, pp. 161–2.

18  Lewis, Amini, and Lannon, *A General Theory of Love*, pp. 78–9.

19  Fisher, Aron, and Brown, "Romantic Love: An fMRI Study," p. 170.

20  Ibid., p. 148.

21  Ibid., p. 149.

22  Ibid., p. 182.

23  Ibid., p. 185.

CHAPTER 6

# I'M DATING MY SISTER, AND OTHER TABOOS

Ought I to date a gorilla, a sibling, or a blow-up doll? For most of us, perhaps, this is not a very interesting question, insofar as most of us think it unlikely that we would ever want to do any of these things. But the question is really just an arresting way of asking a more general question that should be of interest to us all. Namely, to what extent ought the fact that certain behaviors involved in mate selection, sexual activity, and interpersonal romantic interaction – what I will loosely call "dating behaviors" – are considered pathological, influence our decisions with respect to those behaviors? This is an important question, since many dating behaviors are, or have been at various times, considered pathological.

Whether an individual ought to avoid pathological dating behavior depends on how we understand the notions of "ought" and "pathology." Let's start with the former. There are at least two important senses of "ought." One is the ethical sense, in which we say that I ought to avoid doing morally wrong actions and ought to engage in morally right actions. If some pathological dating behaviors are morally wrong – as for instance most people are inclined to think that pedophilia is wrong – then to the extent that we are motivated to do what is right and avoid what is wrong, their moral wrongness gives each of us a reason to avoid those behaviors. The sense of "ought" intended in this essay is *not* the ethical sense. Rather, it is the prudential sense of "ought," according to which what

I ought to do is what is in my narrow self-interest to do, given my own preferences. The two notions of ought are very different. If I am trying to lose weight, then prudentially speaking I ought not to eat chocolate, though clearly there is nothing ethically proscribed about chocolate eating. I ought not, ethically, to cheat on an exam, but if I am confident of not getting caught and I need good marks to pursue my chosen goals, then there might be cases where, prudentially speaking, I ought to cheat. Decision theory is a formal theory that offers a framework for working out which of a range of options one ought, prudentially, to choose on any particular occasion. It tells me to choose the option that will bring me the most expected benefit or, as we say, *utility*.[1] I come to know which option is utility maximizing by knowing what my preferences are (which things I care about) and how I rank those preferences (from most to least desired) and then plugging these two pieces of information into a decision theory formula that will tell me which option yields the greatest expected amount of utility. This essay asks the question whether, in trying to maximize expected utility – in trying to get those things we most prefer – each of us ought to avoid pathological dating.

To be a little clearer, let us distinguish between a reason to avoid, or embrace, a particular option, versus having an all-things-considered reason to avoid or embrace a particular option. I have an all-things-considered reason to choose something, say dating a blow-up doll, just in case that option is the unique one that is utility maximizing. I have *a* reason to date a blow-up doll just in case there are factors that weigh in favor of dating a blow-up doll. Here is the difference. I have a reason to avoid driving into work today, namely that statistically there is some chance that I will get into an accident and be injured. But it need not be that I have an all-things-considered reason to avoid driving into work, because it might be that the convenience and time saving associated with driving outweighs the possibility of being injured, and that driving turns out to be the choice that maximizes utility. When considering pathological dating, therefore, there are two questions we can ask: whether we have a reason to avoid pathological dating, and whether we have an all-things-considered reason to avoid such behavior.

What, then, is pathological dating? The concept of pathology is one that crops up in ordinary discourse as well as in various more specialized discourses. (If you think that "pathological" is really a term of art among the medical and psychiatric professions, then "sick" will do just as well. We often find ordinary talk of behaviors, and indeed people, being sick.) There is no easy answer to the question of what pathology is and thus when something counts as pathological. But within various socio-linguistic communities we certainly find various practices being labeled as pathological. It is not the project of this essay to try and give a full exposition of the meaning of the term "pathology" or the content of the concept "pathological," and fortunately we do not need any such thing to know that the behaviors labeled as pathological will not be considered to count as such solely in virtue of being so labeled. That is, different communities, and different individuals within a community, might disagree about which behaviors are pathological, but we can expect them to agree that behaviors aren't pathological just because they are labeled as such. Rather, if those behaviors are genuinely pathological they are so because of *some* relevant feature, or property, that they have in common.

This claim is very plausible because it is surely part of the concept of "pathology" that a behavior counts as pathological only if *something* like the following is true: the behavior is a manifestation of an underlying illness or disease, or the behavior is a manifestation of an underlying condition of some kind, one that is deleterious to the individual. Since the concepts of illness, disease, and underlying condition are also underspecified, focusing on these concepts will not be enough to tell us which behaviors really are pathological. So one way we might try to figure out the nature of pathology is to examine the set of behaviors that a community counts as being pathological and to find out what, if anything, those behaviors have in common that would make it right to count them as pathologies. Given this procedure, there is scope for making one of three very different discoveries about those behaviors, and which of these we make will impact on what we should think about our decisions with respect to those behaviors.

The first discovery we might make is that there is no property in common between the behaviors that a particular community takes to be pathological beyond the fact that that they are all labeled as pathologies. The second discovery is that there is something in common between the behaviors that are labeled as pathologies, but that the property these behaviors share is not the right kind of property for us to conclude that the behaviors really are pathologies. And the third possibility is that we might discover that the property shared by the set of behaviors labeled as pathological is of the right kind for us to conclude that those behaviors really are pathologies. In what follows I will consider each of these possibilities in turn. I want to suggest that even if it turns out that the sorts of behaviors we consider to be dating pathologies really do have something in common that makes them pathological, this need not give an individual an all-things-considered reason to refrain from engaging in those behaviors.

🐾 KRISTIE MILLER

## Mere Social Conventions

Suppose that in our community romantic relationships with members of another species, romantic relationships with siblings, and romantic relationships with inanimate objects (like blow-up dolls) are all considered to be pathologies. Suppose further that we discover that there is no property that all these behaviors share except for the fact that we label each as pathological. This, I suggest, is the discovery that they are not truly pathological; rather, it is a matter of mere social convention that they are labeled as such. Let us call these behaviors *merely conventionally pathological*. If behaviors like dating a blow-up doll or a gorilla turn out to be like this, then clearly there would be no reason, grounded in the nature of these behaviors as pathologies, to avoid these behaviors. This, of course, is not to say that I would have no reason to avoid, say, dating a blow-up doll or a gorilla. If gorillas tend to accidentally squash people, then that might be a reason not to date them. If blow-up dolls are liable to suddenly deflate and cause injury to those in the vicinity, that would be a reason not to date them. But none of these reasons has anything to do with those actions being pathological.

There is, however, one reason I will quite likely have to avoid behaviors that are labeled as pathologies. Communities often negatively sanction behaviors considered to be pathological, either through legal sanctions or social disapproval. Since such sanctions will, for most people, be costs – that is they will be a source of *disutility* – the existence of these sanctions will give most of us a reason to avoid these behaviors even while knowing that in fact they are not pathologies. This is not to say, however, that such sanctions will give an individual an all-things-considered reason to avoid such behaviors. It is rational for me to choose a behavior that is labeled as pathological just in case the total utility I get from choosing that behavior is greater than the utility I would get from any alternative behaviors that I could choose. If the social costs of choosing a behavior that is labeled as pathological are high, then it might well be rational to choose an alternative behavior that is lower on my preference rankings, since the overall utility of the latter will still be greater than that of the former. So if having a romantic attachment to, say, a sock is high on my preference rankings, and having a romantic attachment to what is considered an appropriate human person is low on my preference rankings, then it will be rational to choose the latter only if the social costs of choosing the sock are really quite high and thus the overall expected utility of the sock choice is lower.

On the other hand, if the chances of being discovered to have what is considered a pathological preference are low, or if I attach almost no cost to any negative sanctions in the community, then it might be rational to choose a behavior that is labeled as pathological even if there are alternative behaviors that I rank almost as highly as the behavior in question. If I marginally prefer dating a sock to dating a person, it will be rational to do so as long as there will be no social (or other) costs associated with the sock choice that will diminish its overall utility. Equally, it might be rational for me to choose a behavior labeled as pathological if I effectively have no alternative choices: if it is my only preference with respect to a range of behaviors and if the utility of choosing that behavior is greater than the utility of abstaining from any such behavior. So it might be rational for me to date a gorilla if gorillas are my one and only preference even if the costs associated with that preference are quite high, just so long as the utility of dating a gorilla is greater than the utility of not dating at all.

## Pseudo-Pathologies

The second possibility I countenanced earlier is that when we consider the set of behaviors labeled as pathological by some community, we might discover that although there is some property that those behaviors have in common (beyond being so labeled), this property is not of an appropriate kind to vindicate the notion that the behaviors are genuinely pathological. So, for instance, suppose polyandry – the practice of one woman having multiple male partners at a time – and all the various practices associated with polyandry were considered pathologies in some community. We now know that polyandry is associated with conditions of extreme scarcity of resources. The proposed explanation for this is that societies are in part organized in a way that maximizes the chances of successfully raising children. Where resources are very scarce, multiple males are needed in order to bring in enough resources to raise a child.[2] If a society has extremely scarce resources, then insofar as it prudentially cares about successful childrearing, it has reason to organize itself around the practice of polyandry and to negatively sanction persons whose preference is, say, polygamy. Assuming that certain claims about polyandry and scarce resources are true, then in the community in question the dating behaviors that are labeled as pathological do have something in common: they are the kinds of behaviors that are antithetical to successful childrearing within that community. So it looks as though we have an explanation for why those behaviors are labeled as pathological – it is not *mere* social convention that they are labeled as such. On the other hand, it does not seem that the property in question that they share is the right kind for those behaviors to be considered genuinely pathological. Whichever way we choose to understand the broad notions of an underlying condition or disease, the notion of "being such as to make it less likely that children will be raised successfully" does not seem to be that sort of condition. We do not, in general, take it that all behavior that minimizes the success of raising children is pathological in some way: we do not, in general, think that contraception is pathological even where this prevents the raising of any children.

Let us call behaviors labeled as pathological that share some feature in common, where that feature is inappropriate for the behaviors to be genuine pathologies, *pseudo-pathologies*. If we understand prudence narrowly as each individual maximizing his or her own utility, then it is no surprise that this kind of discovery about the behaviors a community labels as pathological need not give any individual an all-things-considered reason to avoid those behaviors. The very same sorts of considerations that we encountered with respect to merely conventionally pathological behaviors will equally apply to pseudo-pathologies. Namely, there will be reasons associated with the social costs of engaging in behaviors so labeled, as well as, potentially, any reasons peculiar to a particular behavior. But in the case of pseudo-pathologies there might be additional reasons to take into consideration. For although the behaviors in question are not pathological, they have something in common. In the example under consideration they have in common that they tend to undermine successful childrearing. So an individual in that community might have a reason to avoid *all* of the dating behaviors labeled as pathological if that individual has a preference for successful childrearing. In general, an individual in a community has a reason to avoid such behaviors just in case the individual's preferences in some way coincide with what we might think of as the community's preferences. But even where this is the case, an individual who cares about childrearing might still be rational to engage in pathological dating if her preference for the pathological behavior is higher than that of her preference for childrearing, or if engaging in the relevant behavior does not substantially diminish her chances of child raising. The point, here, is that even if the feature shared by the behaviors labeled as pathological is salient to me in some way and gives me a reason to avoid those behaviors, it need not give me an all-things-considered reason to avoid those behaviors. Equally, it might give me *no* reason at all to avoid those behaviors if the features they share are not ones with respect to which I have a preference.

I have said that this essay is interested in considering what each of us ought to do given that we are considering our own narrow prudential interests. But one might also be interested in what one ought to do, prudentially, where this is understood more broadly to include consideration of the broader interests of one's community. Broad prudential reason, as we might call it, considers the total utility an action brings when summed over all the individuals in a community. If I am concerned with broad prudential reason, I will have reason to avoid behaviors that are *disutilitous* (that is, cause disutility) to the community.

Nevertheless, even when I am considering what I ought, broadly prudentially speaking, to do, it is not obvious that I will have a reason to avoid pseudo-pathological behaviors. The fact that there is an explanation for why certain dating behaviors are negatively sanctioned does not entail that those behaviors cause disutility to the community. Communities living in very resource-poor environments are more likely to survive, in the long term, if they have practices that contribute to childrearing. So a community that has, or once had, a poor resource environment will have an explanation for why it negatively sanctions certain dating behaviors. But it does not follow that the utility of the members of that community, as it now stands, is maximized by those practices. Perhaps the current environment is not resource poor. Perhaps none of the current members of the community care about childrearing or about the survival of the community into the future. Perhaps the community members plan to move to richer pastures. Since what is disutilitous to a community depends on the preferences of the members of that community, it does not follow that behaviors that are pseudo-pathological will be ones that, broadly prudentially speaking, I have a reason, let alone an all-things-considered reason, to avoid.

## Pathologies and Decisions

This leaves us with our third class of behaviors: those that are labeled as pathological and which share a *relevant* property. If there are any such behaviors, they are good candidates to be considered genuine pathologies.

One candidate to be the property shared by genuine pathologies is surely one that is posited by evolutionary biology.

According to what evolutionary biologists call the theory of inclusive fitness, we all behave in ways that, on average, contribute to the successful reproduction of our genes. So one might be tempted to say that behavior counts as genuinely pathological to the extent that it decreases one's inclusive fitness. On reflection that seems implausible, since then any decision that decreases my chances of passing on my genes turns out to be pathological. But using contraception, wearing dowdy clothes, and collecting *Star Trek* figurines, though they undoubtedly decrease my chances of passing on my genes, are arguably not pathological.

More plausibly, we could focus on the kinds of behavior that have evolved as a result of being selected for. Evolutionary psychologists are primarily interested in psychological mechanisms, or modules, that evolved for us to cope with features of the environment of our ancestors, and which are responsible for many of our behaviors. With this in mind, we might suppose that the objective property that genuinely pathological behaviors share is that they result from malfunctioning psychological modules. So, for instance, evolutionary psychologists and biologists have proposed that there exist a number of evolved mechanisms for mate selection.[3] The general idea is that in the past, our female ancestors needed to detect males who could provide resources for childrearing. Those who could successfully detect those males were more successful in reproducing, and thus passed on their mate selection preferences, while those who were poor at detecting those males were less successful at reproducing and thus did not pass on their mate selection preferences. So females in our current population should share some psychological mechanisms that are responsible for detecting mates who are able to best provide certain resources.

Exactly what these mechanisms are, and what sorts of features they track, is controversial. So while the examples I give are fascinating, and are hopefully illuminating in understanding the more general point, I do not want to suggest that any of these examples offer a correct account of any mechanisms of mate selection.[4] With that in mind, here is another example. In the past females not only needed to choose males who would bring resources for childrearing, they also needed to choose males who had "good genes," that is, genes that if passed on to the offspring would make the offspring fitter. Various evolutionary psychologists argue that there are mate selection mechanisms that help females choose males with good genes. For instance, A. P. Moller argues that there is a mechanism that detects what is known as fluctuating asymmetry.[5] He hypothesizes that symmetry in one's features is correlated with better genes and higher fitness. In some animals females choose mates with higher degrees of symmetry, which has led to the idea that in humans, one mechanism of mate selection is symmetry detection.[6] Other postulated mechanisms include mechanisms that track odors and thereby attract females to males who have an odor that is associated with carrying dissimilar immune response genes (MHC genes), thus giving the offspring a better immune system.[7] For instance, women are more attracted, solely on the basis of smell, to men who have dissimilar MHC genes.[8]

The idea is not that any of us consciously looks for symmetry or sniffs out odors, or that we are consciously motivated to maximize our inclusive fitness. Rather, psychological mechanisms have evolved to track certain features, and we have certain preferences because of these mechanisms. Mate selection, then, is the result of a cognitive process that weights the various outputs of different psychological mechanisms and comes to an overall decision.[9] In light of this, we might suppose that dating behaviors are pathological to the extent that they arise from faulty psychological mechanisms that have evolved for mate selection.

Suppose that is so. Then there are at least two reasons why engaging in behaviors that are pathological in this sense might still be perfectly prudentially reasonable. Most obviously, there is little reason to suppose that acting in a manner consistent with the output of these evolutionarily driven internal mechanisms will maximize an individual's utility. The mechanisms in question evolved to enhance reproductive fitness. Some of the ways of enhancing that fitness might involve selecting mates who are reliable, trustworthy, have resources, are prepared to put time and energy into childrearing, and so forth. And some of *these* features might be ones that a particular individual prefers in a mate. But *in general* it need not be that the choices that would maximize an individual's utility will be the same choices that result from weighting the outputs of various properly functioning psychological modules. We have already noted that features that contribute to inclusive fitness need not thereby be features that maximize an individual's utility. The same is true here.

Just to highlight this, consider two quite different examples. Evolutionary psychologists use "good gene" stories to explain why women in committed relationships might be attracted to unreliable, uncommitted males, by noting that mating outside of their relationship allows them to get the good genes of the uncommitted male and the resources of the committed male. There might be a psychological mechanism that underlies that choice. But this does not suggest that it maximizes the utility of any particular individual woman to have an extramarital relationship. There might be significant social and psychological costs associated with such a choice. What is good for our genes, in terms of their probability of reproduction, is not necessarily good for us as individuals. Similarly, the notion that rape might be an evolutionary adaption (as opposed to being a by-product of some other adaptation) has recently been considered.[10] The idea is that in at least some environmental contexts, rape might be an adaptive way for men to pass on genes. This is not to suggest that rape is an ethically acceptable behavior, nor, in fact, to suggest that it is prudentially individually wise. While rape is found in every human society studied, it is also negatively sanctioned in every society.[11] Whether or not rape is an adaptation is controversial. But the point is that even if it were, which perhaps counterintuitively would seem to make rape non-pathological by the current account of pathology, it would not follow that such behavior would be utility maximizing for any individual man given the high costs associated with that behavior in our society. Indeed, even in the absence of social sanctions, such behavior might cause considerable psychological distress to the perpetrator and hence fail to be maximizing, while still being fitness maximizing.

Thus, acting as a result of input from properly functioning psychological mechanisms does not guarantee that the individual will maximize "dating" utility. Conversely, acting in a way that issues from a faulty mechanism will count as acting pathologically, on this view, even if that behavior turns out to be one that maximizes the individual's overall utility. If that is so, then it will frequently be prudent to act pathologically.

## Pathology and Utility

There is one final property that behaviors labeled as pathological could share and in virtue of which they would count as genuine pathologies: if those behaviors are ones that, given human psychology, are likely to yield disutility to those individuals who engage in them. If this is how we understand the notion of pathology, then it raises the question of why anyone would ever act pathologically. For in this sense, acting pathologically appears to go hand in hand with failing to act prudently. But I act imprudently just to the extent that I fail to maximize my own utility given my own preferences. Why would I ever do that? One explanation for imprudence is weakness of will. Suppose I want to settle down in a stable committed relationship with a view to having children in the future, but I also have a yen to date the bad-boy biker who lives over the road. Plausibly, I have first-order desires both to date a committed stable man with a view to having children, and to date the rough biker, and I also have a second-order desire to desire not to date the biker, where I have that second-order desire because I have the first-order desire to settle down. Now suppose that I nevertheless hook up with the biker. This might be as a result of a weakness of will that has led me to act irrationally. I ought, all things considered, to have avoided the biker, but I didn't. One way to think about why I might suffer weakness of will is to notice that there is a difference between maximizing utility in the sense of satisfying my preferences, versus maximizing utility in the sense of maximizing my pleasure, or as we sometimes say, maximizing *hedons*. Biker dating might maximize hedons, but not satisfy my preferences. Indeed, what maximizes hedons very often does not satisfy one's preferences. Now, some of my preferences might include the desire for hedonic utility, and indeed, if that were my most highly ranked preference, then dating the biker would maximize my utility. But if overall my preferences are best satisfied by avoiding bikers, then it is irrational not to do so, despite the fact that dating the biker might seem very attractive because it is hedonically maximizing.

If the conflict between my desire to date the biker and to avoid the biker is not understood as a conflict between preference satisfaction and hedonic maximization, then there is another way we can understand the conflict. Think of a person across her lifetime as being composed of a bunch of different selves each of which exists at a different time. There are my various past selves, my current self, and my various future selves, each of whom have different preferences. If my current self has a strong preference to date a biker, then by doing so she effectively gets the benefit of having that preference fulfilled, and it is some future self that fails to find herself safely settled down and in a position to have children. But if my current self refrains from dating the biker she fails to get the benefit from that interaction, and it is some future self that gets the benefit of being in a situation where she can have children. So if I date the biker despite wanting the stable relationship, we might see this as a case in which my current self maximizes her own benefit – biker dating – and in so doing fails to maximize the benefit to a later self. Whether that choice is rational depends both on the amount of utility to be had from dating bikers versus having children, and how we see the relationship between the two selves in question.

We might think that since each self is the very same person, considered at different times, the interests of each self should have the same weight. If we think that then the decision to date the biker is rational only if the utility to the current self is greater than the disutility to the future self. That is, we just sum the utilities of any choice over all of the selves to determine which action maximizes utility and is therefore the rational choice. What we know, however, is that in fact people tend not to treat the interests of their various selves equally. Rather, they tend to weight the utility of their current self more highly than that of their future selves.[12] That is to say, we tend to care less about the happiness and unhappiness of ourselves in the far future than we do about ourselves in the present and the near future. If this pattern of care were rational, then it might be rational for me to date the biker now, even if the disutility to my future self of finding herself not in a position to have children is greater than the utility to my current self.

There is a genuine question of how to weight the utilities of different stages, or selves, of a single person. Once we weight the utility of these different selves in some manner, however, we should choose the action that maximizes weighted utility across the *whole* person. Given this, if I have reason to think that some behavior is likely to lead to future disutility, I have a reason to avoid that behavior. So if dating behaviors count as pathological because, given what we know of human nature, they are inclined to cause disutility, then I certainly have a reason to avoid such behaviors. But I need not have an all-things-considered reason to avoid those behaviors.

In this circumstance behaviors count as genuinely pathological because of their likelihood of producing disutility. If I have reason to think I have some feature that makes it unlikely that engaging in pathological behavior will produce disutility for me, then I might still be rational to engage in that behavior. For instance, if I think that a behavior is likely to cause disutility by virtue of a psychological feature that people share, and if in addition I have reason to suppose that my psychology is appreciably different from others' in relevant respects, then I could have reason to doubt that pathological behaviors will cause disutility to me. For example, suppose I had statistical evidence that intimate relationships between siblings cause disutility. Suppose I also know that individuals raised in the same home are very unlikely to develop romantic feelings towards one another.[13] Now suppose I came to believe that most siblings who enter relationships are raised together. This would give me reason to think that there is something unusual about the psychology of these individuals, and therefore to give some credence to the idea that it is this psychological feature that is responsible for the disutility. If I were not raised with my siblings, then I might have little reason to think that I would experience the same disutility if I were to date one of my siblings, since I would have no reason to suppose that I share this psychological feature. In general, where I have evidence that engaging in a particular behavior is liable to cause disutility I have reason to avoid that behavior unless I have reason to suppose that I am in an unusual reference class of people for whom the behavior will not produce disutility. Under those conditions it might well be rational to engage in such behavior.

Whether behaviors that we label as pathological turn out to be merely socially conventionally pathological, or pseudo-pathological, or genuinely pathological, it will in no way straightforwardly follow that I ought not to engage in those behaviors. There will be circumstances in which dating a blow-up doll, a gorilla, or a sibling are choices that maximize utility for some individual, and therefore are the rational choice for that person.

## NOTES

1   For a nice introduction to decision theory, see M. Peterson, *An Introduction to Decision Theory* (Cambridge: Cambridge University Press, 2009).
2   J. H. Crook and S. J. Crook, "Tibetan Polyandry: Problems of Adaptation and Fitness," in L. Betzig, M. Borgerhoff-Mulder, and P. Turke (eds.) *Human Reproductive Behavior* (Cambridge: Cambridge University Press, 1988).
3   D. M. Buss, *Evolutionary Psychology: The New Science of the Mind* (Boston: Allyn and Bacon, 1999).
4   For a critical discussion of some of these claims, see S. Downes, "Integrating the Multiple Biological Causes of Human Behavior," *Biology and Philosophy* 20 (2005): 177–90.
5   A. P. Moller, "Fluctuating Asymmetry in Male Sexual Ornaments May Reliably Reveal Male Quality," *Animal Behavior* 40 (1990): 1185–7.
6   See, for instance, S. W. Gangestad and R. Thornhill, "The Evolutionary Psychology of Extrapair Sex: The Role of Fluctuating Asymmetry," *Evolutionary Human Behavior* 18 (1997): 69–88; R. Thornhill and S. W. Gangestad, "The Scent of Symmetry: A Human Sex Pheromone That Signals Fitness?" *Evolutionary Human Behavior* 20 (1999): 175–201; S.W. Gangestad, "Human Sexual Selection, Good Genes and Special Design," *Annual New York Academy of Science* 907 (2000): 50–61; S.W. Gangestad and J. A. Simpson, "The Evolution of Human Mating: Trade-offs and Strategic Pluralism," *Behavioral Brain Science* 23 (2000): 573–644.

7   C. Wedekind and T. Seebeck et al., "MHC-Dependent Mate Preferences in Humans," *Proceedings of the Royal Society London Series B* 260 (1995): 245–9; D. Penn and W. K. Potts, "How Do Major Histocompatibility Complex Genes Influence Odor and Mating Preferences?" *Advanced Immunology* 69 (1998): 411–36; E. Janssen and N. Zavazava, "How Does the Major Histocompatibility Complex Influence Behavior?" *Archive for Immunological Therapy Experimental* 47 (1999): 139–42.

8   Wedekind and Seebeck et al., "MHC-Dependent Mate Preferences in Humans."

9   K. Sterelny, *Thought in a Hostile World* (Oxford: Blackwell, 2003).

10  R. Thornhill and C. T. Palmer, *A Natural History of Rape: Biological Bases of Sexual Coercion* (Cambridge, MA: MIT Press, 2000).

11  Ibid., pp. 140–3.

12  For evidence of discounting, see G. Ainslie and Nick Haslam, "Hyperbolic Discounting," in G. Loewenstein and J. Elster (eds.) *Choice Over Time* (New York: Russell Sage Foundation, 1992), pp. 57–92; S. Frederick, G. Loewenstein, and T. O'Donoghue, "Time Discounting and Time Preference: A Critical Review," in G. Loewenstein, D. Read, and R. F. Baumeister (eds.) *Time and Decision* (New York: Russell Sage Foundation, 2003), pp. 13–86; U. Benzion, A. Rapoport, and J. Yagil, "Discount Rates Inferred From Decision: An Experimental Study," *Management Science* 35 (1989): 270–84; D. Laibson, "Golden Eggs and Hyperbolic Discounting," *Quarterly Journal of Economics* 112, 2 (1997): 443–77.

13  J. Shepher, *Incest: A Biosocial View* (New York: Academic Press, 1983).

CHAPTER 7

# JUST PUSHY ENOUGH

 In one of romantic comedy's iconic moments, John Cusack (as Lloyd Dobler, in the 1989 movie *Say Anything*) serenades Ione Skye (as Diane Court) with Peter Gabriel's "In Your Eyes." Diane has broken up with Lloyd and told him to leave her alone, but Lloyd doesn't comply. Instead, he shows up at her house at daybreak and stands there resolutely, holding his boom box above his head. Though she doesn't immediately admit it, Diane is won over by Lloyd's serenade – and so are we, as viewers. Lloyd's serenade is so charming that we don't stop to consider what he's really doing. He's violating Diane's boundaries, and in more ways than one. He's violating her expressed wish to be left alone. He's showing up uninvited at an ungodly hour – usually an intolerably rude and pushy thing to do. For all he knows, he's waking her up and making a scene (surely the loud music will wake the neighbors, too!). He might even be trespassing on her lawn.

In *The Sure Thing* (1985), John Cusack engages in another instance of charming boundary violation. Daphne Zuniga (as Alison Bradbury) has rejected John Cusack (as Walter "Gib" Gibson), but again he won't take no for an answer. While Daphne is swimming laps in a pool, Gib tries to convince her to tutor him (which will lead ineluctably to falling in love in him). He paces up and down the lane as she swims, and tells a pitiful tale about what will happen to him without her help – he won't get his grades up, he'll get a bad job, and he'll lead a loserly and unsatisfying life.

He's pestering her, and he's trying to give her a guilt trip, a manipulative little tug on her heart-strings. She ignores him and briskly swims on. In a final bid for Daphne's attention, Gib jumps fully clothed into the pool.

Another more recent example of a charming boundary violation is from the American television series *The Office*. Andy Bernard (played by Ed Helms) has asked his co-worker Angela Martin (played by Angela Kinsey) to go out with him, and she's turned him down. Andy is eager to change her mind, so while Angela is working at her desk, and in front of their colleagues, he nervously but energetically serenades her with the song "Take a Chance on Me."[1] Andy's serenade is a clear violation of Angela's many boundaries. Angela is uptight; she insists upon strictly proper conduct (she's the "office stickler," in the words of the boss Michael) and she's very concerned with appearances. She maintains a wide interpersonal berth with her colleagues – she's aloof and secretive about her personal life. Angela meticulously maintains all of these boundaries, and Andy violates them all when he serenades her in front of her colleagues. His serenade is also manipulative – by asking her out in such a public and crowd-pleasing way, he makes it more difficult for her to reject him. Despite all this, Andy's serenade is utterly charming.

We cheer on Andy Bernard, Lloyd Dobler, and Walter Gibson even though we generally frown upon these kinds of boundary violations. Typically, we find it inappropriate to bother people who've told us to leave them alone, to pester and manipulate, to show up uninvited (especially in the middle of the night), to make a potentially embarrassing scene, to physically trespass on someone's property, and to violate someone's personal space (especially while she's sleeping, or swimming, or working at her desk). In some cases, these boundary violations are morally wrong (for example, breaking into a stranger's house, or stalking an ex-girlfriend). At the very least, these kinds of boundary violation are typically rude, annoying, and off-putting.

So why do we find *these* boundary violations charming and untroubling? Part of the explanation is surely the unique appeal of John Cusack and Ed Helms – how could anyone mind having their boundaries violated by such beseeching and adorably vulnerable guys? Another part of the explanation is that our responses to these scenes are influenced by regrettable gender norms and retrograde romantic notions – we find it romantic and fitting for the man to violate the woman's boundaries, despite her protests.

I think, however, that there is a further explanation as to why these particular boundary violations are unproblematic even though these kinds of boundary violations are typically inappropriate and sometimes even morally wrong. In these cases, Lloyd, Gib, and Andy are acting like boundaries don't exist, in the hope that the boundaries will cease to exist. They're acting as if they're in a closer relationship in which those boundaries don't exist (e.g., Lloyd would be welcome to show up unannounced if Diane were his girlfriend) because they hope this will forge the closer relationship. In other words, they're faking it till they make it: faking a closer relationship without boundaries in order to make this closer relationship. In my opinion, faking it till you make it is often appropriate, even when it involves violating boundaries in manipulative and pushy ways.

This opinion puts me at odds with some Kantian moral philosophers – a popular and powerful lot. According to these Kantians, we must always treat people as rational agents. If we want to get someone to date us, or to get back together with us, we must not pull stunts that are designed to manipulate or overwhelm, or to elicit an irrational response. These Kantians are wrong – and luckily so, for the career of John Cusack. Contrary to this Kantian view, many kinds of non-rational and even irrational influence are appropriate. The dividing line between appropriate and inappropriate behavior isn't whether it treats someone as a rational agent. Hence the dividing line between appropriate and inappropriate boundary violations in dating contexts isn't whether they treat someone as a rational agent. There's a more complicated story about what distinguishes appropriate boundary violations from inappropriate boundary violations in dating contexts. In the rest of this essay, I give part of that story.

## The Difference Between Appropriate and Inappropriate Boundary Violations

Not everyone agrees that these kinds of boundary violations are typically inappropriate. Some theorists draw a sharp distinction between violating physical boundaries and all other kinds of boundary violation, and claim that violating physical boundaries is morally wrong, but other ways of violating personal boundaries are permitted.

For example, the English professor and popular writer Camille Paglia maintains that touching someone without her consent is morally wrong, but that all manner of verbally aggressive behavior is appropriate in the

ANNE BARNHILL

pursuit of romance and sex. In a discussion of dating, seduction, and date rape, Paglia writes:

> Surely, for the good of the human species, we want to keep men virile and vigorous. They should feel free to seek sex and to persuade reluctant women. As a libertarian, I believe that we have absolute right to our own body and that no one may lay a hand on us without our consent. But consent may be non-verbal, expressed by language or behavior – such as going to a stranger's apartment on the first date, which I think should correctly be interpreted as consent to sex. "Verbal coercion" is a ridiculous concept: I agree with Ovid that every trick of rhetoric should be used in the slippery art of love.[2]

Paglia is a notoriously controversial writer and she stakes out an extreme position. On the other extreme are the aforementioned Kantian moral philosophers who maintain that many kinds of verbal behavior are morally wrong. These moral philosophers are followers of German philosopher Immanuel Kant, and they interpret Kant's famous injunction to *treat others as ends in themselves and never as mere means* as an injunction to treat people always as rational agents. This means that we must not manipulate people, or trick them, or try to influence them non-rationally in any other way, or try to exert control over them rather than letting them be guided by their own reason.[3] For example, listen to philosopher Thomas Hill's interpretation of Kant: "Since the exercise of rationality is something to be cherished, in trying to influence others one should appeal to their reason rather than try to manipulate them by non-rational techniques."[4] And Kantian philosopher Christine Korsgaard seconds that interpretation of Kant:

> To treat others as ends in themselves is always to address and deal with them as rational beings. Every rational being gets to reason out, for herself, what she is to think, choose, or do. So if you need someone's contribution to your end, you must put the facts before her and ask for her contribution. If you think she is doing something wrong, you may try to convince her by argument but you may not resort to tricks or force.[5]

Neither the Paglian view nor the Kantian view yield the correct conclusion about boundary violations; the truth is somewhere in between these extremes. Sometimes it's inappropriate to manipulate, to violate someone's personal space, or to touch someone without her consent; and sometimes it's perfectly all right. For example, having sexual intercourse with someone who hasn't consented is a physical boundary violation that is always morally wrong. But unexpectedly putting your hand on someone's knee is a physical boundary violation that's only *sometimes* inappropriate; in some contexts, it's a perfectly appropriate attempt to initiate a physical relationship. To give another slightly different example, some instances of manipulation are appropriate but others aren't. Imagine a variation on the "Take a Chance on Me" serenade from *The Office*: Andy Bernard isn't seeking a date with Angela, but is trying to persuade her to loan him money. If he's just seeking a loan, it seems inappropriate to serenade her publicly, given that it will embarrass her and manipulate her by putting her on the spot. Nevertheless, it seems all right for Andy to violate Angela's boundaries in those same ways to get a date.

So when exactly is it appropriate to violate boundaries? The answer to this question is complicated, as there are many varieties of boundary violations and the moral rules governing each variety are different. Here I focus on just one species of boundary violation, which I call *prospective boundary violation*.[6] Prospective boundary violation, as I define it, is ignoring or violating an interpersonal boundary that doesn't exist in a closer relationship, in order to establish that closer relationship. Prospective boundary violation is strategic – you're strategically violating boundaries in order to destroy those boundaries, not just violating boundaries carelessly or for the fun of it.

To get a handle on the difference between prospective boundary violations and other boundary violations, consider these two cases:

*Nosey Questions*: Kenny gets along with his neighbor Maria, but has no interest in becoming better friends with her. He has often seen her in the company of a man. One day he asks her, out of curiosity, "Is that your boyfriend?" Maria says, "Yes, it is." Kenny asks, "How long have you been together?" Maria says, "Six months." Kenny asks, "How's the sex?"

*Becoming Friends*: Kenny is friendly with his neighbor Maria and wants to become better friends with her. He thinks that they could become close friends, once he breaks the ice. He has often seen her in the company of a man. One day, he asks her, "Is that your boyfriend?" Maria says, "Yes, it is." Kenny asks, "How long have you been together?" Maria says, "Six months." Kenny asks, "How's the sex?"

In *Nosey Questions* Kenny asks an intrusive question just to slake his own curiosity. But in *Becoming Friends* Kenny asks an intrusive question in order to establish emotional intimacy between him and Maria so that they'll become friends. Kenny treats Maria as someone already a friend, in the hope that she'll play along and become his friend. Kenny violates an interpersonal boundary – the boundary against talking about sex that exists between people who don't know each other well – in order to destroy that interpersonal boundary. People who are friends don't have that interpersonal boundary between them, so to become friends that boundary must somehow be destroyed.

John Cusack's serenade in *Say Anything* is, similarly, a violation of interpersonal boundaries that's meant to destroy those interpersonal boundaries. When Lloyd and Diane were dating, there weren't boundaries against showing up uninvited, or expressing love, or invading each other's personal space, or disturbing each other's sleep (Lloyd and Diane had been lovers). Now that they're broken up, those boundaries have been reinstated. Lloyd's boundary-violating serenade is a bid to break down those boundaries and reestablish their relationship. The same is true of Walter Gibson's poolside plea and Andy Bernard's serenade.

Lloyd, Gib, and Andy's boundary violations are all examples of prospective boundary violation – ignoring or violating an interpersonal boundary that doesn't exist in a closer relationship, in order to establish that closer relationship. What makes the boundary violation appropriate in these cases is that it's meant to establish a closer relationship. If the boundary violation were done for certain other reasons – if Kenny were just curious about Maria's sex life, or Andy were just trying to get Angela to loan him money – then it would be inappropriate.

## Why Does Prospective Action Work?

When Lloyd Dobler and Andy Bernard get the girl, it makes sense to us. We intuitively understand that violating boundaries – and more generally, acting like you're in a closer relationship with someone than you actually are – can help to establish a closer relationship. But why exactly does it work? Why does acting like he's in a closer relationship with a woman work to establish that closer relationship, rather than just confuse and alienate her?

It works because she'll often play along with it. For example, Maria might play along with Kenny's intrusive questions by telling him about her sex life. In telling Kenny about her sex life, they have one of the central experiences of close friendship – sharing intimate details. By having this experience, Maria might come to feel closer to Kenny, in the way that friends feel close – to trust him, and to feel comforted by having him as her confidant. In this way, Maria's feelings catch up with her actions: her feelings of friendship catch up with her action of sharing intimate details. We have a phrase for this phenomenon: we call it *faking it till you make it*.

What I'm concerned with here is faking a close relationship in order to make a close relationship. But we fake it till we make it in other ways, too. We fake warmth in order to make warmth: you don't feel warmly towards your boss but you want to, so you act warmly toward him and that makes you feel more warmly toward him. And we fake distance in order to create distance: you have a close friend who makes extreme emotional demands and you want to be more emotionally distant from her, so you act distant and that creates emotional distance. We fake it till we make it in other activities, too, not just in relationships with other people: you want to be a confident public speaker, so you act confident when you give a public lecture, and that makes you feel more confident.

Faking it till you make it is a common strategy and a time-tested one. Aristotle recommended that we act virtuously, even if we don't think or feel as the virtuous person does. Over time, Aristotle counseled, we will be habituated into virtuous thoughts and feelings by performing virtuous actions. It's an interesting feature of human psychology that this kind of habituation works – that our thoughts and feelings do sometimes catch up with our actions. Prospective boundary violation is a way of faking it till you make it, and it must rely upon this feelings-catch-up-with-actions feature of human psychology: by acting as if boundaries don't exist, we come to feel that they really don't exist.

In close relationships, people don't maintain the interpersonal boundaries that they maintain with strangers and acquaintances. So violating a boundary – acting like that boundary isn't there – is a way of acting like you're in a closer relationship already. When someone plays along with what you're doing – when she, too, acts like the boundary isn't there – she might come to feel that the boundary isn't there. So by acting like you're in a closer relationship, you bring it about that you're in a closer relationship.

But violating boundaries is a high risk strategy for establishing a closer relationship. When you violate someone's boundaries – for example, you ask her intrusive questions, or you show up uninvited at her house, or you jump into the pool, or you serenade her in front of her colleagues even though she's intensely private – you are interfering with how she's chosen to control herself and to control what happens to her. What happens to her is now under your control and not her own control, to some extent. This might make her feel closer to you and receptive to your next move or, alternately, it might put her off entirely. Depending on how you handle the situation, you might build a closer relationship or forever destroy the possibility of one. If she tells you the troubling details of her sex life and you ridicule her, she's probably not going to trust you or like you anymore. But if you're sensitive and helpful, then she might come to trust you, feel closer to you, and open up to you in the future. By treating her in ways characteristic of a closer relationship, you've created a test for yourself: a test of whether or not you're worthy of a closer relationship. Depending on how you treat her, you prove yourself worthy or unworthy of being close to.

## Rules on Prospective Boundary Violation

What makes Lloyd Dobler's, Walter Gibson's, Andy Bernard's, and Kenny's boundary violations appropriate is that they're meant to establish a closer relationship. If the boundary violations were done for some other reasons – if Kenny is just curious about Maria's sex life, or Andy is just trying to get Angela to loan him money – then they would be inappropriate. Does this mean that any prospective boundary violation – that is, any boundary violation that's meant to establish a closer relationship – is appropriate? No, certainly not. There are rules governing prospective boundary violation:

*Rule 1:* You must not harm someone when you violate her boundaries.

However, making her a little embarrassed or annoyed is all right.

*Rule 2:* You may treat someone as if you're in a somewhat closer relationship, but not a very much closer relationship.

For example, suppose you're on a first date and you want to establish a sexual relationship with your date. So far, both of you have awkwardly kept your distance. You need to break the ice. Unexpectedly putting your hand on her knee might be an appropriate boundary violation that breaks the ice and helps to establish a sexual relationship. Unexpectedly forcing her to have sex with you, however, isn't an appropriate way to establish a sexual relationship.

> *Rule 3*: You must genuinely want to be in the closer relationship that your boundary violation might help to establish.

This is the rule that we most often violate.

We sometimes unwittingly violate this rule because we're self-deceived about our desires for closer relationships. For example, it seems to you that you want a romantic relationship with someone, but you're deceiving yourself; really you just want to have sex with her. Also, there's a great temptation to pretend we want closer relationships, because acting as if you want a closer relationship with someone is an effective way to get her to do what you want. For instance, an effective tactic for salespeople is to act as if they like customers and want to be friends with them. This makes the customer respond in kind and treat the salesperson as a friend – as someone to be trusted and cooperated with. But the salesperson doesn't want to be the customer's friend – she's just pretending in order to make the sale. (We might say that the salesperson has engaged in fake faking it till you make it.)

> *Rule 4*: The closer relationship that you hope to establish by violating boundaries must be the kind of relationship the other person would plausibly want to have.

Sometimes we want a closer relationship with someone that she wouldn't want. In these cases we shouldn't violate her boundaries in pursuit of a relationship we know (or should know) she wouldn't want. For example, Maggie is strapped for cash and hopes to establish a benefactor-recipient relationship with a rich acquaintance, Tina. So Maggie takes money from Tina's wallet when Tina isn't looking. Maggie has committed a prospective boundary violation that succeeds in establishing the closer relationship (the benefactor-recipient relationship), which is a closer relationship than Maggie genuinely wants to establish. But however successful, Maggie's boundary violation is clearly morally wrong because Tina wouldn't want to be in that closer relationship and Maggie should know that.

A more commonplace example is trying to establish a straight (or gay) romantic relationship with someone who's only interested in gay (or straight) romantic relationships. You shouldn't violate a gay (or straight) person's boundaries in a futile bid to establish a straight (or gay) relationship – it's inappropriate, not to mention a waste of your time.

In some cases, a moment's reflection will make it clear that someone doesn't want the kind of closer relationship you want. But in other cases it's difficult to discern whether someone wants a closer relationship, both because we have limited understanding of other people and because we're apt to be self-deceived.

## Conclusions

How does John Cusack always get the girl? It's not by scrupulously respecting her boundaries. It's by violating her boundaries – but in a strategic and morally permissible way. He doesn't act aggressively willy-nilly, he doesn't disregard her feelings, and he doesn't use her. Rather, he figures out how to push the limits in a way that doesn't harm her (Rule 1) and doesn't push the limits too much too fast (Rule 2). Also, he's genuine about wanting to have a relationship with her (Rule 3), and he's perceptive enough to realize that he has a real shot (Rule 4).

## NOTES

1  You can watch the scene at www.hulu.com/watch/83434/the-office-andy-serenades-angela. I'm sorry that the three paradigm examples of charming boundary violation I've found all feature young, white, middle-class straight people, and that they're examples of men violating women's boundaries. But such is the stuff of mainstream film and television.
2  Camille Paglia, *Vamps and Tramps* (New York: Random House, 1994), pp. 35–6.
3  According to philosopher Christine Korsgaard's interpretation of Kant: "We are not only forbidden to use another as a mere means to our private purposes. We are also forbidden to take attitudes toward her which involve regarding her as not in control of herself, which is to say, as not using her reason." Christine Korsgaard, *Creating the Kingdom of Ends* (Cambridge: Cambridge University Press, 1996), p. 141.
4  Thomas Hill, *Dignity and Practical Reason in Kant's Moral Theory* (Ithaca: Cornell University Press, 1992), p. 50.

5   Korsgaard, *Creating the Kingdom of Ends*, p. 142. Korsgaard elaborates on the point: "Any attempt to control the actions and reactions of another by any means except an appeal to reason treats her as a mere means, because it attempts to reduce her to a mediate cause. This includes much more than the utterance of falsehoods. In the *Lectures on Ethics*, Kant says "whatever militates against frankness lowers the dignity of man." It is an everyday temptation, even (or perhaps especially) in our dealings with those close to us, to withhold something, or to tidy up an anecdote, or to embellish a story, or even just to place a certain emphasis, in order to be sure of getting the reaction we want. Kant holds the Socratic view that "any sort of persuasion that is aimed at distracting its listener's attention from either the reasons that she ought to use or the reasons the speaker thinks she will use is wrong" (ibid.).

6   Prospective boundary violation is an instance of what I term *prospective action*. I develop the concept of prospective action and discuss the moral rules that govern it in an unpublished paper, "Taking Liberties."

CHAPTER 8

# BUY MY LOVE

On Sex Workers, Gold Diggers, and "Rules Girls"

In their wildly successful dating guide, Ellen Fein and Sherrie Schneider make their readers a promise: "Follow *The Rules*, and he will not just marry you, but feel crazy about you, forever! What we are promising you is 'happily ever after.' A marriage truly made in heaven."[1] As a 1996 *New York Times* Bestseller, *The Rules: Time-Tested Secrets for Capturing the Heart of Mr. Right* spawned multiple sequels, including *The Rules II: More Rules to Live and Love By* (1998), *The Rules for Marriage: Time-Tested Secrets for Making Your Marriage Work* (2002), and *The Rules for Online Dating: Capturing the Heart of Mr. Right in Cyberspace* (2002). Referred to as "the original dating bible" by *American Woman* magazine, these dating guides created a movement of followers called "Rules Girls," who believe that Fein and Schneider will lead them down the aisle into marital bliss.

Despite its widespread popularity, *The Rules* was not uncontroversial. *The New York Times* itself exclaimed, "Rules Girl? In 1996? Get real."[2] British psychologist Patricia Boynton states: "Where we find publications like *The Rules* that are harmful to women, we need to be more vocal about why they don't work."[3] Following these critiques, we believe that dating philosophies like *The Rules* seriously influence women to stop thinking about what they as individuals actually want from romantic relationships and force them to live out their quest for love in a way that is conformist to the most oppressive of traditional gender norms. We are led to ask: What would following *The Rules* mean for the ways in which people experience and negotiate relationships, intimacy, and sex?

Although some of the rules seem quite reasonable, the authors insist that *The Rules* are a total system, where all rules must be followed in order to ensure romantic happiness. In this essay, we will specifically focus on "Rule 4: Don't Meet Him Halfway or Go Dutch on a Date" and "Rule 12: Stop Dating Him If He Doesn't Buy You a Romantic Gift for Your Birthday or Valentine's Day," which explicitly address the relationship between money and romantic intimacy. We will argue that these sort of conventional rules about dating blur the ethical line between romance and sex work. Through a comparison of sex workers, "professional girlfriends" (women who date men with the goal of getting them to pay for their lives), and Rules Girls we will show that only when there are no explicit rules surrounding the exchange of time, sex, and money can authentic romantic relationships be found.

While providing a definition for an authentic intimate relationship is beyond the purview of this essay, these relationships are certainly not characterized by objective rules about the exchange of time, sex, and money. Perhaps they are characterized by ongoing equal negotiations or a sense of reciprocity. Perhaps by the sense that both partners enjoy spending time with one another, without the implication that one should pay for the other's time or reward them for having sex. While the Rules Girl is motivated by non-business-like goals such as "true" love, she approaches relationships in a characteristically business-like way. The Rules Girl does not focus on emotional factors or compatibility in seeking out and developing relationships. She ignores the generally subjective indicators of love and commitment in favor of objective manipulations of interpersonal relationships. The object is to perform a relationship that looks like what *The Rules* tells you it should look like. The object is to get married to the first decent man who comes along.

In contrast, sex workers are not concerned with building romantic relationships with clients. Rather, they explicitly exchange money for their time, company, and sexual activities. The terms "sex worker" and "client" denote the obvious business nature of this relationship. The explicit business exchange involved between a sex worker and a client is most clear when both the client and the sex worker view the exchange as purely business.

A more complex case occurs when a client requests that the sex worker provide him with a "girlfriend experience." Within this girlfriend experience, the sex worker will act as if she is on a date with the client by sharing a drink, cuddling, and kissing (at an extra charge) before subtly moving into sexual intercourse. The client will often return for subsequent dates (though only if he had a nice time and connected with the sex worker). Through this continued "dating" the client will build on the relationship he believes he is forming with the sex worker. Even if the client believes he is in a non-business relationship with the sex worker, few outsiders would agree. The case of this kind of client demonstrates that merely going on "dates" cannot be the sole characteristic required to constitute an authentic romantic relationship. In short, this version of the sex worker-client relationship provides evidence that merely *believing* that you are in a relationship does not mean that you *are* in a relationship. Regardless of your opinions about the ethical implications involved in sex work, we assert that most readers would agree that a sex worker and a client are not engaging in "dating" and their relationship, despite the beliefs of the client in this case, are purely financial, not romantic. The clear and explicit exchange of money for time and sex seems to counteract the client's personal beliefs.

While the "girlfriend experience" provided by a sex worker is clearly not a case of an authentic intimate relationship, women who date men with the goal of having the men pay for their lives (whom we will call "professional girlfriends" but are also known as "gold diggers") present a more complicated case. Professional girlfriends seem to blur the line between authentic relationships and being paid for sex. While we prefer the term "professional girlfriend" to "gold diggers" for analytic accuracy, the term professional girlfriend should not be interpreted to mean a woman whose formal and explicit employment is "being a girlfriend." A professional girlfriend is professional in the sense that she dates in order to secure a higher standard of living than she could afford on her own. In their critical examination of African-American female social scripts, Dionne P. Stephens and Layli D. Phillips state:

> Gold Diggers are depicted as purposefully selecting male partners based on the lifestyle or affluence that they can provide. A man and a dollar sign are seen as being one and the same as the Gold Digger views the man's worth according to the balance of his bank accounts or the cash in his pocket. As long as the money is available, the Gold Digger will make herself available.[4]

While Stephens and Phillips depict professional girlfriends as motivated solely by finances, professional girlfriends tend to engage in monogamous relationships, often for long periods of time. The fact that professional girlfriends engage in long-term monogamous relationships presents a significant difference between them and the "girlfriend experience" that sex workers provide. Also, the exchange of money for sex and time is much less formalized; there is no predetermined hourly rate of exchange. The most significant difference between a sex worker and a professional girlfriend, for the purposes of this essay, is the fact that a relationship between a professional girlfriend and her "partner" receives significantly more social recognition and validation than the exchange between a sex worker and her client. The professional girlfriend and her partner go out together and are publicly intimate. She may publicly identify her partner as her "boyfriend" and talk about their relationship with others. To the outside eye, they appear to genuinely care about each other. As far as many others can tell, the professional girlfriend and her partner are engaging in a real relationship.

The public perception that the professional girlfriend and her partner are engaged in a real relationship does not, from our point of view, mean that there *is* an authentic intimate relationship occurring. We do not believe that the relationship between a professional girlfriend and her partner is an authentic relationship because the professional girlfriend is motivated by the financial security and rewards offered by her partner for her company. She desires money, designer clothes, fancy restaurants, and expensive vacations, not her partner for himself. If the financial rewards were to end, so would the relationship. Often, the threat of ending the relationship due to her financial constraints is used by the professional girlfriend to extort more money and more gifts from her partner. Like the enamored client of the sex worker, the partner of the professional girlfriend pays for her expenses out of desperation and to assuage potential loneliness. Through these threats the partner becomes aware of the implicit financial exchange that is necessary to sustain their relationship.

While this implicit financial exchange remains clandestine in the case of most professional girlfriends and their partners, if this financial exchange were to become public knowledge, few outsiders would continue to view their relationship as authentic. Once the financial exchange is exposed, the relationship between a professional girlfriend and her partner is hard to distinguish from the relationship between a sex worker and her client. We believe that since few readers would be comfortable asserting that the sex worker and her client are engaged in an authentic intimate relationship, those same readers would be uncomfortable stating that the professional girlfriend and the partner are engaged in an authentic intimate relationship. Therefore, it seems that monogamy, public recognition of the relationship, and the (perhaps mutual) belief on the part of the partners that they are in fact in a relationship are not enough, from our perspective, to constitute an authentic, intimate relationship in the case of the professional girlfriend and the man she chooses to finance her life. If monogamy, public recognition, and the belief that a relationship exists are not enough to constitute an authentic relationship, what is?

Fein and Schneider promise their readers, through following all of their dating rules, that they will be led to an authentic intimate relationship with Mr. Right. Fein and Schneider also hold that *The Rules* will only help their readers find their dream man if they follow all of them; women should not just pick and choose from *The Rules* the ideas that they believe will work for them. While it is important to remember that *The Rules* is a total dating system, we will focus on the two rules that explicitly address the role of money within dating and relationships. These two rules strike us as difficult to practice while searching for or maintaining an authentic intimate relationship because they approach dating and relationships with many of the same characteristics and attitudes as sex workers approach their clients and professional girlfriends approach their "sugar daddies." Before highlighting why we take particular issue with rules 4 and 12, it is important to be clear exactly what Fein and Schneider mean by them and how they fit into the complete *Rules* "philosophy."

Rule 4 states, "Don't Meet Him Halfway or Go Dutch on a Date." Throughout *The Rules* Fein and Schneider argue that men, by nature, need challenges; thus, if pursuing a woman is too easy, they will lose interest and she will end up alone. Men must pursue women, they must do all the work in setting up the date, make all the phone calls and pay for everything; without these gestures a man will not fall in love with a woman and will eventually lose interest. In order to facilitate their *Rules* method of "playing hard to get," Fein and Schneider argue, with Rule 4, that part of giving a man a challenge is to insist that he bear the entire financial burden of the dating experience, especially, but not exclusively, for the first three dates. They state, "Love is *easy* when the man pursues the woman and pays for the woman most of the time."[5] Even if the woman is more financially secure than the man, she must remain committed to having him pay for the dates. Fein and Schneider believe that women should not pay for anything on the first three dates, even if it makes them quite uncomfortable to do so: "It's nice of you to care about his finances, but remember that he is deriving great pleasure from taking you out. Why deprive him of the joy of feeling chivalrous?"[6] Since women are not allowed to reciprocate financially, they are encouraged to be grateful about the date that their partner has organized and paid for: "actually the best way you can repay him is by being appreciative. ... Don't criticize the place or the food or the service, even if they are plain awful. ... See all the effort and expense he is putting into the date."[7]

While Rule 4 covers how to negotiate the financial costs of going on dates, Rule 12 concerns gift-giving. Rule 12 is titled, "Stop Dating Him if He Doesn't Buy You a Romantic Gift for Your Birthday or Valentine's Day." Fein and Schneider insist that Rule 12 is not about how much the gift costs but what type of gift it is. Despite this insistence they do seem to have their minds on one thing: "What kind of present can you expect to receive on your birthday when a man is in love with you? Ideally, jewelry." And they continue: "This is not a rule for gold-diggers; it's just that when a man wants to marry you he usually gives you jewelry."[8] The pre-occupation with jewelry is part of an overall concern that the kind of presents a woman receives from her male partner denote the breadth and depth of his love for her. They preach: "In general, *The Rule* is that when a man loves you he just wants to give you things. Anything."[9] Fein and Schneider caution that women shouldn't accept just anything; they should only remain with men who give them romantic gifts on important occasions. By romantic, Fein and Schneider mean the stereotypical gifts such as flowers, chocolate, candy, and, of course, jewelry. They do insist that the cost of the gift is irrelevant; what matters is that the gift is roman-tic, not practical: "Again, this is not being gold-diggers or princesses wanting to be doted on all the time. It's about determining whether a man is truly in love with you and, if not, going on to the next."[10] Apparently, romantic gifts mean men love you; practical gifts like espresso machines and rare books do not.

The purpose of *The Rules* is to establish a dynamic between a woman and a man where the man feels in pursuit of the woman. By creating this pursuit dynamic, Fein and Schneider believe that women will find and capture the man who wants to marry them. Rule 4 fits directly into the total system of *The Rules* because, if followed, this rule makes the man feel like the initiator. Fein and Schneider believe "men really feel good when they work hard to see you. Don't take that away from them."[11] Given that Rule 4 insists that the man pay for the entire dating experi-ence, it leaves them in control. It is the man's budget that determines where the couple goes, what activities are involved, and when the date ends (usually, when the cash runs out). It also places the man in charge of the direction of the relationship because different activities mean certain things. For example, there are clearly different connotations to going on a simple picnic with homemade food versus going to a fast-food restaurant, even though the budget may be approximately the same. Rule 4 helps establish the overall dynamic of female pursuit and male control in the relationship.

While Rule 4 contributes to the overall pursuit model, Rule 12 tests whether a man is pursuing because he loves a woman or if he is pursuing for the fun of the pursuit. Rule 12 states that if a man gives love-objects (i.e., chocolate, flowers, candy, jewelry), then he is in love. If he gives practical gifts (i.e., a new laptop, designer luggage, antique furniture, a toaster), he is "in like," perhaps as a sister, but certainly not as a wife. Rule 12 is to help women measure whether any particular relationship is heading for marriage or whether it is best to cut their losses and continue their search for their future husband. Fein and Schneider write, "*The Rule* is that if you don't get jewelry or some other romantic gift on your birthday or other significant occasion, you might as well call it quits because he is not in love with you and chances are you won't get the most important gift of all: an engagement ring."[12] Therefore, the overall goal of following *The Rules* is to find a husband. Rules 4 and 12 provide one way of measuring success in terms of finances and gifts; he commits to you if he travels to see you and saves the money to spend on you and he loves you if he gives you gifts that he doesn't buy for his sister.

Unlike the sex worker or the professional girlfriend, Rules Girls are more interested in the emotional connection than the financial benefits. However, we do not believe that Fein and Schneider or their rules will help women find authentic intimate relationships or "true" love. First, we have major issues with the entire project of *The Rules*. *The Rules* indoctrinate women to believe that successful relationships cannot be equal. Rather, according to Fein and Schneider, women who manipulate men into thinking that the men are in control characterize successful relationships. If you believe that Rules Girls are not oppressed and are active participants in the creation of a "Rules" relationship, then the men are manipulated. Alternatively, if you believe the men are really in control, then the women are arguably oppressed. Either way, the situation is hardly that of equality. We will not be concentrating on this forceful critique here; the lack of equality in *The Rules* has been critiqued elsewhere.[13]

Before proceeding to the overall argument about sex work and dating, it is necessary to establish why this distinction is usually drawn and if it is important. The *Oxford English Dictionary* defines business as "a person's official or professional duties as a whole; stated occupation, profession, or trade" or, more generally, as "action which occupies time, demands attention and labor; *esp.* serious occupation, work as opposed to pleasure or recreation."[14] While dating and relationships can "occupy time and demand attention," they are fundamentally different from business because business is pursued primarily for monetary gain and reward, whereas the rewards from an authentic intimate relationship should not be monetary, but emotional.

Here, then, is a key difference between sex workers, professional girlfriends, and Rules Girls; the sex worker and the professional girlfriend's behaviors are characteristic of business because they seek monetary not emotional rewards, whereas the Rules Girls seek emotional rewards through marriage. In fact, Fein and Schneider never state that the rewards of dating according to *The Rules* should be monetary; thus, they could argue that they are not suggesting that dating should be approached as a business. What Fein and Schneider promise is explicitly emotional reward: a lifetime of happiness with Mr. Right. The method that Fein and Schneider insist is the only way to achieve this emotional reward, however, is through dedicated commitment to perform the method of dating defined by their rules.

We believe that *The Rules*, while not arguing that dating should be business, puts forward an approach to dating that is explicitly business-like. Business-like can be defined as "of persons and things: suitable for business, befitting business; apt for business, practical, methodical, systematic."[15] Since "business-like" is a way of describing actions and things, what becomes relevant is not whether you would consider yourself to be engaged in dating, but rather *how* you date. Despite Fein and Schneider's claims to the contrary, *The Rules* advocate a stringent and systematic method for approaching dating. If you approach dating in this systematic and methodical way, you are engaging in a business-like relationship. We believe that business-like relationships and authentic intimate relationships are inherently different.

The above two rules, along with other aspects of Fein and Schneider's dating advice, treat dating like business because their rules implore women to see themselves as products, to view their worth in terms of the cost the man bears in dating them, and to use gift-giving to measure success. First, they argue that women should approach their quest to find

KYLA REID AND TINASHE DUNE

Mr. Right in terms of marketing a product. Fein and Schneider argue that women should preoccupy themselves with cultivating a particular external image. Women should always wear makeup, grow their hair long, and wear feminine clothes. Fein and Schneider caution "don't leave the house without wearing makeup. Put lipstick on even when you go jogging" and advise "if you have a bad nose, get a nose job."[16] This image cultivation is akin to a business marketing campaign because women are encouraged to change their external image to make themselves more attractive to men. Women are packaged in feminine clothes, long hair, and makeup to make them more attractive to potential suitors in just the same way retail products are packaged to be attractive to potential buyers. It is irrelevant to Fein and Schneider whether a woman personally identifies with this ultra-feminine image; what is important is that she will catch a man.

Fein and Schneider are not concerned solely with the external packaging of women. They also believe that women must *perform* femininity as well. It is not as if you appear feminine to attract a man and then reveal your individuality later; rather, you must continuously act the part of the product that you are selling. Fein and Schneider write: "Don't be a loud, knee-slapping, hysterically funny girl ... . You may feel that you won't be able to be yourself, but men will love it."[17] The goal is not to find a man who wants to have a relationship with you, but a man that wants to be with this ultra-feminine, doll-like version of you. When *The Rules* clash with other personal values or needs, then Rules Girls choose to do *The Rules*. The need to "put *The Rules* first" is evident in the discussion surrounding sex and intimacy; they ask: "But what if you like sex a lot too and denying yourself is just as hard as denying him? Does that mean you can sleep with him on the first or second date? Unfortunately, the answer is still no. You will just have to exercise a bit of self-restraint and character building."[18]

The unflinching dedication to marketing one's self according to *The Rules* can be paralleled to the ways in which sex workers alter their personalities and physical appearance. Sex workers will adopt different names and different personas while interacting with clients. They will don wigs, makeup, and clothing to attract more or higher status clients. The appearance and performance of a sex worker's persona is designed to increase profits, not to develop a relationship with the client based on who the sex worker actually is. Similarly, Rules Girls are supposed to alter their appearance and personality in hope of getting married, not in hope of developing a relationship with a partner based on who she actually is. Instead of viewing relationships as ongoing negotiations in getting to know someone, Fein and Schneider view relationships as marketing campaigns with the end-goal of marriage, albeit one made in heaven.

Second, since men pay the entire cost of dating, *The Rules* suggest that women should view their company as a fair exchange. It is not as if they are merely taking advantage of the man; he is paying for her time and company. According to Fein and Schneider, "He feels the money he spends on the food, the movie, and the cabs is the price of being with you and it's worth every penny."[19] This financial exchange – her time for his money – is very much akin to financial exchanges that occur in the business market, such as the exchange between a sex worker and her client. This similarity leaves us concerned about what viewing paying for dates in this way could mean for the ways women think of their personal worth. In sex work, one's financial worth is based on experience, physical appearance, and willingness to provide specialized services (e.g., light bondage or role play). In short, sex workers expect to be financially compensated for unique skills, experience, and assets. Transferring this to *The Rules*, would it mean that women who consider themselves valuable on the dating market should expect to be taken to a fancy restaurant and the opera rather than a fast-food restaurant and rented movie? And will a Rules Girl feel better about her worth if she goes on a more expensive date? While Fein and Schneider insist that dates should be geared to a man's budget, thinking of your worth in terms of expecting the man to pay in the first place does not eliminate these problematic questions.

Third, Fein and Schneider see the giving of romantic gifts in similar ways as employees view bonuses in the business market. Individuals in the business market may receive bonuses for good performance. Managers who increase profits and productivity can receive free tropical vacations or financial incentives. Investment bankers can receive large financial gifts at the end of a successful fiscal year. Sex workers receive tips for good service. While these bonuses are not guaranteed, it is through these bonuses that workers know that they are valued. Similarly, a romantic gift serves the same purpose for the Rules Girl. While love-objects are not guaranteed, they demonstrate to the Rules Girl that her male partner is in fact in love with her. Her male partner *values* her. A romantic gift is a sign that he is in love with *her*, not anyone else. She then feels more secure in her relationship and begins waiting for the most significant love-object, the engagement ring. Viewing one's worth in relation to material "stuff" is problematic in terms of personal relationships. For

KYLA REID AND TINASHE DUNE

example, your employer, through giving you bonuses, does not reflect a deep emotional attachment to you, but is merely expressing gratitude for your usefulness. Similarly, the presentation of love-objects does not necessarily denote love, especially since Fein and Schneider seem to have no concern that these gifts be tailored to your personal likes and dislikes. Wouldn't it be a clearer expression of love if the gifts given on Valentine's Day and special holidays were tailored to the person and the relationship? While value in the business market can be measured in terms of the year-end bonus, it seems inauthentic to measure how much a potential partner loves with the yardstick of the value of love-objects received.

The parallels between the Rules Girl and our earlier examples of sex workers and professional girlfriends need to be made more explicit. Like the sex worker, there are clear expectations about the financial exchange on the part of Rules Girls. Rules Girls expect and in fact insist that men pay for dates in order to keep dating them. Sex workers expect and insist that their clients pay them for their time and sexual services. In fact, sex workers expect to be paid extra for kissing in a way similar to how Rules Girls, in an ideal *Rules* relationship, can expect to be bought "roses after ... sex."[20] Both Rules Girls and sex workers have clear expectations about men paying for their time and these expectations create a business-like environment for both relationships.

Rules Girls are similar to professional girlfriends because both measure the success of their relationship in terms of objects. For a professional girlfriend, her relationship is successful, from her perspective, if her sugar daddy pays for an expensive quality of life. The relationship of a Rules Girl is thought to be successful if her male partner buys her love-objects, culminating in the gift of the ultimate love-object, the engagement ring. Also, both professional girlfriends and Rules Girls are concerned with increasing their status through their relationships with men. The professional girlfriend is interested in the increasing financial and social status afforded by nicer clothes, fancier restaurants, newer cars, and better apartments. The Rules Girl is interested in the increased social status of being a married woman. In fact, *The Rules* preach that the only ultimate goal for women is marriage. The easy comparison between Rules Girls, professional girlfriends, and sex workers should be disconcerting for anyone who is actually seeking an authentic intimate relationship.

So what if you already thought *The Rules* were ridiculous? What if you agreed with us from the beginning that they miss the point? Regardless of whether or not you are a Rules Girl, we all engage in some form of

*The Rules* when we date. For example, many men and women have been socialized to believe that men should, at the very least, pay for the first date. Without this gesture, often both men and women get confused about each other's intentions. *The Rules* philosophy endorses the giving and receiving of red roses because roses are often socially interpreted to express feelings of love. Considering that it is often socially expected that women should only consent to sex after a declaration of love, men may choose to give red roses or even say that they love women in order to manipulate them into having sex with them. In fact, both men and women can take advantage of each other when dating rules are manipulated. *The Rules* is just the most extreme example of the uncritical and manipulative actions we all engage in when dating. In fact, if you disagree with *The Rules*, you should disagree with most social conventions surrounding dates.

We are left concluding that we should all be more critical about the social expectations in relationships and dating – for instance, who pays, what gifts we give and receive, and what money means – if we want to avoid uncomfortable parallels between our dating selves, sex work, and gold digging.

## NOTES

1   Ellen Fein and Sherrie Schneider, *All The Rules: Time-Tested Secrets for Capturing the Heart of Mr. Right* (New York: Grand Central Publishing, 2007), pp. 8–9.
2   Jill Gerston, "So Many Rules, So Little Time," *New York Times* October 23, 1996; available online at www.nytimes.com/1996/10/23/garden/so-many-rules-so-little-time.html (accessed July 11, 2009).
3   Patricia Boynton, "II. Abiding the Rules: Instructing Women in Relationships," *Feminism and Psychology* 13, 2 (2003): 242.
4   Dionne P. Stephens and Layli D. Phillips, "Freaks, Gold Diggers, Divas, and Dykes: The Sociohistorical Development of Adolescent African-American Women's Sexual Scripts," *Sexuality and Culture* 7, 1 (2003): 18–19.
5   Fein and Schneider, *All The Rules*, p. 40.
6   Ibid., p. 40.
7   Ibid., p. 41.
8   Ibid., p. 69.
9   Ibid., p. 71.
10   Ibid., p. 71.
11   Ibid., p. 40.
12   Ibid., pp. 69–70.

13 See T. S. Zimmerman, K. E. Holm, and M. E. Starrels, "A Feminist Analysis of Self-Help Bestsellers for Improving Relationships: A Decade Review," *Journal of Marital and Family Therapy* 27, 2 (2001): 165–75; Boynton, "II. Abiding by The Rules"; M. Tyler, "Sex Self-Help Books: Hot Secrets for Great Sex or Promoting the Sex of Prostitution?" *Women's Studies International Forum* 31 (2008): 363–72.
14 *The Oxford English Dictionary*, 2nd edn. (Oxford: Oxford University Press 1989). The *OED Online* is available at www.dictionary.oed.com/cgi/entry/50029998 (accessed July 10, 2009).
15 Ibid.
16 Fein and Schneider, *All The Rules*, p. 21.
17 Ibid., p. 22.
18 Ibid., pp. 78–9.
19 Ibid., p. 40.
20 Ibid., p. 145.

PART III

# ROLLING RIGHT ALONG

Dating Like a Pro

CHAPTER 9

# AGAINST MATCHMAKING

If you are a single, adult male as I am, chances are you have had the unpleasant experience of being set up or "matched" by a friend (or family member). Single, adult women no doubt fall prey to the same sort of unpleasantness and I'd be willing to bet that for any argument we could offer against matchmaking from a strictly male point of view, there is a parallel argument that applies to females, but seeing as I am a member of the former category and not the latter, it seems appropriate to focus a bit more closely on the perspective of we guys.

Whichever side of potential matches you find yourself on, imagine the following scenario. You receive a call from your friend or family member and in a voice that does a noticeably poor job of concealing her (or his ... most likely her ... okay let's be honest ... most definitely her) excitement (see figure 9.1), she tells you, "Oh, I have someone who would be just perfect for you!" Unsurprisingly, this ominous claim is almost always followed by the equally ominous suggestion, "How 'bout I set you two up?!" Suddenly, your throat feels dry. Your heart rate jumps. Your sweat glands begin to do whatever sweat glands do. One of your worst fears is coming true. Your friend or family member is trying to play matchmaker, and she is utterly convinced that you are one half of the perfect match.

If you are quick on your feet, or if you have a bit of luck shine upon you, you will quickly think of some excuse for not being set up. You are just *so* busy these days – that Xbox won't play itself. You just aren't in a

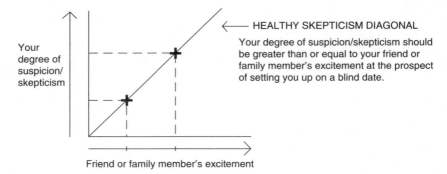

Your degree of suspicion/ skepticism

←—— HEALTHY SKEPTICISM DIAGONAL

Your degree of suspicion/skepticism should be greater than or equal to your friend or family member's excitement at the prospect of setting you up on a blind date.

Friend or family member's excitement

FIGURE 9.1

good emotional place right now – that last girl your friend or family member set you up with six months ago really did a number on you. Your friend or family member will either believe that these excuses are sincere and legitimate or, in rare cases, they will correctly interpret your excuses as polite requests to refrain from attempting the match. Still, if you aren't so quick on your feet, if you aren't so lucky, it's going to happen. You are going on a blind date. The match is going to be made.

Despite the negative, visceral reaction you have displayed in response to your friend or family member's best efforts at finding you a mate – someone to perhaps spend the next four or five decades with – you are or hope to be a thoughtful, reflective person who doesn't simply take all of life's experiences at face value. Thus, you find yourself asking, "Am I just making a big fuss over nothing? Would it really be so bad to let my friend or family member set me up on a date?" To be frank, these are not the types of questions that presently concern me. The reason for this is that I can simply tell you that *no*, you are not just making a big fuss over nothing and *yes*, it really would be so bad to let your friend or family member set you up. What I am presently concerned with is offering a charitable, if not defensible, explanation of this sort of reaction. Of course, I'm not interested in defending the sweating or jump in heart rate. On the contrary, I hope to offer a rational defense of your (and my) adversity to matchmaking.

Presumably, there are at least two explanations for these sorts of reactions, which may or may not be mutually exclusive. The first explanation is that you are simply reacting to your fear of the awkwardness of dating *in general* and have mistakenly picked out your friend or family member's attempt to set you up as the object of your annoyance, fear, or disdain.

After all, when the dating process occurs in a more natural environment, stretched out over a longer period of time, any accompanying anxiety tends to come in smaller, more bearable doses. In contrast, when your friend or family member informs you of her intention to set you up, it hits you all at once. Boom! You are going on a blind date. Matchmaking's unique concentration of unpleasantness might explain the fact that you have no desire to be matched despite the fact that you tolerate and even welcome the prospect of dating in general.

Still, there is a second explanation for the negative, visceral reaction that perhaps you (and certainly I) have that may be compatible with this first explanation, but that is not so accommodating to your friend or family member's hopes (nay, dreams) of setting you up with whomever it might be that is just *perfect* for you. It is that matchmaking might very well get in the way of your happiness. Yes, that's right – *happiness*. This is admittedly a bold claim, but it is defensible if we take a certain approach to answering questions of ethics (i.e., how we ought to live). It's defensible if we take a virtue theoretic approach to ethics, which says that the only, or most easily achievable, way for you to achieve happiness or to be happy is for you to fulfill your function, or to act in accordance with your nature. As I'll hope to show, matchmaking is to be avoided because it is *unnatural*.

What could be more contrived or more unnatural than a blind date that has been set up by your friend or family member? Nothing. Matchmaking (at least, of the sort here described) will disallow you fulfillment of your function or to live in accordance with your nature – maybe not as a "man" (at least, in the biological sense), but certainly as a *guy*. Since a guy is the type of thing you are (or at least, that I am), the unnaturalness of matchmaking works against us in our pursuit of happiness.

## Happy Dating

In order to understand virtue theory (so that we may finally condemn our friend or family member's best efforts), we'll first have to introduce the notion of *telos*, or purpose, or function. It's pretty simple really. The function of a knife is to cut. The function of an automobile is to get you to where you need to go in a timely and comfortable manner. A function is what something does, or how it is to be evaluated given the type of thing that it is. A knife is a cutting type of thing; an automobile is a transportation type of thing. These are what these things do; what they are.

What type of thing are you? It's not just inanimate objects or artifacts that have a function. According to Aristotle, the function of man (e.g., we guys) is to obtain *eudaimonia*.[1] For our purposes, we can translate Aristotle's *eudaimonia* as simply "happiness" so long as we make the following qualification. There are at least two popular uses of the term "happiness" and only one of them will do as a translation of *eudaimonia*.

Imagine that you're on a first date (a first date that may or may not have been the result of matchmaking). Your waiter – picking up on the subtle, awkward cues that tell him that he is waiting on a couple on their first date – decides to help mark the occasion by offering you a free hot-fudge sundae (to share; multiple-dessert markers are to be saved for anniversaries). Upon receiving your free dessert, you let your date know that you are now "happy" and in a sense, you are. We can call this type of happiness hot-fudge happiness. It's a fleeting, moment-in-time sort of happiness. It's the type of happiness that will vanish as quickly as it arrived if you lean in for a goodnight kiss and are met with nothing more than a disapproving glare. You might say that hot-fudge happiness isn't *really* happiness; it is, well, "happiness."

Contrast hot-fudge happiness with this other sort. Bill and Fran had their first date nearly six decades ago and began their marriage not long after. Sitting on their porch, moments from their simultaneous passing after long, fulfilling lives, Bill turns to Fran and says, "Franny, I sure am happy." The type of happiness that Bill has expressed to his wife Fran is closer to the notion of Aristotle's *eudaimonia*. It's a flourishing life sort of happiness. It's the happiness that only accompanies a well-lived life. Hot-fudge happiness is okay in its own right, but what we really care about in life is *eudaimonia*, truly living well.

The main difference between *eudaimonia* and hot-fudge happiness is that *eudaimonia* isn't a feeling. In contrast to *feeling* well, *eudaimonia* is more comparable to something like health. Health is a complex set of features that may or unfortunately may not be true of your body. *Eudaimonia* is a complex set of features that may or may not be true of your life. Just as there is typically a feeling or sense that accompanies health, there is typically a feeling or sense that accompanies *eudaimonia*. The sense of achieving *eudaimonia*, however, is not identical to *eudaimonia* itself (i.e., you could be a happiness hypochondriac).[2]

In a similar way that given the type of thing it is, a knife's function is cutting, in a similar way that given the type of thing it is, an automobile is meant for transporting, your function is to achieve *eudaimonia*. That is what you are; that is what you are meant for. If this is the case, then everything you do is to be judged with your achievement of *eudaimonia* (i.e., *true* happiness) in mind. If an action helps you achieve true happiness, then it's a good action, if it detracts from your ability to achieve true happiness, then it's a bad action. This is true even for matchmaking, both matching and allowing oneself to be matched. So, does matchmaking lead to true happiness, hot-fudge happiness (i.e., "happiness"), or none of the above?

## The End of Matchmaking

Why do your friends or family members attempt to match you? Why do you on occasion begrudgingly allow them to do so? Presumably, it's the same reason that you do anything and it's the same reason your friends or family members do anything. You are ultimately hoping to achieve true happiness, as are they. The question then seems to be, how exactly is matchmaking supposed to lead to your (the matchee's) happiness? It's not as if being matched – even successfully – can simply grant true happiness. For that matter, there are no actions it would seem that are just supposed to immediately and inevitably make us happy. As much as we guys might hate to admit it, eating a perfectly prepared steak, attending a game in box seats, or even sexual intercourse isn't a good for us in and of itself. They are only good because they potentially fulfill some need in us that left unfulfilled might stand in the way of making us truly happy. As your friend or family member might point out, the end or goal of matchmaking is to help you achieve happiness by allowing (i.e., forcing) you to meet and get to know that one special person who can help you in your daily life in the way only a romantic partner can. If you are a candidate for being one half of the *perfect* match, your friend or family member might point out that you cannot or at least have not achieved this end without her help, so she feels obliged to intercede (whether you like it or not).

Admittedly, it is possible for matchmaking to achieve this end. There is no doubt a person or two will pick up this book and find themselves modestly offended even by this chapter's title because their very successful relationship or marriage was the result of matchmaking. Let's hope that their friends or family members don't pick up this book, as they will almost certainly be offended by the suggestion that their best efforts are unwanted or unwarranted. Nevertheless, I'm confident that there are plenty of happy marriages that are the result of matchmaking. I'm even willing to bet (as a sincerely uninformed Westerner) that there are plenty of *arranged* marriages that are more than successful, flourishing. If this is so, what's with all the fuss? Why come down so hard on matchmaking and all those friends or family members who claim to have it as a significant part of their skill set?

The problem with matchmaking is that while it can be successful in bringing together two people who complement each other – perhaps an integral part in achieving true happiness for many – it does so by ignoring all of the other important aspects of a guy's psyche, of his person. Finding your one true love may be an important end in achieving true happiness, but it's certainly not the *only* end; it's not the only need guys have with regard to their quest for happiness. Finding a match on your own or with the help of your friend or family member is only good because it can potentially lead to your true happiness, a complex set of features that will hopefully be true of your life. Matchmaking as usually done by all the friends or family members of the world ignores this fact and it is in this sense that matchmaking is artificial, or unnatural. It forces the two halves of the *perfect* match to focus their love life too narrowly, as if it were the ultimate goal. It forces a focus on romance in such a way that other aspects of their lives may go underdeveloped.

Being successfully matched might fulfill an important need that can help you achieve happiness, but if this end can be achieved while taking your whole person into account, that would certainly be preferable.

## Dating Lessons from the Animal Kingdom

Matchmaking is unnatural. It has a tendency to get in the way of your ultimate function: achieving *eudaimonia*; true happiness. In support of this claim, we'll step out of the realm of awkward first dates and try to take a lesson from the animal kingdom (which I'm willing to bet could offer us a good number of interesting dating analogies).

Imagine two bears; we'll call them Zoo-bear and Wild-bear. Also imagine that both bears live exactly where their names imply. Now consider the lives that both bears lead. Zoo-bear lives in relative comfort, needn't worry about any harms that might exist outside the zoo's walls, and perhaps most importantly, he is fed any and all meals he requires without lifting a single paw. In contrast to Zoo-bear, Wild-bear lives in whatever environment he himself can find, deals with all of the dangers of nature that exist beyond the walls of the zoo, and also most significantly, eats only that which he can track down on his own. What is the significance of the difference between the lives of Zoo-bear and Wild-bear? The main difference, I would contend, is that Wild-bear has a shot at achieving happiness that Zoo-bear does not; not human happiness but bear happiness. As far as I know, Aristotle never spoke of bear-*eudaimonia*, but I suspect that if he did, he would have said that bear-*eudaimonia* is similar or parallel to human *eudaimonia*, it's simply for bears. Nevertheless, Wild-bear can lead a fulfilled, flourishing life because he is living in accordance with his nature in a way that Zoo-bear is not.

If there *is* such a thing as bear-*eudaimonia*, it is only or most easily achievable in an environment that allows bears to exercise all aspects of their nature. The Zoo-bear doesn't get the (both literal and figurative) exercise he needs to live a fully flourishing bear life. Bears need to hunt. Bears need to roam. Without these activities his muscles atrophy, he becomes lazy. Zoo-bear doesn't have the same shot at happiness that Wild-bear does because his zoo life only meets his hunger and safety needs. It is still a positive good thing that Zoo-bear eats and that he is safe, but how much better off would he be if those aspects of his life were fulfilled in such a way that his whole person (i.e., his bear-ness) were fulfilled? In other words, it's good for Zoo-bear that he is safe and fed, but it would be better for him if he achieved these ends on his own.

What exactly do the bears have to do with dating or matchmaking? Can you guess who the Zoo-bear is? Who the Wild-bear is? Like bears or most any other member of the animal kingdom, there is a complex algorithm that constitutes what it will take for guys to achieve *eudaimonia*: true happiness. In many cases part of the equation is finding a mate, but in no cases does the hunt for a mate represent the entirety of the equation. Guys need to develop their own social skills; they need to accomplish certain things on their own. As old fashioned, archaic, or even chauvinist as this may sound (or be), there is a sense in which men need to hunt, men need to roam. Without these activities, their social muscles atrophy; they become lazy. Thus, when your friend or family member oh so graciously offers to lend her matchmaking services to you, she is playing the role of Zoo-bear's zoo keeper, who feeds Zoo-bear his fish while neglecting the other aspects of Zoo-bear that need to be fulfilled for his own bear flourishing. In other words, it is good for your romantic needs to be met so to speak, but it would be better for you if you accomplished this end on your own. Human beings (not just guys) have a tendency to flourish when they make it a habit of fulfilling their most significant ends on their own. Insofar as matchmaking stands in the way of this, it is unnatural, unhelpful, and unwarranted.

## For Friends or Family Members

As you may have already noted, I have been kind of harsh to a good number of friends or family members out there. But this chapter would be incomplete if we didn't point out that many – if not most – of the friends or family members who attempt to make all of those perfect matches have only the best of intentions. As Aristotle himself pointed out, a significant factor in achieving happiness is investing one's self in the life of others.[3] Your friend or family member who is giving it her all to set you up with the perfect match does so because she wants to achieve her own *eudaimonia*; but a significant part of what it will take for her to achieve this is for her friends and family members (i.e., you) themselves to be happy. Because of this, and because she believes that you ending up with your perfect match is an invaluable part of your success in life, it is to be expected that she would try her hand at matchmaking.

Herein lies the problem. Your friend or family member wants you to be happy, and she has perhaps correctly identified part of what it will take for you to obtain happiness, but she has forgotten that what it will take for you to achieve happiness is a complex algorithm. You will have to develop yourself, accomplish your own tasks, and maybe even woo your romantic interests unassisted. If she really wants you to be happy (and she does) it would be more advantageous for the both of you if she takes into account your whole person, and all that it will take for you to achieve happiness. She'll then allow you to play a larger role in your own successes, thereby making it easier to live in accordance with your nature.

So what should we say to the friends or family members who *really* want to match us? Those who really do have the best of intentions and want to see us happy? If she really does know two halves of the perfect match, of which you are one, should she just keep it to herself? Must she just leave it up to chance that you hunt and roam, and find your perfect match? Here's a surprising answer from a guy who has just written an essay against matchmaking: not necessarily.

JOSHUA S. HETER

For all the friends or family members out there who are just sure about those perfect matches, who just can't help themselves when it comes to playing matchmaker, I suggest that instead of taking an active role and officially setting up your friends or family members, it would be more beneficial to take a more passive approach and find a way to merely introduce them. Bring them into a mutual social circle and let things progress *naturally*. If this opportunity passes without a match occurring on its own, it is more than likely that the belief that there was a perfect match was a mere illusion. Pushing the issue further will only get in the way of everyone's *eudaimonia*. If we revisit the bear analogy, the more passive matchmaker is less like an enabling zoo keeper, who meets the bear's more basic needs perhaps at the expense of his overall wellbeing, and more like the director of a vast wildlife sanctuary who assists the bears in meeting some of their basic needs, but not in such an intrusive way that their bear-*eudaimonia* is threatened.

It's perfectly acceptable, if not recommended, if not obligatory, to assist our friends and family members in their own attempts at achieving happiness. It's best, however, that we do so without butting in, without intruding. At least for guys, in our quest for *eudaimonia*, as well as our quest for love, we have to do certain things on our own.

## NOTES

1   Aristotle makes this claim conditionally (i.e., "if he has a function"). See Aristotle, *Nicomachean Ethics*, Book I, Chapter 7.
2   For more on this point, see Martha Nussbaum, "Non-Relative Virtues: An Aristotelian Approach," in Peter French, Theodore Uehling, Jr., and Howard Wettstein (eds.) *Midwest Studies in Philosophy* Vol. 13 (Minneapolis: University of Minnesota Press, 1980), pp. 32–50.
3   Aristotle, *Nicomachean Ethics*, Books VIII–IX. The term used by Aristotle to refer to the types of relationships that are significant in our quest for *eudaimonia* is *philia*, and it seems to be best translated as something more than simple "friendship." Perhaps it is closely related to our "friend or family member" role.

CHAPTER 10

# HITTING THE BARS WITH ARISTOTLE

## Dating in a Time of Uncertainty

What does a man do when he suddenly finds himself single? In some ways there have never been more choices available. He can hang out in bars getting slowly smashed, Bogart style, in the hope that Ingrid Bergman might walk through the door. He can go into the singles scene and meet other equally desperate people and maybe even hook himself a stalker. Alternatively, for those who lack social skills, or are too hideously disfigured and malodorous to go out in public, there is always the Internet. But this wealth of choices belies one fact: we live in a time of profound confusion. The old ways of being a man have gone, unlamented and unlikely to return. The SNAG (Sensitive New Age Guy) never really existed outside the imagination of women's magazine editors and nobody really trusted him anyway.

The truth is that no straight man with a modicum of decency really knows what to do. Most of us have tried to do what mothers, sisters, and female friends have taught us, and be nice. We paid lots of compliments, bought gifts, meals and drinks, and generally tried to offend as little as possible, in the hope perhaps that we might bore women into submission. All the time we felt a gnawing unease that the old saw was true and that women really did prefer jerks. We know that partly because we watched our mothers, sisters, and female friends dating them.

Into this vacuum has stepped the Online Seduction Community, aka The Game, with the avowed aim of turning Average Frustrated Chumps (AFCs) into Pick-Up Artists (PUAs). The Game was spawned in the early days of the Internet and spread its message through newsgroups and word of mouth. Its bible in those early days was the *Layguide*, which (for those whose ears are not attuned to subtle innuendo) was dedicated to teaching men how to obtain casual sex. The Game's message is a combination of the banally obvious: "Try not to scare girls by declaring your love on a first date" to the downright Machiavellian: "Create an air of mystery by never answering a direct question."

In the last decade, The Game has mushroomed. There has been at least one bestselling book: *The Game* by Neil Strauss, which is currently being made into a film, and a reality television series: *The Pick-Up Artist*, in which awkward and geeky AFCs are turned into PUAs before our eyes.[1] Many American sit-coms now have a PUA character – for example, Barney in *How I Met Your Mother* and Russell in *Rules of Engagement* – and some of their distinctive techniques have been referenced or parodied in several popular shows. For those enigmatic figures running the operation The Game is a multi-million dollar enterprise and has already led to one significant intellectual property dispute.[2] There has also been an important and interesting shift in the tone of the enterprise from teaching a series of tricks to get women into bed to something more approaching self-help or life coaching.

The growth of the PUA has met with a hostile response in some quarters.[3] But what is striking about that response is that rather than simply mocking the gullibility of the men who buy into it, the overwhelming tone reveals a worry that the techniques being taught might actually work. This tells us something fairly profound and troubling about contemporary dating and in what follows I want to consider what we might learn from The Game. I also hope to sketch out an alternative based, somewhat loosely, on the teachings of Aristotle, which might enable men to achieve a modicum of success on the dating scene without becoming manipulative jerks. My suggestion is that The Game, at its best, teaches men to mimic the conduct of Aristotle's *Megalopsūche* – the magnanimous or great-souled man. Similarly, the infamous success of the jerk owes less to inherent female masochism than it does to the fact that the jerk inadvertently mimics the magnanimous man. My conclusion is that the truly ethical thing to do is to try to become what others mimic.[4]

# Of Jerks and "Nice" Guys

For something so closely related to the survival of our species, dating is a surprisingly tricky business, or so it seems these days. Some of this diffi-culty stems from the larger difficulty of modern urban living. Communities and personal relationships are fragmented, work places increasingly greater demands on personal time, and the traditional ways of meeting a mate are less feasible or less attractive than they once were. With these difficulties come opportunities for some. The modern urban landscape provides rich pickings for those uninterested in a serious relationship. But for anyone who looks to form more robust bonds, the difficulties may seem insurmountable. Most of us get by on the basis of introduc-tions by mutual friends and colleagues, but this often turns out to be a lottery. As one ages, the pool of available singles gets ever drier.

The rise of feminism and its accompanying socioeconomic changes mean that women are quite rightly unprepared to settle for what their grandmothers too often endured. It is no longer sufficient for a man to be a good provider. Today's women demand a much broader range of qualities and characteristics than those of previous generations. If it sometimes appears to many men that women are unclear about what they want, what they do not want is pretty obvious. Yet, given the high value most women apparently place upon caring, kindness, sensitivity, and emotional intelligence, the continued success of the jerk seems para-doxical. Of course, a lot depends upon what one means by "success" here and any evidence would be largely anecdotal, but like all clichés, the idea that "nice guys finish last" has a ring of truth to it. I hazard that every reader knows at least one attractive, intelligent woman with a jerk addiction.

If one were to ask that woman she would doubtless deny that her beloved is a jerk, or even if she were to concede his jerkish qualities she would point to all of his other admirable qualities that outweigh them. True as this might be, given the fact that there are hundreds of men out there with all of these admirable qualities and few of the jerkish ones, a puzzle remains. The standard response is to blame women and, like Freud, bemoan this deep seated feminine irrationality. A more honest solution may be to wonder not what is so attractive about jerks, but rather what makes nice guys so deeply unappealing.

A moment's reflection upon how we typically use the term "nice" is illuminating. The expression is a placeholder, used when we can think of nothing better to say about a person. The nice guy, like parsley, is noticed only in his absence. To call someone nice is to imply that he lacks any particular distinction. A nice person is neither witty nor especially charming. While a nice person is probably not offensively stupid, it is also unlikely that he possesses any great intellectual merit. We would not describe Ludwig Wittgenstein, Bertrand Russell, or Martin Heidegger as nice.

The nice guy's problems run deeper. As the psychologist Robert Glover suggests in his book *No More Mr. Nice Guy*, the term "nice" ought to be uttered in a heavily ironic tone of voice.[5] The "nice" guy's niceness is an artifice, an attempt to obtain what he wants but lacks the insight or the *cojones* to ask for directly. His acts of kindness are indirect requests for reciprocation. When, as usually happens, he fails to obtain what he desires, his niceness often turns to resentment. Indeed, nice guys often harbor a thinly veiled contempt for women. Nice guys number heavily among perpetrators of domestic violence and abuse and even those who do not sink so low force their partners to live with surly resentment and a lingering feeling of guilt. Since he is so nice and does so much to please her, how come she finds him so irritating?

Supplication seldom has aphrodisiac effects. The average nice guy is about as attractive as cold porridge. Feeling unworthy and unable to receive, he is also unable to genuinely give. Little wonder then that many women prefer the attractions of the outlaw biker or unemployed rock star to that of the average nice guy. In love, as in so many other areas of life, the nice is the enemy of the good.

The term "jerk," by contrast, never comes unmodified; he is always a certain kind of jerk. He is the witty jerk, the charming jerk, the athletic jerk, the brilliant professorial jerk, or the jerk that plays in a band. He offers excitement and above all he does not supplicate. His charms may be illusory. His self-containment is actually self-absorption. His apparent indifference masks a genuine lack of care. He is, after all, a jerk. For all that, he represents a challenge to those women who are used to being pursued by nice guys.

Nice guys observe the apparent success of the jerk with despair. For some, it merely exacerbates their fear and contempt for women; others seek to emulate the jerk's achievements by becoming jerks themselves. Some may succeed in this endeavor, but for most the effort is futile. They take on the jerk's more unpleasant characteristics without really getting the point. The very act of trying to be a jerk means that they remain within supplication mode. The jerk's disregard for others' approval is the key to his success; it is pointless therefore to try to act like a jerk in order to obtain approval. The best that one can achieve is to become a somewhat unsavory nice guy.

Most men who fall within the nice guy category would not want to become jerks even if they could and in many cases their motives are pure. They would like to have some of the jerk's appeal without behaving in abusive or manipulative ways. They would like to be more effective in dating while remaining ethical. Such men form the primary target market for the purveyors of The Game.

## Gurus of The Game

Anyone dipping his toes into the bizarre world of The Game quickly finds himself in an alternate reality. It has its heroes: "Mystery," "Style," "David deAngelo"; an esoteric vocabulary: "sarging" (going out to meet women), "negs" (ambivalent compliments which border on insults), "kino" (physical contact), "wingman" (a male or sometimes female accomplice); and a series of techniques only available to the initiated: "C&F" (cocky and funny), "AMOG destroyers" (techniques deployed to neutralize or distract the "Alpha Male of the Group"), "accelerating kino" (increasing physical contact). Participants share their experiences in "field reports" circulating on the Internet that recount successes and failures and offer commentary and feedback to novices as they progress from AFC to full-blown PUA.

Each of the gurus has a distinctive set of techniques, which he guards closely. This is a business enterprise after all. "Mystery" emphasizes "peacocking," that is, wearing flamboyant clothing to draw attention to oneself in bars and nightclubs. David deAngelo advocates "C&F," making comments cocky but funny and intended to convey confidence, intelligence, and indifference in roughly equal degrees. Despite largely superficial differences, the various methods are based upon a common approach to the world of dating. On the surface, this seems little more than the old-fashioned view that men need to be self-confident in approaching women and not seek approval. However, the gurus will tell you, advising someone that they can improve their dating skills by becoming more confident is rather like telling them to improve by improving. Confidence, it is argued, comes through success and not the other way around. Instead of general advice, the gurus offer specific tips on how to dress, the effective use of voice and posture, the proper ways in which to approach a woman, and how to behave on dates.

Some of the tips offered sound somewhat trite, until one realizes that their main targets are men who have had little experience with dating. For instance, men are discouraged from acting in any way that makes them seem needy, such as staring at a woman for a long time without actually approaching her. Others are highly counterintuitive. For instance, the dating gurus advise men not to offer compliments and in some cases to be ambivalent to the point of insulting in their comments. An example of such a "neg" might be to initially draw attention to a woman's shoes, only to follow it up with the comment that they look "comfortable" or that the style is "very popular." The rationale behind such a strategy, which the gurus insist should only be used on exceptionally attractive women, is to mark the man out as someone different from the crowd who will not go out of his way to seek the woman's approval simply because she is attractive. The principle behind this idea draws heavily on neuro-linguistic programming. A "neg" introduces cognitive dissonance and changes the frame of reference such that the woman hearing it is supposed to then unconsciously seek the approval of the man who has slighted her. Another technique in this vein is to adopt a qualifying frame toward the woman in which she has to prove herself rather than the reverse. Men are encouraged to act as if they are interviewing potential dates and looking for reasons to reject them.

Many of the gurus draw explicitly on the pseudo-science of evolutionary psychology. The aim, they suggest, is to portray oneself as an Alpha male toward whom women are evolutionarily "programmed" to feel sexual attraction. Much of this cashes out in terms of how the aspiring PUA acts in social situations. He should do or say nothing that makes him seem of low social status – for example, boasting about his achievements. He should move slowly and with determination and eliminate verbal and other ticks. He should demonstrate leadership qualities, particularly when confronted with a mixed group in which there might be another potential Alpha male. Instead of openly challenging the other Alpha male, he should act as he would toward an equal.

In recent years the emphasis has moved away from external tricks and techniques and more towards a concern with self-development. Picking up women in bars ceases to be an end in itself and becomes part of a wider project of self-improvement. Many gurus flirt with New Age ideas, partly in recognition of the fact that no set of tricks can fully compensate for a deep-seated lack of self-esteem, and partly through a realization that a life dedicated to meeting women in bars is rather vacuous. Indeed, it seems odd that a movement whose intention is to make men less approval-seeking measures its success entirely in terms of whether they obtain the approval of attractive women.

Is The Game in fact successful? It is difficult to obtain any independent non-anecdotal evidence. Much of the material available is produced by those with a vested interest in shifting product. There is also the problem of confirmation bias. Even if the adoption of some strategy leads a man to be more outgoing and confident and thus meet more women, it is not necessarily the case that the method is responsible. Suppose that he were sold some magic beans and carried them in the belief that this would help his chances in the dating game. If he acted upon this belief and achieved a modicum of success, we would probably not attribute it to the power of the beans. Moreover, any serious analysis would require some understanding of what counts as "success" here. There is a world of difference between smoothtalking a woman into spending the night and establishing a serious relationship.

Be that as it may, given the success of The Game as a cultural phenomenon, regardless of whether it lives up to its much-vaunted claims, it is worthy of attention. What does the growth of this movement tell us about contemporary dating and what response is appropriate? In the next section, I turn to the work of Aristotle, a thinker not known for his romantic conquests, in the hope of throwing light on this question.

## Aristotle: My Wingman

Aristotle is the Philosopher's Philosopher. His work spans every field of human endeavor, from metaphysics and natural philosophy through to ethics and aesthetics. A keen observer of the natural world, he was an equally insightful commentator on human affairs. The opening preamble of his masterly *Nicomachean Ethics* has seldom been surpassed in its sensitivity to the complexities of human social life. In human affairs, he argues, "in arguing about what is for the most part so from premises which are for the most part true we must be content to draw conclusions that are similarly qualified."[6] Circumspection when generalizing about people is the mark of an educated mind.

An Aristotelian will therefore treat with caution claims such as those advanced by the dating gurus that their techniques can enable any man to achieve success with any woman. Leaving such hyperbole aside, can Aristotle shed any light on the vexed issue of dating in the new millennium? Aristotle's own views were heavily colored by the prejudices of his time. He would, for instance, have been baffled by the rise of feminism. Nevertheless, many of his central ideas have stood the test of time. In what follows, I will focus on two areas of his ethical and political thought: his account of character and his analysis of friendship, both of which have direct relevance to the topic at hand.

The issue of character is closely related to the concept of social proof, which figures heavily in the work of the dating gurus. In any social interaction with strangers, we need to work out very quickly whether they are trustworthy. Social proof is a set of verbal and non-verbal cues that provide the information necessary to make an evaluation of a stranger's trustworthiness. For the most part, men potentially pose a much greater physical and emotional risk to women than conversely. For that reason, interactions with strangers are fraught with danger. The simplest solution would be to ask. But as we all know, people lie and the most dangerous are often the best liars. Women on the dating scene need to become adept at ascertaining social proof.

Consequently, the dating gurus propose, women, especially very attractive women, who are veterans of the dating scene have developed highly honed skills for filtering out unsuitable suitors. For that reason, the gurus teach a series of techniques intended to circumvent these filters. Novices are taught to avoid any action that could be taken to indicate low status. They are told to eschew direct approaches that might appear needy, to approach in a casual non-committal way and to avoid compliments or offers of drinks. The aim of this is to demonstrate that they have the kind of character that many women find attractive.

We are, of course, discussing a relatively unusual situation. Through most of our history we have formed relationships based upon close community relationships. Where choice was exercised at all it tended to be mediated by those relationships. The anthropological record suggests that free choice in partners is the exception rather than the rule; the sociological one indicates that even in our own culture our choices are not as unconstrained as we would like to believe. Meeting strangers in clubs and bars is then a peculiar experience and it is therefore not surprising that few lack the skills to do so effectively. Those who have acquired this unique set of skills may lack other important personal characteristics.

Given this fact the problem of social proof looms large. How can we, in conditions of relatively anonymity, ascertain whether a person is someone with whom we might wish to pursue a relationship? Here is a problem for anyone attempting to negotiate the complexities of the modern urban landscape. For women, however, the risks are, in general, higher. Women can be harmed by men – physically, emotionally, or financially – in ways and to a degree that men cannot be similarly harmed by women. For that reason the ability to determine trustworthiness is of paramount importance. The renowned "women's intuition" can thus be understood less in terms of some mythical communion with a higher reality and more in terms of a heightened sensitivity to those cues, verbal and non-verbal, which demonstrate or, more precisely, reveal character.

The nice guy recognizes this and most of his actions are intended to demonstrate that he presents no threat whatsoever. For that reason, he emphasizes his soft and sensitive side. He pays lots of compliments. He seldom volunteers his opinion and when he finds that it conflicts with hers, he will gladly modify it, even in matters of great seriousness. The effect is at best soporific and at worst emetic.

By contrast the jerk and the PUA display a studied indifference to the opinions of others. In this respect they resemble the type of character described by Aristotle as the magnanimous or great-souled man. Many women revolted by the supplications of the nice guy find this attractive. The question that is posed is whether it is possible to adopt some of the more positive attributes of jerks and PUAs without taking on their more unpleasant characteristics.

Let us therefore consider the nature of the magnanimous man. Aristotle suggests that the magnanimous or great-souled man has a high degree of self-containment. One theme that has increasingly been stressed in the recent dating literature is that the aspiring pick-up artist should foster an attitude of "indifference to outcomes." This idea draws heavily upon New Age thinkers such as Eckhart Tolle or David Deida, but antecedents can be found in Aristotle, who suggests that the magnanimous man is properly concerned with honor and all else only insofar as it contributes to his honor. Aristotle frequently describes the magnanimous man as "imperturbable." Thus, while he may take pleasure in his achievements and conquests, he should not allow himself to be misled by them. He should regard them as fitting acknowledgments of the status he knows himself to merit.

Aristotle also describes the appropriate demeanor of the magnanimous man. His advice eerily prefigures that given by the dating gurus. His "gait is measured, his voice deep and his speech unhurried."[7] These physical characteristics reveal his indifference to the things that do not really matter in life. Knowing what is truly important in life means that he is unworried by trivialities. While he is skilled at social interaction and takes appropriate pleasure in the friendships that he forges, he is not dependent upon the favor of anyone. He has a healthy estimation of his own worth. In case this be confused with conceitedness, Aristotle makes clear that this requires a degree of self-knowledge. The magnanimous man has just as much self-regard as his abilities and accomplishments entitle him. Moreover, it is an important aspect of this self-knowledge that he recognizes that he only deserves honor insofar as he is good. Magnanimity requires a full complement of the virtues. The magnanimous man should be brave, honest, loyal, appropriately generous, and so on. These characteristics distinguish him from either the jerk or those aspiring pick-up artists who simply aim to manipulate women into satisfying their desires. He is haughty only towards the haughty, gracious towards those in an inferior position. He does not engage in flattery, but neither does he unintentionally offend. Equally, he is relatively immune to flattery and insult. He will accept compliments when they represent a just assessment of his worth, but will neither seek them nor be overly excited upon receiving them. If they are true, he knows their truth already. Although Aristotle does not make this explicit, it seems reasonable to suppose that the magnanimous man will take sincere and truthful criticism in the spirit in which it is intended.

In modern psychological parlance we would say that the magnanimous man has a healthy self-esteem. Because of this he is not a hostage to the approval of others. While he shares at a superficial level many of the more attractive features of the jerk or the PUA, his superiority lies in the fact that he genuinely possesses a good character. His self-containment is not the same as the jerk's self-absorption. He values friendships, including those erotic friendships which he forms with women, while at the same time does not make them the central focus of his life. In this he differs significantly from the dating gurus and their students. If he succeeds or fails in the dating game, he takes this in his stride.

How does one become magnanimous? Aristotle insists at several points that one attains virtuous character by acting in a virtuous manner. He draws an analogy between ethical conduct and the mastery of a craft: "Men will become good builders as a result of building well and bad ones as a result of building badly."[8] Similarly, "it is the way that we behave in our dealings with other people that make us just or unjust, and the way that we behave in the face of danger, accustoming ourselves to be timid or confident, that makes us brave or cowardly."[9] In the same way, then, someone aspiring to magnanimity should start to act in a magnanimous way. Perhaps it is possible that at least some of the men attracted by the teachings of the dating gurus will acquire the character of the magnanimous man and this would be no bad thing.

## After The Game

Some attracted by The Game are simply seeking hedonistic gratification. They see dating as an end in itself, measuring their self-worth by reference to the quantity of "9s" and "10s" that they can successfully hook. It is clear from reading the message boards and email lists, however, that many men who are drawn to The Game are looking for serious relationships. Their rationale is that by increasing the number of women they date, the greater their likelihood is of meeting The One.

Can such men learn anything from Aristotle? I believe they can. Aristotle's discussion of the various types of friendship and the role that they play in the Good Life offers a model for the kinds of relationships we should foster. This requires a creative reading of Aristotle. From what we know of Ancient Greek men, it seems that relationships with women figured relatively low on their list of priorities. Friendship was understood to be primarily between men who were equal in status. At first sight, this seems to exclude the possibility of genuine friendship between men and women. Nevertheless, I believe that there is a more charitable reading possible, in which social and political equality is a necessary condition for friendship and that consequently genuine friendship between sexual partners is possible to the extent that such equality is present. Indeed, based upon such a reading, one of the objectionable features of the longstanding oppression of women has been the manner in which it frustrates the possibility of genuine friendship.

In his discussion of the magnanimous man, Aristotle introduces an important qualification. While stressing his independence in general, Aristotle acknowledges that it is entirely appropriate for the magnanimous man to be dependent upon his friends.[10] This is in keeping with Aristotle's claim elsewhere that a life without friendship, even if it were characterized by all sorts of other attainments, would be significantly impoverished. Of all the Ancients, Aristotle is most emphatic in his insistence upon the fact that humans are necessarily social animals. Thus, relationships including friendships are not merely an optional extra, but are constitutive of a fully human life.[11]

Of course, it might be remarked that there are friendships and there are *friendships* and only some of these are conducive to a flourishing life. Aristotle recognizes this and broadly distinguishes between three classes of friendship, all of which are characterized by the fact that the parties have an attitude of good will (*eunoia*) towards one another. Without this attitude there is no friendship, but merely an association. Even with the presence of good will, not all friendships are of the same status. There are those friendships entered into largely as a matter of convenience. Such friendships are typically those that we have with our work colleagues and business associates. They exist for as long as both parties obtain whatever external ends they entered into the association to fulfill. Then there are friendships that rest upon a basis of mutual pleasure. We may, for instance, find the other amusing or physically attractive. While he regards such friendship as generally superior to those of utility, friendships based upon mutual pleasure are vulnerable to the vicissitudes of fortune. Physical beauty fades and what one once found amusing may come to irritate.

The highest form of friendship is that which one enters into for no other purpose than the joy that that friendship brings. Of such friendships, Aristotle writes, it is as if there were one soul shared between two bodies. The emotion that such friends share is a mutual and disinterested appreciation of each other's good qualities. Such friendships are strong enough to withstand anything that time and fate throws at them. It is such friendships that form the pinnacle of a life well lived.

Clearly, such an ideal is a strenuous one and it would be hard to find real world examples that fully live up to Aristotelian strictures. Real friendships often embody a combination of different elements: utility, pleasure, and disinterested appreciation may all come to play a greater or lesser role as the friendship develops. Most problematic are those friendships whose primary or at least initial motivation is erotic. The popular romantic comedy *When Harry Met Sally* articulates a common thought when Billy Crystal's character proclaims that men and women simply cannot be friends, since such erotic friendships seem perpetually imperilled by the imperatives of sexual desire.

In a slightly less pessimistic mood, we might concede that the highest form of friendship is even less common between men and women than it is between persons of the same sex. This should doubtless be a cause for regret. Nevertheless, human life is characterized by a plurality of goods and even if we rarely attain the highest goods, this need not mean that our lives are impoverished. Even the inferior varieties of friendship remain friendships, albeit transient ones. As Rosalind Hursthouse rightly notes, friendships between colleagues may end when one of them changes jobs; that notwithstanding, there remains an important distinction between colleagues who are friends and those who are simply colleagues.[12] Equally, a friendship whose primary motivation is sexual desire may be full of transient joys, but they remain joys nonetheless.

Lest we become too pious, I think it is important to recall that a thinker as wise and worldly as Aristotle would recognize that relationships driven only by sexual desire and lacking the appropriate spirit of concern and good will towards the other are arid. Nevertheless, relationships bereft of sexual attraction can be equally soul destroying. The goods and pleasures that constitute a fully human life are many and various. The joys and pains that surround the business of dating and relationships form a small but indispensable subset of these.

## NOTES

1  Neil Strauss, *The Game: Penetrating the Secret Society of Pick Up Artists* (London: IT Books, 2005).
2  *Rosen v. Mystery Method, Inc.*, No. 07 C 5727, 2008 WL 723331 (N.D. Ill. Mar. 14, 2008) (Kocoras, J.).
3  Deborah Netburn, "Danger: Pickup Artists Ahead." *LA Times* August 31, 2005; available online at www.latimes.com/features/lifestyle/cl-et-game31aug 31,0,1782296.story (accessed July 29, 2009).
4  I am grateful to my Aristotle Special Topic students at the University of Notre Dame Australia, especially Justin Keogh, for the original idea that prompted this essay.
5  Robert A. Glover, *No More Mr. Nice Guy: A Proven Plan For Getting What You Want In Love, Sex and Life* (Barnes and Noble Digital).
6  Aristotle, *The Ethics of Aristotle*, trans. J. A. K. Thomson (London: Penguin, 1961), p. 65.
7  Ibid., p. 158.
8  Ibid., p. 92.
9  Ibid., p. 92.
10  Ibid., p. 157.
11  Ibid., p. 258.
12  Rosalind Hursthouse, "Aristotle for Women Who Love Too Much," *Ethics* 117 (2007): 329. I am deeply indebted to Hursthouse for this article and for her collegial friendship. I suspect she will not endorse all of my arguments here.

CHAPTER 11

# I'VE NEVER BEEN ON A DATE
# (YET SOMEHOW I GOT MARRIED!)

No, I'm serious. And just to head off the obvious explanations: there are no mail-order brides or arranged marriages involved, no *Hangover*-style wake-up-married-after-a-night-of-debauchery incidents and no marriage of convenience because my boss needed a green card. It's just that I got to the altar without ever having been on a *real* date. Sure, I've been in several relationships, I just never dated beforehand.

I've had "date nights" with my wife, and probably when I was in other relationships. But I don't think these count as dates. A real date involves two people getting together in order to see whether they want to do it again.[1] People in committed relationships can't really date because when they go out for a night on the town there is no sense in which this is a "try-out." They might not have a good evening, but at no point should they think to themselves, "Well the evening didn't work out, I guess this is the last time I see this person." If something along those lines did happen, it would be because of much deeper issues. Besides, real dates do not have the weight of a lifelong commitment on them. A couple who goes out on the town to see if they can make their marriage work has done something that transcends a simple date.

This may seem like an exceptionally restrictive definition of a "real date," but actually it fits with common experience. When someone says to me that they are "dating" someone I take that to mean that they are not in a committed relationship. Someone in a serious relationship might use the word "dating," but I think that is more of an artifact of language. We don't have many words to describe committed relationships that are not marriages because for a long time that wasn't something that people were expected to do.

If you look up "date" in the dictionary you'll find a lot of different definitions, most having to do with periods of time. The *Oxford English Dictionary* gives one definition of "date" as "a social or romantic appointment or engagement." An appointment is usually a one-time thing. If you keep an appointment regularly that begins to become something else. Dating is a fairly recent phenomenon that began in the twentieth century.[2] Prior to that men courted women according to very specific rules of etiquette. Dates might lead to "going steady," but dating was an alternative to the old system of courtship – an opportunity for young people to socialize with the thought that this could be a potential romantic partner.

All of this may seem like stacking the definition, but there are important insights to be gained by engaging in some philosophical analysis of my experiences. I think most people would agree that ending up in a committed relationship is the brass ring of dating. Somehow I got hold of that ring without going through the usual steps. Wouldn't it be great to figure out how to get the prize without going through some of the hassle?

## Mind Games

I doubt I'm the first person to suggest that dating is a mind game, but I'm probably the first to mean it literally. The important caveat to my claim that I've never been on a real date is that I have not been in a situation where I was trying out to be someone's boyfriend. "Trying" reflects an intention and it is very important that one has that intention in order to be on a real date.

The behaviors of dating, such as eating dinner together, going to a movie, and/or having a coffee, are indistinguishable from non-dates if we don't take intentions into account. Parents could do all of these things with their children, but it is not a date. Even if we specified that the people involved not be blood relations, it's still possible for platonic friends to go through all of these motions. That is, unless you ascribe to the belief that you can scratch any platonic friend and find some very un-platonic desires lurking underneath.

We can put this *When Harry Met Sally* philosophy aside, because the point is that dating is an intentional activity and no intentional activity

ANDREW TERJESEN

can be defined solely by its behaviors. This philosophical point can be traced back to the medieval philosopher Peter Abelard (1079–1142). It might seem backwards to consult the "Dark Ages" for some philosophical insight on dating, but if it's any consolation Abelard was probably the mack daddy of his time.[3] In a work on ethics called *Ethics* (a title reflecting either a lack of imagination or the belief that this was the definitive work on the topic – knowing Abelard's arrogance, the latter is more likely to be true), Abelard argued that sin was determined by the intention of the actor and nothing else.

One of Abelard's examples is a classic. Imagine that someone comes home drunk and accidentally crawls into the wrong bed. She has sex with the person in the bed only to discover in the morning that it was her next-door neighbor instead of her husband. Although the behavior (sex with someone who is not her spouse) seems like adultery, it isn't, because the drunken person was ignorant that she was having sex with the wrong person. She therefore lacked the intention to commit adultery. On the flip side, if she had gone home with the intention of committing adultery and accidentally slept with her spouse she would still have committed adultery.

The same is true of dating. All of the physical actions that compose a typical date could be replicated by someone who has no intention of going on a date. The crucial element in being a date is that the person involved has the intention of keeping an appointment to engage in some activities that are meant to explore the romantic possibilities with the other party. One advantage of thinking of a date this way is that the definition of a date can be flexible enough to adapt with the times. In the beginning, a date was a two-person affair, but nowadays it is much more common to go out on a date as part of a group. Even though the behaviors are very different, the intention is the same, although I admit that group dating complicates matters, as it will not always be clear what the couplings are within the group.

## Is It or Isn't It?

So, in order to have a date it is crucial to have the intention of exploring the romantic potential of the person you are dating. But, you might wonder, if there are no physical aspects of dating that can be used, how can we ever tell if someone is out on a date with someone else? This might seem like only an abstract philosophical question, but how we answer it has implications for everyday life. Not only would it help us figure out when we are being a "third wheel," but also a theory of dating intentions would be of great use in sorting out some of the messiness of modern group dating. Otherwise one could end up with love triangles or rhomboids or even dodecahedrons (if you're socially active enough).

Determining someone's intentions – effectively, reading a mind – is no easy task. Yet we do it on a regular basis, even if we're not always right. If we had a theory of how we "mindread," we might be able to better understand why we make the mistakes we do and perhaps even correct them. The heart of the problem is that we can't see someone's intentions the way that we see how many glasses are on the table. Unless we have the power of telepathy or empathy, we will never have access to the inner-workings of someone's mind. We can't know for certain what someone is thinking, but we do by-and-large have a pretty good idea when someone is in pain or angry with us. Sometimes we can even tell when pain is faked in order to get our sympathy. (For some reason the fake orgasm is much harder to detect for the male of the species.) How do we do it?

Philosophers have wrestled with this question for a long time and the best answer is one that we find exemplified in the work of Bertrand Russell (1872–1970). Russell, like Abelard, demolishes the stereotype of the philosopher who is too involved in the world of abstract ideas to really understand human passions. In his lifetime, he was married four times and had countless affairs (some of them simultaneously). He's a philosopher who knows a thing or two about dating. Russell argues that we are able to "mind-read" through the use of analogies between our own experiences and those of others.[4] For example, if I'd ever been on a date and I was late, I should be able to tell whether my date is annoyed with me or not by observing her behavior. If she is scowling, I reason that she is angry based on the fact that when I feel myself scowl it is at times when I know that I am angry. Similarly, if upon arrival I see her tapping her foot repeatedly or she speaks abruptly to me, I surmise that she has lost patience with me, as these are all behaviors I engage in when I feel that time is being wasted.

By noticing similarities between my behaviors and the behaviors of others, I can infer from something I am certain about (that my behaviors were caused by a particular mental state) to something that is probably true (that others' behaviors were caused by the same mental state as mine). The thing about analogical reasoning is that it cannot guarantee that its conclusion is true. Just because two things are very similar does not mean that they share exactly the same features. At best, reasoning by analogy gives us a justification for our beliefs about someone else's mental states. That's why two reasonable people can misunderstand a situation. Bill interprets Hillary's behavior as "playing hard to get," but really she is not interested in him. Nevertheless, for all its imperfections, analogical reasoning is the best method we have for figuring out the intentions of another person. That it is not perfectly reliable explains why there can be so much confusion about how our partner feels about us, especially when we are first getting to know each other and don't have much experience together.

## It Takes Two

Using analogical reasoning I could have good reason for thinking that someone wants to go out on a date with me. Both people, however, must intend for the evening to be a date in order for it to be a real date. If it were possible to unilaterally declare a date, then all of us will have been on dates and never have known it. Dating is a mutual activity, but that means that the intention to go out on a date must be shared. But how do two different people share an intention?

Having the same intention is not the same as sharing an intention. For example, both Barack and John might have the intention of becoming President of the United States, but they don't have the shared intention of being President. Both of them intend to be the only President and both of them intend for the other not to be President. In order to have a shared intention, it must be the case that we are coordinating our actions in order to realize the same goal.

Remember, dating is not simply a physical activity, so it would not be enough for two people to coordinate in order to make sure that the evening is pleasant in order to count as a date. In order for the date to be a shared intention both parties must be regarding it as a try-out. This means that not only must it be both Meg and Tom's intention that it is a date, but each of them must be aware that that is the other's intention. Otherwise, both of them could go to the movies wishing it were a date but thinking the other person is not really interested.[5] If so, it would be the comic misunderstanding that is the bread and butter of romantic comedies that keeps the movie rolling along until the end when they real-ize that they want to be with each other.

Even the requirement that both Meg and Tom recognize the other's intention is not enough to have the shared intention that they go out on a date. Tom might know that Meg is interested in dating, but not think that she realizes he wants to date her. In that case, until he makes his inten-tions clear they don't have a shared intention to go on a date. Now, Tom doesn't have to make an explicit declaration of interest if he thinks Meg knows that he intends for their evening to be a romantic engagement.

Meg and Tom's intentions would be coordinated (and therefore shared) if all of the following were true: Meg intended to go out on a date with Tom, Tom intended to go out on a date with Meg, Meg knew that Tom's intention was to date her, Tom knew that Meg's intention was to date him, Meg knew that Tom was aware of her intention and Tom knew that Meg was aware of his intention. Under these conditions, Tom and Meg would be able to work together on making the date a romantic evening, as they would know that it is the shared goal of the other.

Unfortunately, as we've all probably experienced, we can be mis-taken in our reading of someone else's thoughts. As we've seen, this is because our beliefs about what other people are thinking are the result of analogical reasoning, which only yields probable conclusions.[6] That means Tom will be somewhat unsure if he has read Meg right. It would be better if he has good reason to think that he has good reason for thinking that Meg shares his intentions. To achieve this, Tom would not only need to have good reason to think that Meg was aware of his inten-tions, he would also need to have good reason to think that Meg was aware that he was aware of her intentions. Of course, he could only be confident about that if he had good reason to think that Meg was aware that he was aware that she was aware that he was aware of her inten-tions. As you might have already guessed, the nature of analogical rea-soning means that this might not be enough either and the vicious cycle of "I know that you know that I know that you know . . ." continues. What we have here is what philosophers call an infinite regress, because there does not seem to be an end to the demand for more evidence that we are right in how we read the other person's intentions. This might sound crazy, until you're the person spending all night trying to figure out if he or she's really that into you. Every time you think you've got "conclusive" proof, you'll second-guess yourself and begin the cycle anew. And if you're not sure what is going on, it's hard to call that a shared intention.[7]

ANDREW TERJESEN

## The Talk

There is one way to avoid the infinite regress and that's to be explicit at the very beginning. Uncertainty grabs hold of us because we're trying to figure out what someone else is thinking by reading his or her behavior. If someone told you what he was thinking you wouldn't need to rely on analogical reasoning to figure it out. Tom could say to Meg, "So, it's a date?" and she'll have the opportunity to clarify things then and there by saying "yes" or "no."

It's a simple solution as long as you ignore the possibility that the word "date" can be ambiguous. "It's a date" could mean "It's an appointment," as we do sometimes use the phrase in non-romantic circumstances. Also, the solution works only if we're sure that we're not being lied to. We think, based on analogical reasoning, that people say what they believe is true as long as there are no clear advantages in telling a lie. But that analogy holds imperfectly – you might be dealing with a pathological liar, for example. Finally, this simple solution requires us to be willing to put everything on the table and risk the possibility of rejection before the date has even happened. My own experiences lead me to infer that many people would rather delay the possibility of rejection for as long as they can and therefore would not use the d-word when arranging an outing with someone they are interested in.

Even if we do avoid the d-word at first, at some point every potential couple has to have the dreaded "Talk" when they define the relationship. This is the conversation every new couple has that starts with the question, "So what exactly is this?" The Talk is inevitable because it is the only way to try and put an end to the infinite regress that occurs when we try to infer how someone feels about a relationship with us. Relationships and the feelings that they involve are far too complex for us to get through by analogy. There are too many possible ways in which we might have misunderstood our partner's intentions for us to have any certainty about the conclusions of our analogical reasoning.

Technically, the Talk is still a form of analogical reasoning. In this case, we're making an analogy to when we say things like "I want to spend more time with you" in the context of a serious conversation and the fact that we are sincerely reporting our desires. There's something odd about that previous sentence. Romantic relationships seem too important to say such things lightly, at least for a person with anything approximating human emotions. (Hopefully, one is observant enough to recognize when the speaker is a cad or a manipulator who is not interested in a real relationship but only the side benefits.)

The emotions involved in the Talk explain why it is such a dreaded occurrence. Since few people have the courage to risk going first, much of the Talk can involve trying to entice the other person to spell out their feelings first. Of course, the other wants you to do the same. So the initiation of the Talk becomes an exercise in brinkmanship until someone accidentally tips his or her hand and everything falls into place. In addition, one party may not be at the same level of attachment as his or her partner and will want to be careful not to say something that would cause that person to feel rejected. At which point, you get such political-style rhetoric as "I don't want to put a label on things," "We have a good thing going," and "Ditto." In fairness, this person might actually believe that he or she is moving towards the same level of relationship but is not there yet.

In the end, the Talk will establish what level the relationship is at and where the couple wants it to go from there: be it a continued non-exclusive relationship, an exclusive relationship (at which point they're no longer dating), or something else. Or it could simply spell the end, as the couple realizes they did not have an accurate sense of one another's intentions and feel that this is not the type of relationship either or both of them wanted.

## The Friend Zone

Of course, once two people realize they are interested in dating each other it does not retroactively transform all the previous times they went out – but were unsure of what was happening – into dates. Prior to the Talk, or whatever causes them to realize they share intentions, each held a torch for the other, but together they were not coordinating their actions in a manner that would count as a date. It's even possible that both were doing everything possible to disguise their intentions (out of fear of rejection), so that to any outside observer whatever they were doing did not look like a date.

One reason to think that this philosophical analysis of dating (as shared intentions to explore romantic possibilities) is on the money is that it also explains other phenomena related to dating. As we've already seen, it explains why unilateral dating is impossible by definition and it explains the significance and difficulties of the Talk. Plus, it helps us to better understand how it is that someone can fall into the "Friend Zone."

When we first meet someone, it is impossible to have any shared intentions. At that point any relationship could go in all sorts of directions. Nevertheless, if you spend time with a person whom you're interested in you have to be wary of the signals you're sending. Play it cool and you might give the other person the impression that you're not interested. Or if you're interested in someone who tends to second guess herself you'll need to be much more explicit in your intentions: make some sort of grand romantic gesture or simply have the Talk as soon as you can. Otherwise you may have inadvertently created the impression that you share an intention with the other person to simply become a friend.

All the physical activities associated with dating (even the ones that seem very exclusive to dating can nowadays be part of other kinds of relationships – Friends with Benefits anyone?) are designed to create connections between people. These connections, however, do not have to be romantic connections – that's why the same physical activities can be engaged in by family members, platonic friends, and so forth. The Friend Zone is located in the fuzzy area where the shared intention to date meets the shared intention to get to know someone. Spend too much time in that fuzzy area without sending out clear signals and you'll never leave the Friend Zone. This can happen because the other party has decided to suppress their romantic interest since you seem uninterested; for fear of ruining a good relationship with the awkwardness of dating; because the other person might have started a relationship with someone else since your weren't available; or simply because you have unwittingly made yourself into someone that it would be "gross" to date – a kind of social incest.

The Friend Zone became a popular phrase because of an episode of *Friends* when Ross was crowned "Mayor of the Friend Zone." In that context it represented defeat: Ross had failed to make his interest in Rachel clear and he detoured into the Friend Zone as a result. But I think that it's a mistake to think of the Friend Zone as a trap one falls into.[8] Any strong romantic relationship is a form of friendship and one has to build the friendship up early on if one expects to have the kind of committed relationship that is the end goal of dating. People pass through the Friend Zone on the way to dating and more. Some people have trouble getting from the friend part to the dating part, but that is by no means the end of the story. After all, it eventually worked out for Ross and Rachel.

## Do You Like Me? Check Box, Yes or No

After a few outings, my future wife and I had the Talk. In our case, we were already interested in something more committed than dating, so we jumped immediately to the Longer Talk. I suspect that as one gets older (we were both in the second half of our twenties), it takes less time to figure out if someone is a serious prospect for a long-term commitment. However, I don't think that was the only reason we jumped from getting to know each other to a relationship. I think we also bypassed the dating stage because our interactions had already begun to form a solid friendship. We realized we had lots of similar interests and, most importantly, a shared sense of humor. Once it became clear through the Longer Talk that we also were physically attracted to each other, there seemed little point in merely dating. That would've been moving backwards. Instead, we jumped forward into a committed relationship.

What happened with my wife was not unique in my experience. In all my relationships I've jumped into "going steady" after an initial awkward period. On reflection, I think that is because my uncertainty about whether we were dating (which meant we weren't dating at that time) led me to focus on cultivating a friendship with these women instead of thinking of ways to "get in their pants." By embracing the Friend Zone I made it possible for those relationships to skip the dating phase.

One lesson to be learned from my experience is the importance of being as upfront as possible when trying to date someone. When we were in elementary school, a note with a multiple-choice question seemed a good way to start. Given the lack of standard dating rituals these days, it would be a good idea to find a more mature version of the elementary school note.

But there's a much more important lesson here. Assuming that the goal of dating is finding a committed partner, then my experiences show the value of focusing on cultivating a friendship with the person you're interested in. The Friend Zone is not a dead-end, it's the most important step in getting to a relationship.[9] Once it is clear that you enjoy someone's company and take an interest in their wellbeing, the physical attraction is relatively simple to figure out. Become good at being someone's friend and you'll become a Zen master of dating – getting what you want out of dating without ever having to do it.

ANDREW TERJESEN

# NOTES

1   See chapter 4 for another take on the definition of a date. John Rowan and Patricia Hallen seem to agree that dating is about testing things out before making a more serious commitment. However, they say this can happen unconsciously. I will argue that we have to be conscious of going on a date for it to count as a *real* date.

2   For a more detailed examination of how much things have changed in the twentieth century and why, you should take a look at Beth Bailey's *From Front Porch to Back Seat: Courtship in Twentieth-Century America* (Baltimore: Johns Hopkins University Press, 1989).

3   Abelard is more often remembered for his tragic relationship with Heloise and the way it ended (with his castration). However, he was also an important philosopher in his time. His insights about the importance of intention in judging actions can be found in Book I of his *Ethics*, in Peter Abelard, *Ethical Writings*, trans. Paul Vincent Spade (New York: Hackett, 1995).

4   For the full argument, see Bertrand Russell, *Human Knowledge: Its Scope and Limits*, Part I, Chapter 6. Although originally published in 1948, Routledge published a reprint (most recently in 2003).

5   I must admit that my wife disagrees with me on this point. She claims our first date happened when we saw *Gladiator* together and spent time walking my dog after lunch with her sisters. Her point is that it was obvious because she brought her sisters to the movie to meet me. My argument is that it may have seemed obvious to her, but I wasn't sure what was going on. At the time, I thought it was just as likely that someone I had had some interesting conversations with wanted to see a Russell Crowe movie, and I hated going to movies by myself. So I didn't think of it as a date. As a form of relationship building I think it is crucial that dates be bilateral decisions (or multilateral if that's your thing).

6   The problem goes even deeper. As the philosopher David Hume (1711–76) noted, we actually have no good reason for thinking that the future will follow from the past. For example, just because a billiard ball hasn't passed through solid objects in the past is not proof that it won't do so in the future. He explores what has become known as the "problem of induction" in his *Enquiry Concerning Human Knowledge*, Section 4.

7   This is probably why for many millennia courtships have been very formal affairs. If there were unambiguous dating rituals (and I don't think it's written anywhere that bringing your sisters is a dating ritual), then the problem of being reasonably certain that you're on a date is avoided.

8   Although all parts of this essay have benefitted from the attention and helpful comments of my editors (Kristie and Marlene), my ideas concerning the nature of the Friend Zone evolved enormously in the editorial process and

they deserve all credit for these insights and my more nuanced conclusions based on them.

9 Aristotle (384–322 BCE) in the *Nicomachean Ethics*, Book VIII, describes true friendship as wishing the good for each other. I think that's a pretty good description of marriage and long-term relationships as long as you spice it up with some sex.

CHRISTOPHER BROWN AND DAVID W. TIEN

CHAPTER 12

# MORALITY, SPONTANEITY, AND THE ART OF GETTING (TRULY) LUCKY ON THE FIRST DATE

For the reflective single adult, certain questions about dating become especially salient when preparing for a first date. Should I put my best foot forward? What should I do if it becomes obvious that we're not hitting it off? How proactive or guarded should I be about having sex? It might seem that the answers vary, depending on what one hopes to get out of the first date. We contend, however, that the answers – respectively (and quite crudely): "It depends," "Call it a night," and "Not particularly" – are the same for all cases, provided that one's motives going into the first date are of the right sort.

We'll begin with our account of the wrong sorts of motives, which is based on arguments from the moral philosophy of Immanuel Kant. It may comfort some readers to know at the outset that we reject Kant's notoriously austere views on sex. But, to preempt premature sighs of relief, it should be noted that, according to our account, many (perhaps most) people who do date should not date. For those with the right motives, we advocate an approach informed by insights from Asian philosophy, recent research in psychology, and good old common sense. We argue that the most effective pursuit of the permissible dating goals essentially involves "being in the moment." The key is to maintain a certain state of consciousness, similar to what many contemporary philosophers and psychologists call "flow," and widely discussed in ancient Asian philosophy, particularly by Zhuangzi. Once we have clarified the approach, we will return (with more refined answers) to questions about first dates.


## The Kantian Gate

It may seem quite silly to suppose that Immanuel Kant could be a source of anything that resembles sound dating advice. Kant never married or even courted, and biographers agree that he most probably never had sex, and quite possibly never developed any romantic interests at all. (Besides, what kind of advice – on *any* worldly matter – could one reasonably expect from a sickly, obsessive-compulsive, eighteenth-century Prussian who never traveled beyond a stone's throw from his hometown?)[1] It's not too surprising that, in his philosophical texts, Kant was as explicit as one could be that procreation is the only morally acceptable end of sexual activity, and then only in a marital context.[2] Just as explicit, and hardly more surprising, was his condemnation of all of our sensuous desires.[3]

There is good reason to suspect that Kant's arguments for quite a few of his philosophical positions were little more than rationalizations of his own psychological quirks. (Of course, Kant would hardly be unique in this regard.) Suspicions aside, his arguments for the above views are deeply flawed. We'll spare readers the details, but suffice it to say that the foundational principles of Kantian morality do not, and cannot, impose anything as monkish as the prohibitions Kant advocated. Still, there's much to be said for the foundational principles themselves, and we'll be explaining what one of them can tell us about morality and dating. The principle we have in mind is the so-called Formula of Universal Law, and we'll show that it provides a moral rule on who may date and who should not. We also intend to suggest that this rule, which we'll call the Kantian Gate, gets things right.

Let us start with a word or two about the Formula of Universal Law. Translated from the original German, it states, "Act only in accordance with that maxim through which you can at the same time will as a universal law."[4] Roughly, it calls upon us to examine our maxims, that is, our personal action-guiding principles (or, quite simply, our motives), and to ask whether we would want everyone to always act in accord with them. If one of my maxims is such that I *would not* want everyone always acting in accord with it, the Formula of Universal Law implies that I shouldn't act on it either. For example, suppose I generally refuse to help others unless there's something in it for me. But suppose also that I do want others to help me, at least in certain kinds of situations, even when there's nothing in it for them. (In other words, suppose also that I am in fact a rational human being!) Then my maxim of not helping others unless there's something in it for me is one that I cannot "will as a universal law." For, obviously, I can't want everyone to generally refuse to help others unless there's something in it for them and at the same time want people to help me even when there's nothing in it for them. I'd then be wanting two things that are, in the strictest sense, mutually exclusive. So, given that I'm to act only on maxims that I *can* will as universal laws, I should abandon the maxim in question and be willing to make at least some genuine sacrifices for the sake of helping others.[5]

This example illustrates a noteworthy aspect of the Formula of Universal Law. The reason I cannot will the maxim in question as a universal law is that I would not want others to always act on that maxim *in their treatment of me.* So, the Formula of Universal Law in effect generates something much like the Golden Rule. It is this: if you do not want others to always treat you in accord with a certain maxim, then you should not act on that maxim yourself. Notice, however, that the Golden Rule is explicitly about actions ("Do unto others . . ."), whereas the Kantian counterpart is concerned with the maxims that motivate actions. This is no trivial point, partly because it's often quite difficult to be clear about what motivates one to act in one way rather than another. In addition, our maxims are often a good bit more complex than that of the above example. And, of course, it's no secret that even the most mature adults may sometimes fool themselves about what their true motives are. Applying the Formula of Universal Law requires a good bit of self-knowledge and honesty, to make sure one does not oversimplify or sugarcoat one's maxims. This isn't just to avoid keeping maxims one should abandon. It's also to avoid abandoning maxims that are really perfectly fine, or even good, but which one hasn't fully understood.

So, let's now start talking about dating maxims. There are two questions you'd need answers for if you want to fairly precisely understand your dating maxims. First, what, ultimately, do you aim to get out of dating? Second, what are you prepared to do to get it? Now, most of us will find it pretty difficult to answer either question completely. For example, suppose your answer to the first question is, "To get to know someone I'm interested in." This is a common answer, largely because it's a safe one, but it's rarely even close to the whole story. Remember, the question is about what you *ultimately* want out of dating. So, unless all – really *all* – you want out of a date is to satisfy your curiosity (which would be pretty curious itself), the complete answer would say something about *why* you want to get to know the person/people you (would) date. A more explicit answer would be along the lines of, "To see if s/he's a good fit, given the kind of interests in her/him I have." And it's only when you start spelling out what those interests are that you're getting to the heart of the matter. Another common initial response goes, "Just to spend more time with . . ." Often, this is in fact the complete answer, or pretty close to it. And when it is, we (the authors) would say "Good!" for reasons we'll explain later in this essay. When it's not, though, it's just another instance of safe shorthand. In order to work toward a complete answer, one has to keep asking, "But why do I want *that*?" Eventually, having answered this, asked it again, and so forth, you'll get to a point where all one can honestly say is, "I just do." Chances are, you'll then have identified your most fundamental reasons for dating, or, your *dating ends*.

Although we don't think all dating ends are created equally good, we do think that there are very few dating ends that are inherently bad. For the most part, it's the second question (above) that's crucial in determining whether a dating maxim is to be acted on or not. In other words, we don't think it matters so much what you ultimately want out of dating, but rather what lengths you're willing to go to, and what kinds of things you're willing to forgo, to get it. And, as we shall see, a dating maxim that involves even the most mundane dating end(s) can be made bad by the approaches one is willing to take. For example, dating for the sake of securing a life partner seems unobjectionable, but if one is willing to lie at every turn, coerce, and demean in order to secure it, then one definitely should not be dating. On the other hand, we'll also explain how a maxim involving one or more questionable dating ends can be permissible if, for example, one is unwilling to pursue these in anything short of a completely respectful way.

Of course, there are some dating ends which in fact *are* inherently bad, and which cannot possibly be part of any morally permissible dating maxim. Perhaps the most obvious example is a dating end that involves inflicting what one considers to be genuine harms on another person – simply for the sake of inflicting harm. Explaining the wrongness of this fundamentally malicious end is hardly necessary, but doing so will serve to introduce the Kantian Gate.

CHRISTOPHER BROWN AND DAVID W. TIEN

We've seen that the Formula of Universal Law generates the following rule: if you do not want others to always treat you in accord with a certain maxim, then you should not act on that maxim yourself. Applying this rule, we find that any maxim including the above dating end is a maxim that no human being should act on. Nobody wants others to harm him or her simply for harm's sake. (Even those poor souls who want to be harmed don't want this *for its own sake*; they believe it serves some further purpose, e.g., getting what they (think they) "deserve.") So, since we don't want others treating us in accord with any maxim that includes a fundamentally malicious end, none of us should ever act on such a maxim. Of course, then, anyone who has a *dating* maxim with this end should not date. They cannot will their dating maxim as a universal law, since they want *their* date(s) *not* to act on that maxim. So, the general rule here is this: unless you *do* want your date(s) acting on your own dating maxim, or at least *wouldn't mind* it, you should not date. This is the Kantian Gate.

Now, it's worth pointing out that what makes the malicious dating end *inherently* bad is the fact that *nobody* wants to be on the receiving end of it. This is probably true of a few other possible dating ends. And if there are any ends, dating or otherwise, that *everyone* wants to be on the receiving end of, these could be inherently *good*. But most dating ends are neither inherently good nor inherently bad. Again, for the most part, it's not the ends that make dating maxims bad; it's the approach.

For example, deception, in one form or another, manages to find its way into many people's dating approaches. And, although Kant was wrong to say that lying is *never* permissible, the salient point here begins with the fact that most of us have a problem with others deceiving us to get what they want from us. If you do have a problem with it, you should have just as much of a problem with deceiving others to get what you want from them, whether it's sex, a free dinner, or a long-term relationship. That said, it does seem that something short of complete honesty is sometimes understandable, perhaps even called for, especially when one is first getting to know someone. On these matters, the general verdict we get from the Kantian Gate is this: unless you wouldn't mind your date(s) falling as short of complete honesty as you're inclined to fall, you should not date. And we'd be quick to point out what this means for those who are inclined to deceive whenever they can get away with it, for the sake of sex or any other dating end. To them, the Kantian Gate says: you should be willing to put up with any date of yours deceiving you whenever s/he can get away with it, for the sake of *her/his* dating ends – which may be quite different from yours, and even incompatible with much of what you generally want out of life. But we doubt that anyone really is so willing. Similar verdicts apply for approaches involving extremely opportunistic coercion or manipulation, regardless of what one's dating ends are. Many who take one or more of these approaches in their pursuit of their dating ends *would mind* it if their dates took the same approach in the pursuit of theirs. So, the Kantian Gate bars them from dating.

But let's now assume that your dating maxims do in fact get you through the Kantian Gate. Your dating ends aren't inherently bad, and your approach is one you wouldn't mind being taken by any of your dates. The question we'll turn to in the next section is whether your approach can be improved upon. More specifically, is it the best one for achieving your dating ends? Of course, we can't survey all of the permissible ends, but, as luck would have it, it doesn't really matter. What we'll be doing is describing an approach, which, we believe, is not only uniquely enjoyable, but also the very best way of achieving any permissible dating end. You could think of it as a "tweak" to your existing approach, but we'd suggest rebuilding your entire dating approach around it.

## Dating as Flow and Cultivated Spontaneity

At some point in our lives, most of us have had the feeling of being completely engrossed in an engaging dialogue with a new acquaintance. During such experiences we lose ourselves in the conversation and leave behind any awkward self-consciousness. We feel entirely at ease expressing ourselves in a way that feels comfortable, natural, and authentic. We feel emotionally "connected" with someone who understands us. It is as if our interlocutors could finish our sentences and we theirs. Hours pass by in minutes. And it is thrilling.

This is an approximate description in the context of dating of what is meant by – borrowing a term from Mihalyi Csikszentmihalyi – "flow."[6] Our contention is that achieving "flow" in dating experiences is a sufficient condition for effectively and genuinely connecting two individuals in a manner that allows both parties to "be themselves" truly and sincerely.[7] At a more advanced level, one can learn, practice, and master the elements involved in dating and thus achieve a kind of Daoist cultivated spontaneity in dating situations.

In this section, we will first analyze the relevance and philosophical significance of Csikszentmihalyi's concept of "flow" to dating. Then, we will explore the ideal of cultivated spontaneity in Chinese philosophy, particularly in the philosophy of the *Zhuangzi*, and how it pertains to the achievement of advanced dating skills, which would enable one to date successfully a wider range of people than one would without such skills and enlarges one's options for finding suitable romantic partners.

As a caveat for what follows, in the face of a remarkable dearth of academically rigorous empirical research on the social phenomenon of dating, we must admit that much of our argumentation is based on armchair theorizing and wholly unscientific field research by our colleagues, peers, and ourselves. We trust, though, that our conclusions will, upon reflection, resonate at some level with your own experience and intuitions.

In his *Flow: The Psychology of Optimal Experience*, Mihalyi Csikszentmihalyi makes a landmark contribution to the academic study of "flow." He summarizes the result of years of research on how people feel when they most enjoy themselves and why. He and his research group at the University of Chicago teamed up with researchers from around the world to interview thousands of people in many different fields. They asked people to wear an electronic pager. Whenever the pager signaled, the subjects were to record what they were doing and how much they enjoyed it. The pager was activated by a radio transmitter throughout the day at random intervals. Over a hundred thousand records formed the body of data upon which Csikszentmihalyi drew his conclusions.

People reported the highest levels of happiness and satisfaction when they were engaged in three sorts of activities. Among the highest-rated activities were eating meals, especially in the company of others, and, perhaps unsurprisingly, sex. The biggest discovery was that most people valued, even above food and sex, a certain kind of experience – a state of total immersion in a task that is challenging yet closely matched to one's abilities. This was what the researchers called "flow" – "the state in which people are so involved in an activity that nothing else seems to matter; the experience itself is so enjoyable that people will do it even at great cost, for the sheer sake of doing it."[8] It is akin to what high-performance athletes, musicians, and surgeons call "being in the zone."

If we define "dating" as an activity two people engage in together with the intention of getting to know each other better for romantic interests, then we can ask whether this state of flow can also occur during the activity of dating. Csikszentmihalyi has identified seven elements of the flow experience, all of which can be found in the context of dating.

First, there is a challenging activity that requires skills. In his discussion of this component, Csikszentmihalyi mentions the case of socializing, which is very similar to dating:

> Socializing might at first sight appear to be an exception to the statement that one needs to use skills to enjoy an activity, for it does not seem that gossiping or joking around with another person requires particular abilities. But of course, it does; as so many shy people know, if a person feels self-conscious, he or she will dread establishing informal contacts and avoid company whenever possible.[9]

What is required for this first condition is that the activity be challenging enough that we are not bored, but not be so challenging that meeting it lies beyond our present abilities. In socializing, we find more enjoyment from interlocutors who teach us new things or help us to see things from novel perspectives. This quality is what marks a social interaction as engaging or stimulating. Nobody likes talking to a blank wall.

Second, there is a merging of action and awareness, which means that people in the state of flow become so engrossed in the activity that they lose a sense of themselves as separate from the actions they are performing; the activity becomes spontaneous and almost automatic. In dating, the activities include not just the complexities of flirtatious conversation, but also eye contact, body language, and managing logistics – where to go and when to go there. When one is in the dating flow, one doesn't need to think about when to shoot a flirtatious glance or how to tease the date playfully, one just does it naturally. When one is not in the moment and is self-conscious about one's words and actions, no amount of calculated movements or planned scripts will matter; many people will detect the lack of authenticity.[10]

Third, there are clear goals and immediate feedback. In athletic competition the goals are relatively straightforward and the feedback is obvious. In ice hockey, for example, the ultimate goal is to get the puck into the opposing team's net as many times as possible, and we can know almost immediately whether a shot has scored. What about in dating? The goal could be to "put one's best foot forward" while becoming better acquainted with one's date, or it could be to attract the date romantically while representing oneself truthfully. How do we know whether we are succeeding in attracting our dates? What feedback is available? Examples include whether your date reinitiates conversation when you stop talking, whether your date holds deep eye contact with you even when neither of

CHRISTOPHER BROWN AND DAVID W. TIEN

you is talking, whether your date is smiling and laughing at things you say, whether your date continually compliments you, or whether when your date says or does something, he or she looks to you for your reaction. All of this information constitutes important and immediate feedback indicating your date's interest or lack of interest.

Fourth, there is a complete focusing of attention on the task at hand, leaving no mental energy or space for irrelevant information. If, on a date, you find your mind wandering to your grocery list or the assignments due tomorrow, you are probably not enjoying yourself. If, instead, you are so captivated by the conversation with your date that you don't notice anyone else around you or any events occurring nearby, then you have probably fulfilled this condition of flow.

Fifth, there is a marked lack of that sense of worry typical in many situations in normal life about losing control. A dancer expressed this feature thusly: "A strong relaxation and calmness comes over me. I have no worries of failure. What a powerful and warm feeling it is! I want to expand, to hug the world. I feel enormous power to effect something of grace and beauty."[11] What the dancer is reporting is not the objective presence of control, but her perception that control is possible. She may fall or break her leg, but she is convinced that she is in control and that her skills play a major role in the outcome. Applied to dating, a skillful dater is so confident in her social value and in her control in presenting herself that she is not worried about whether her date likes her, but only about whether she likes her date, which makes her seem all the more attractive.

Sixth, there is a loss of self-consciousness. This is related to the fourth element. The flow experience is not about a passive obliteration of the self because in fact flow often involves a very active role for the self. A violinist must be extremely sensitive to every movement of her fingers and must be listening intently to the sounds entering her ears. Loss of self-consciousness does not mean a loss of self or of consciousness, but of a loss of consciousness of the self. One is not thinking about oneself executing the play; one just executes the play. In skillful dating, one is not self-consciously thinking about oneself telling a charming story; rather, one loses oneself in the telling of one's story, in listening to one's date tell a joke or share a secret, and in the social interaction as a whole.

Seventh, there is a transformation of the perception of the passing of time. Usually, people report that time seems to pass much faster, though occasionally with physical activities people report that time seems to slow down. Perhaps this quality is the most easily understood when applied to dating. As the adage goes, "Time flies when you're having fun."

Clearly then, all seven components of flow are characteristic of enjoyable and successful dates. Moreover, if one achieves the state of flow while on a date, one also accomplishes three goals that are often required for successful dating: (1) one has an immensely pleasant time, as or more enjoyable than a good meal or sex; (2) one acts out of one's authentic and natural self, free from self-conscious posturing, deception, or artifice; and (3) one presents oneself in the best possible light and acts as one's best self. Hence, approaching dating as a flow activity is likely one's best strategy.

Achieving a flow state in dating situations, however, can sometimes be difficult. Often, there are arbitrary social norms impeding us from acting unselfconsciously. If we were free from negative social programming, maybe we could be more attractive naturally. In addition, there certainly are social skills that are not intuitive and that we can learn, practice, and master just like any other skill. This implies a two-step process.

An excellent model is available in Chinese philosophy.[12] In an insightful study of the values of spontaneity, Philip J. Ivanhoe turns to Chinese philosophy to help articulate two views of spontaneity – untutored spontaneity and cultivated spontaneity.[13] On the theory of "untutored spontaneity," exponents of which include the text of the *Dao De Jing*, one seeks ways to identify and eliminate impediments that were artificially imposed and blocking the free flow of one's natural-standing tendencies. In the case of "cultivated spontaneity," advocated in early Confucian texts such as the *Xunzi*, there are no such desirable natural tendencies to set free. One of the primary goals in developing cultivated spontaneity is to acquire the right kind of standing dispositions. As Ivanhoe summarizes: "Some type of explicit training – a kind of socialization or enculturation – is needed in order to establish even the possibility of spontaneity. Instead of a paring away of obstructions, one aims at building up the right constellation of abilities, habits, sensibilities, and judgment."[14] While most of the Chinese philosophers Ivanhoe examines take one side or the other, one prominent Chinese philosophical text,[15] the *Zhuangzi*, has a hybrid view in which there is first a negative project of paring away limiting or wrongheaded beliefs or practices, debilitating habituation, or the general ill-effects of deleterious socialization, which frees up one's prereflective intuitions and tendencies. And then there is a positive project involving a sustained course of practice to train oneself to act in accord with one's natural inclinations and predispositions.[16]

Over two thousand years before Csikszentmihalyi came upon his insight about flow, the *Zhuangzi* depicted a similar state using terms bearing a close resemblance to modern descriptions of flow, as can be clearly seen in the *Zhuangzi*'s "knack stories."[17] While the message of the *Zhuangzi* was originally and primarily about moral, spiritual, or religious self-cultivation, the general theory and framework of the *Zhuangzi*'s method can also be applied effectively to dating.

According to the *Zhuangzi*, the negative aspect of this method involves shedding one's social programming and over-reliance on traditional ways of thinking. The process begins by identifying and then overturning one's rigid preconceptions about the way the world, life, and society should be. The *Zhuangzi* presents this as a therapeutic task consisting in training both the body and the mind through the techniques of "forgetting" (*wang*) and the "fasting of the heart and mind" (*xinzhai*).[18] This constitutes the purgative aspect of the *Zhuangzi*'s method.

The eventual goal is to free up one's intuitive grasp of the general patterns underlying the events and activities in the world. This is a process of gradual cultivation resulting in the acquisition of a sort of skill regarding how to live. In addition to the aforementioned process of undoing pernicious socialization, there is a positive project. We must train ourselves to recognize the patterns and processes inherent in the world and learn to live in harmony with them; in short, we are to accord with the *Dao*. Ultimately, we are to attain the openness and flexibility needed to deal with novel situations and vicissitudes of life while still staying in tune with our natural tendencies and innate intuitions.

Few people are so lucky as to be able naturally to attain that state of flow on a consistent basis with dating partners from diverse walks of life. To achieve this ability, most of us would have to undergo some sort of training process, which for many people would involve both negative and positive phases.

Those among us who are shy, insecure, or socially awkward are often held back by limiting beliefs imposed by others and by the surrounding society. Examples include thinking that you are not good enough just as you are and that to get people to like or accept you, you must first try to please or impress them; that sex and sexual desire are dirty and evil things and subjects to be ashamed about; and that you do not deserve nor do you have permission to date exceptionally desirable people. Debilitating beliefs inculcated by society need to be overthrown to enable you to achieve flow in social interactions and to be truly your best self. This is the purgative aspect.

In addition to undoing the shackles of harmful social education, there is a positive project of learning how to present actively your best self and to connect with other people emotionally. Most of the formal education systems around the world have neglected to teach such social skills. In our formative years, many of us lacked mentors in the social arts to teach us how to win friends and influence people and how to attract and charm the opposite sex. Developing these social skills constitutes the positive project.[19]

Although mastering these social skills involves the acquisition of abilities we did not previously have, the goal is to enhance and display to best effect those attractive qualities of ourselves that were already present. This is how the negative and positive phases of cultivation work in tandem. Just as in the *Zhuangzi*, once we are free of the harmful obscurations, we begin to act in accord with the *Dao*, so too once we overcome these limiting beliefs imposed by society, we are already freeing ourselves to become our more attractive, ideal selves. Hence, if we want to be skillful and successful daters, able to enter into the flow state consistently with a wide range of people, including those with whom we seemingly have little in common, our best strategy is to engage in a *Zhuangzi*-style two-part method of self-cultivation.

Unfortunately, for most of us, getting to the point where we can consistently enter into the flow state would take a good bit of time. And those of us who've not yet reached this point will probably find it difficult to maintain flow throughout a first date. Our recommendation is to strive for it nonetheless. The crucial step, we believe, is to allow yourself to be engrossed, as completely as you can manage, in the activities of each moment. You want to put your best foot forward? We see no better way. And if it's not your best foot you're putting forward when you're in a state of flow, it probably means that your best foot is a fake – in which case you should revisit the Kantian Gate! Not hitting it off with your date? Then, at least for the moment, you're not able to achieve flow with her/him. And if you don't see a way of turning things around, it's not clear why you should keep the date going. Better to politely call it a night and find better use of your time. And what about sex? A preoccupation with sex (pro or con) is all too likely to get in the way of really connecting with your date – even if s/he is similarly preoccupied. So, on the one hand, if you're more interested in sex than in achieving a real connection, this reveals something about your dating ends. And if you don't care whether your date has similar ends, then, according to the Kantian Gate, you should not date. On the other hand, if you're guarded about sex, you should ensure that the person you're dating understands this, so that there's no need to be guarded during the date. Preoccupations need to be

CHRISTOPHER BROWN AND DAVID W. TIEN

resolved in order to free up the mind to focus more fully on the moment. That's when you have a shot at achieving flow. That's when you have a shot at getting *truly* lucky on the first date.

## NOTES

1 Our point here is perhaps overstated. For an admirably comprehensive account of Kant's life and its relations to his philosophical works, see Manfred Kuehn, *Kant: A Biography* (New York: Cambridge University Press, 2001).

2 See Mary Gregor (ed. and trans.) *Immanuel Kant: Practical Philosophy* (Cambridge: Cambridge University Press, 1999), pp. 426–8, 494–5, 548–50.

3 Ibid., pp. 55, 59, 79.

4 Ibid., p. 73.

5 This example is Kant's. See Gregor, *Immanuel Kant*, p. 75.

6 Mihalyi Csikszentmihalyi, *Flow: The Psychology of Optimal Experience* (New York: Harper Collins, 1990). This is the classic formulation of Csikszentmihalyi's theory of flow. For his later work that expands on this theme, see his *The Evolving Self* (New York: Harper Perennial, 1994) and *Creativity: Flow and the Psychology of Discovery and Invention* (New York: Harper Perennial, 1997).

7 See Joshua Knobe, "Ordinary Ethical Reasoning and the Ideal of 'Being Yourself,'" *Philosophical Psychology* 18, 3 (2005): 327–40.

8 Csikszentmihalyi, *Flow*, p. 4.

9 Ibid., p. 50.

10 For a good introduction to the literature in neuroscience and psychology on why and how people pick up on social cues at an unconscious bio-chemical level, see Daniel Goleman, *Social Intelligence: The New Science of Human Relationships* (New York: Bantam, 2006).

11 Csikszentmihalyi, *Flow*, pp. 59–60.

12 See Philip J. Ivanhoe, "The Values of Spontaneity," in Yu-kam Por, Julia Tao, and Philip J. Ivanhoe (eds.) *Taking Confucian Ethics Seriously: Contemporary Theories and Applications* (Albany: State University of New York Press, 2010); Philip J. Ivanhoe, "The Theme of Unselfconsciousness in the *Liezi*," in Ronnie Littlejohn and Jeffrey Dippmann (eds.) *Riding the Wind with Liezi: New Essays on the Daoist Classic* (Albany: State University of New York Press, 2009), pp. 129–52; Edward Slingerland, *Wu-wei as Conceptual Metaphor and Spiritual Ideal in Early China* (New York: Oxford University Press, 2006); Roger Ames, *The Art of Rulership: A Study of Ancient Chinese Political Thought* (Albany: State University of New York Press, 1994); and Joel Kupperman, *Learning from Asian Philosophy* (New York: Oxford University Press, 1999), pp. 26–35, 79–89.

13  Ivanhoe, "The Values of Spontaneity," p. 9.
14  Ibid.
15  Ibid., p. 4, note 11.
16  Karen L. Carr and Philip J. Ivanhoe, *The Sense of Anti-Rationalism: Zhuangzi and Kierkegaard's Religious Thought* (New York: Seven Bridges Press, 2000).
17  See Carr and Ivanhoe, *The Sense of Anti-Rationalism*, pp. 96–8. While a full exposition of the *Zhuangzi*'s theory of self-cultivation and his knack stories in terms of flow is beyond the scope of this paper, interested readers can begin by consulting Paul Kjellberg and Philip J. Ivanhoe, eds., *Essays on Skepticism, Relativism, and Ethics in the Philosophy of Zhuangzi* (Albany, NY: SUNY Press, 1996).
18  Ibid.
19  The actual details of this positive project, such as how to demonstrate your desirable qualities without bragging, rest beyond the scope of this essay.

# PART IV

# ANOTHER WORLD
Cyber-Rendezvous

CHAPTER 13

# DATING AND PLAY IN VIRTUAL WORLDS

**"Is this man cheating on his wife?"**[1]

Ric and Sue Hoogestraat were growing apart. Ric was spending his evenings and weekends on a new hobby, an interest his wife Sue did not share. And through his new hobby, Ric met Janet. They began to hang out, to build hobby projects together, and to go shopping together, all behind Sue's back.

What drew the attention of the *Wall Street Journal*'s Alexandra Alter is that Ric and Janet had never met in the flesh. Their shared workroom, their dates, and their eventual marriage were all virtual, carried out in a virtual world called *Second Life*.

In this essay we will explore the philosophy and ethics of dating through the lens of virtual worlds. To the eye, a virtual world looks quite similar to a three-dimensional video game. The player controls a 3D representation of herself called an avatar, which inhabits a 3D world. Unlike a game, however, many virtual worlds do not have rules, scores, or winners and losers. Instead, the virtual world allows players to dance, role-play, build buildings, chat with friends, attend concerts, and so on.

The methodology of this essay is inspired by Michael Heim's seminal essay, "The Erotic Ontology of Cyberspace."[2] Heim describes the virtual world as a "metaphysical laboratory." Because everything inside the virtual world, from the laws of physics to physical appearance, is generated or mediated by a computer program, the virtual world allows us to experiment with our very perceptions of reality. How does our perception of reality change if we can fly (as in *Second Life*)? What if our consciousness can exist in four places at once, carrying on four conversations (as when one opens four *Second Life* clients, running four different avatars)? What if the computer system is garbling, delaying, or modifying our communications in subtle ways?

The question posed by Alter's article "Is this man cheating on his wife?" is an *ontological* question. Ontology is the overarching discipline of philosophy that studies the nature of reality and being. Because virtual worlds cause us to question what is real, we say that they pose an "ontological risk" or create "ontological uncertainty."

The other common usage of *ontology* is for philosophy that studies the inherent necessary qualities of an object. In this sense, the ontology of dating tells us what dating "looks like" and how to distinguish it from other similar concepts, like hook-ups or marriage. Computer scientists have also appropriated the term and are in the process of building gigantic computerized "ontologies," which are computer databases that describe all concepts in the English language in terms of their parts, qualities, and relations to each other.

The question "Is this man cheating on his wife?" is central to our understanding of the ontology of cyberspace, but it is also a question about the ontology of dating. Virtual worlds provide a new context and a new lens for the study of dating.


## "Just a game"


One common reaction to cyberspace is to treat it as *entirely* "not real." This could lead one to argue that Ric was not cheating on Sue.

The argument is that Ric and Janet never met in the flesh, never had any physical intimacy, and never intended to. Dutch (Ric's avatar in *Second Life*) and Tenaj (Janet's avatar) are not people, but characters in a game. Many popular games revolve around a male character with a female love interest. For example, at the end of *The Legend of Zelda II*, the player's character Link kisses Princess Zelda, but we would not say that the player is cheating on his wife.

In *Second Life* players take on a wide variety of roles. Some play horses (complete with a saddle so that anthropoid characters can ride), some play dragons, some play the role of a child in a family, and some play sophisticated war games. In each case the player is playing a role and is very conscious that the role they play is separate from the self. One might argue that Ric and Janet are *playing* the roles of lovers, but are not *really* lovers.

This argument centers on a key ontological fact of virtual reality, that what it *looks like* is not the same as what it *is*. One classic work in this area is Julian Dibbell's "A Rape in Cyberspace."[3] Dibbell tells the story of a "rape" that happened in a text-based virtual world and chronicles the community's attempts to come to grips with this violation.

It is also easy to see, however, why Sue would be skeptical of this argument. To argue that Ric *was* cheating on Sue, we need only point out that some very real intimacy appears to be forming, and that what Ric and Janet did goes far beyond harmless role-play. There are strong reasons to doubt the previous claim that Ric and Janet view their avatars, Dutch and Tenaj, as merely roles to play. Dutch looks almost identical to Ric (though younger) and "Tenaj" is "Janet" backwards. The players and their avatars are looking-glass images of one another, with the computer screen playing the role of the mirror. Furthermore, the analogy to *The Legend of Zelda* seems inappropriate because the Zelda games are one-player games that follow rigid scripts. There is no choice but for Link to kiss Princess Zelda, so the act of kissing the princess is not an act of the player's will that can be morally condemned. The same is not true in *Second Life*. Real people control both characters, and there is no external script compelling their behavior. Hence we should reject the idea that players in virtual worlds are *just* playing a role. The roles are not prescribed as in a play, but instead are constructed by the players.

We now know (with the benefit of hindsight) that Ric was indeed cheating on Sue. Shortly after the *Wall Street Journal* article appeared, Ric dumped Sue, Janet dumped her children at her mom's house, and Ric and Janet ran off to get married. Their further escapades are chronicled in a short feature story from the Canadian Broadcasting Corporation called *Strangers in Paradise*.[4]

However, this does not settle the ontological questions raised by the case. Is virtual dating really dating? Is virtual cheating really cheating? And if so, what does this tell us about the nature and ethics of dating in the real world? In what follows I hope to demonstrate how virtual worlds can function as a lens through which to inspect such ontological questions.

## Play and Dating

A certain spirit of playfulness runs very deeply in most virtual world cultures. This is so much the case that the news media were fascinated, for a time, by anyone using SL (*Second Life*) for anything *serious*.[5] Those participating in the dating culture in RL (real life), however, do not consider dating a frivolous activity. Dating consumes time, money, and emotional energy. A date goes far beyond an evening's entertainment; dates are replayed and analyzed over lunch, email wordings are scrutinized, and deep meaning read into the number of, or time between, text messages. Hundreds of books have been written on the topic, and dating websites like eHarmony and Match.com have become cultural institutions. Dating is *serious business*.

Given the inherently playful nature of virtual worlds, why is virtual dating so successful? I propose that this is because dating is itself inherently playful. This claim may seem quite uncontroversial, but, as we will see, the word "play" brings with it a tremendous amount of philosophical baggage.

Scholars in video game studies and education are in the process of (re) discovering the work of Johan Huizinga.[6] Huizinga's book *Homo Ludens*[7] analyzes the relationship between play and culture. Roughly speaking, *Homo ludens* means "man the player," a construction that Huizinga contrasts with *Homo sapiens*, which can be interpreted as "man the thinker."

Huizinga, an anthropologist, argues that everything we think of as "culture" arises in and through play. His book is full of examples of playful cultural institutions, such as athletic tournaments, legal trials, betrothal rituals, the theatre, and so on. He further argues that "play" precedes culture and even precedes sentience, noting that animals engage in playful behaviors.

We will focus on two of Huizinga's descriptions of the qualities of play, which taken together provide a very satisfying ontological definition of play. (The reader should, of course, bear in mind that the definitions of both "play" and "game" are hotly contested.) Huizinga says:

> Summing up the formal characteristics of play we might call it a free activity standing quite consciously outside "ordinary" life as being "not serious," but at the same time absorbing the player intensely and utterly. It is an activity connected with no material interest, and no profit can be gained by it. It proceeds within its own proper boundaries of time and space according to

fixed rules and in an orderly manner. It promotes the formation of social groupings which tend to surround themselves with secrecy and to stress their difference from the common world by disguise or other means.[8]

He goes on to say:

The play-mood is one of rapture and enthusiasm, and is sacred or festive in accordance with the occasion. A feeling of exaltation and tension accompanies the action, mirth and relaxation follow.[9]

One immediate problem with Huizinga's definition is that he seems to be saying that some activities are play activities and others are something else (presumably "work"). This interpretation is problematic because, of course, play and non-play activities cannot always be separated. Work activities can be undertaken in a spirit of play and professional athletes play a game for their living. It is my view that Huizinga understood this; he seems to use "play," "the spirit of play," and "the play-mood" interchangeably. So when he talks about the "formal characteristics of play" he is talking about the characteristics of "the play spirit," not just providing a litmus test to determine whether (or not) some particular activity is (or is not) play. Huizinga would undoubtedly say that the play spirit inhabits, to a greater or lesser extent, most human endeavors. This is why his book is called *Homo Ludens*.

It is also important to note that Huizinga does not view play as "pointless." In his critique of Huizinga, Roger Caillois says that "play is an occasion of pure waste,"[10] and he appears to take this as part of his definition of play. Huizinga's text at first seems to support this view, saying that play is "connected with no material interest." This is not the same, however, as pure waste. Huizinga indicates that play has *non-material* utility, in that it promotes the "formation of social groupings" and generates feelings of "rapture and enthusiasm."

Indeed, it is tempting to think that the goal of play is "fun," especially in the context of the electronic game industry, but this is another red herring. Play allows us to simulate experiences both visceral (as with a player leaping off a cliff in *World of Warcraft*) and emotionally cathartic (as with Greek tragedy) that many would not describe as "fun." Huizinga goes to great lengths to avoid making claims about the purpose of play, or to list the psychobiological reasons behind play. Instead, his goal is to demonstrate that play and culture are naturally and historically linked.

To what extent does the play-spirit (as described by Huizinga) infuse dating? Several parts of Huizinga's definition are easily applied to dating. Certainly, an ethical dater expects "no profit" from a date. One who dates for material profit is termed an escort, Casanova con man, or prostitute. It is also a common experience that a good date will be "tense" and "rapturous." After a good date we gush with humor and enthusiasm, and feel simultaneously energized and relaxed. Dating "promotes the formation of social groupings" that "surround themselves with secrecy" and "stress their difference from the common world." The "goal" of dating is to form an intimate pairing. Such pairs stress their separation from the world by giving each other secret nicknames, and communicate their special bond to each other by trading gifts.

More interesting is the claim that dating "proceeds within its own proper boundaries of time and space." Huizinga says that play takes place in a separate space (mental or physical) marked off from the rest of the world, which he calls the "magic circle."[11] There is no more perfect example of the dating playground than the restaurant One if By Land, Two if By Sea in New York City. It has been voted the most romantic restaurant in New York, as well as the best place for Valentine's Day dinner. The sharp contrast in colors between the rose-colored walls and the white tablecloths, and the single taper candle lighting each table, naturally mark off a sacred and separate space for the dating couple. It is easy to see how this could feel like a "magic circle."

It is also the case that dating follows a prescribed pattern or set of rules. In her book *Hooking Up*, Kathleen Bogle calls this the "dating script," which again reinforces the idea that a date is something that is played.[12] Some of the rules of dating apply to a single date, just as some of the rules of soccer apply to a single match: the woman should offer to pay, the man should reject this offer and insist on paying, and no mention should be made of ex-girlfriends or ex-boyfriends. Some of the rules apply to the entire "season": on the first date meet in a neutral place, no sex before the third date, no shared bank accounts until marriage, and so on.

The most troubling parts of Huizinga's definition, for our purposes, are the claims that play is "not serious" and that it is "outside the sphere of necessity." It is important not to misunderstand Huizinga's use of the words "serious" and "earnest" in *Homo Ludens*. He does not mean that play is not *important*, and he in fact says that play events are among the most important events in our lives. He describes play as rapturous and exalting. Instead, he views "seriousness" as that habit of mind that explicitly rejects the play-mood.

Searching for a life partner is certainly *important*, but doing so in a spirit of *seriousness* is not compatible with the dating script. The serious-minded dater believes he or she is trying to "know" the prospective partner. Serious daters interrogate their dates with questions; they evaluate their height, weight, number of desired children, political background, and so on. But when dating happens in a spirit of play, the natural result is the *building* of a relationship.

This distinction, between *knowing* and *building* (or making) is crucial in understanding the way that virtual world natives view dating. Tom Boellstorff, in his ethnography of SL,[13] says that those who reject virtual world dating "confuse episteme with techne." These words are derived from Greek verbs. Roughly speaking, *episteme* is "knowing" and *techne* is "making." This brings us back to the ontology of dating in virtual worlds. Though virtual world dating presents a challenge to *episteme*, it fully supports *techne*, and even enhances it by promoting *ludus* (play).

On top of all of this, we must keep in mind that dating is not *necessary*, not even for finding a mate. As Bogle points out in her book, dating is only one possible script for finding a romantic partner. The dating script exists in parallel with other romantic scripts such as "calling," hooking-up, arranged marriage, co-habitation, and so on. Dating is but one system or script for finding a mate, and it is a particularly playful one.


## A Ludic Understanding of Dating


The purpose of this discussion is to demonstrate that the "play spirit" inherent in virtual worlds is not necessarily at odds with the institution of dating. Indeed, we see that the play-spirit (as defined by Huizinga) permeates dating. We reject the claim that dating is "too serious" to trust to the virtual world. The purpose of dating (if there is one) is to *make a relationship*, not to *get to know the other person*. And play is something that, by its nature, creates social groupings, and leads to the feelings of rapture and awe that we describe as "being in love."

Let us return, briefly, to the story of Ric and Janet. The obvious ontological uncertainties created by dating in SL make great fodder for writers. This fascination with broken relationships in virtual worlds reinforces what Boellstorff describes as "a widely disseminated dystopic narrative [that] portray[s] virtual worlds as engines of isolation, the pastime of techno-hermits firmly ensconced in lonely rooms, consoled only by the deceptively warm flicker of a computer screen."[14] The techno-hermit narrative portrays virtual dating as purely play, purely pretend, and totally pathetic. The arguments I have presented here are meant as an antidote for this. "Real" dating is inherently playful and virtual dating is more than just play. As Boellstorff found, virtual world dating "transform[s] actual-world intimacy [and] create[s] real forms of online intimacy."[15]

We have seen that the playful nature of a virtual world is compatible with dating, which is also a playful pursuit. I do admit, though, that there is an ontological risk in dating in a virtual world. It seems that building a relationship via cyberspace makes it more difficult to know what is "real" in a relationship. I will argue, however, that precisely the same *type* of ontological risk exists in the real world. In fact, in some specific real-world places (for example, bars on the Sunset Strip) the likelihood that the other person is a "fake" are as high, or higher, than in virtual worlds.

Let us try once again to put this argument into Huizinga's framework:

> The player who trespasses against the rules or ignores them is a "spoil-sport." The spoilsport is not the same as the false player, the cheat; for the latter pretends to be playing the game and, on the face of it, still acknowledges the magic circle. . . . The spoilsport shatters the play-world itself . . . [and] therefore he is a coward and must be ejected. . . . It sometimes happens, however, that the spoilsports in their turn make a new community with rules of its own.[16]

In dating, a *cheater* is one who seeks certain kinds of intimacy (often sex) outside a supposedly monogamous dating relationship. But what of the *spoilsport* of dating? The similarities between the communities of spoilsports that form around virtual worlds and around the dating culture are striking.

In order to understand the function of spoilsports in virtual worlds, I wish to introduce three archetypes of virtual world hackers: wizards, script kiddies, and griefers. Virtual worlds give rise to a particular kind of spoilsport called a "griefer." These are players of the game who are not playing to win the game, but instead derive pleasure from causing grief, ruining the game for others. Griefers in SL, for example, love to disrupt public events. They have a variety of "weapons" at their disposal that allow them to make loud and annoying noises, trap other players millions of meters in the sky, or crash the game's servers. In *World of Warcraft* they kill non-player characters (quest givers, food vendors, healers, etc.) in beginning towns, making it impossible for new players to get started in the game. In *EVE Online* they have taken advantage of bugs and lag in the game client to destroy a powerful mother-ship using only cheap "starter" ships. A "wizard" (of a system like a game or virtual world) is someone who discovers the true rules of the world that are hidden from lesser beings and can manipulate these hidden rules to accomplish seeming miracles. The wizards are often capable of feats that even the creators of the world did not foresee, because the wizards exploit bugs and unintended features in the system. In SL, for example, many commonly used building techniques, like short-range teleporting and invisible avatars, were apparently unforeseen by Linden Lab (the creators of SL). Most wizards enjoy being recognized for their achievements, and post or publicize their exploits so that others may use them.

Whether fair or not, the wizards tend to be blamed when their creations go awry. Many of the innovations of these virtual world hackers can be used to crash the world, circumvent its intellectual property protections, or trap or control other avatars. Even if the wizard who first discovers and exploits such a hack is not a sociopath, there inevitably comes a time when the hack becomes public knowledge. The sociopathic elements in the world then make use of the hack to wreak havoc and grief.

In the 1990s such bottom-feeding "hackers" came to be called "script kiddies." The script kiddie is like the Sorcerer's Apprentice: he uses the knowledge received from the master, often with no understanding or skill, and often with chaotic results. Some griefers are wizards, but many are merely script kiddies attempting to emulate the true dark wizards.

Julian Dibbell's description of griefer culture[17] demonstrates a high degree of congruence with Huizinga's description of the spoilsport. The griefers have indeed "made a new community," loosely organized on somethingawful.com and the /b/ forum of 4chan.org. They have organizations in many virtual worlds, for example the GoonFleet in *EVE Online* and the PN in *Second Life*. It is also true that other virtual world residents despise the griefers, and well-known griefers (like Plastic Duck in SL) have been permanently "ejected."

Interestingly enough, griefers characterize their activities not as anti-play, but as another form of play, or another game. For example, Dibbell reports one GoonFleet member declaring, "You may be playing EVE Online, but be warned: We are playing Something Awful." This griefer is pointing out another way that the ontological uncertainty of virtual worlds leads to both conflict and play. The GoonFleet takes advantage of the *seriousness* of other *EVE Online* players to generate their own play.

They are true spoilsports in that they do not respect the magic circle, the rules, or the goals of the game. They specifically target those who take the rules and narrative of the game most seriously.

Of course, not all spoilsports are griefers. A child who turns over a checkerboard and refuses to finish the game is a spoilsport, but not a griefer. The griefer can be characterized as someone who is still at play, but who treats the other players in the game not as co-equal, but as game pieces to be toyed with. This leads me to critique the very term "griefer." In the end, it is not "causing grief" that characterizes the griefer's motivation, but instead the ability to "play the emotions" of other people. So let us call them "players," that is, they are "players of people" instead of "players of the game."

## The Wizards of Dating and Their Hangers-on

With this in mind, I contend that there are "griefers" of the dating world and that they are not the same as cheaters. A man who secretly dates two different people (while pretending to be monogamous with each) is a cheater. But if he seeks intimacy with both, dates both, and treats both romantically, then he is not a spoilsport and is not subverting the game. Instead, the griefers of the dating world are the ones we call "players."

Neil Strauss's book *The Game* is an introduction to the "wizards" of the dating world, the pickup artists.[18] Just as a computer hacker studies the hidden inner-workings of computer systems, a true pickup artist studies the hidden inner-workings of the human mind and sex drive. Strauss describes a society of pickup artists that formed online just after the start of the millennium. Through a combination of pop psychology, traditional psychology, creativity, and endless experimentation, these men developed algorithms for attracting and picking up women.

In his alter ego as the pickup artist Style, Strauss himself became a wizard of women, developing new routines and new tactics for meeting women. Style (and his mentor Mystery) shared their techniques with aspiring pickup artists through online forums, just as virtual world wizards do. They became mini-celebrities and took on apprentices and students. The pickup community split into competing factions and many of the founders were driven out, a pattern that can also be observed in the Goon community in SL.

Style eventually realized that he was creating a cult of script kiddies, though he did not use this term. In a post to an MSN group used by pickup artists, he said:

> Most of the [pickup artists] I know are social robots. . . . They have learned to socialize almost entirely through rules and theories they've read online and learned in workshops. . . . After a great twenty-minute set with many of these social robots, a woman begins to realize that they don't have anything more going for them.[19]

A "set" is essentially an algorithm for meeting a woman and getting a first date with her. Style presents himself as an innovator, a true wizard, and a writer of sets. The social robots he complains about are the script kiddies of the dating scene. They obtained the sets and subroutines that Style posted online, and they executed them with some degree of success, but their lack of true understanding led to unpredictable and unsatisfying results. And, just as with hacking, the actions of the script kiddies eventually resulted in the destruction of the magic itself. Style recounts how, at the height of the pickup artist movement, his magic stopped working.[20] The women in the bars had already heard all of his material, inexpertly spouted by the social robots. They were inoculated against the magic by familiarity with it, and it lost its power.

The same thing happens to the bugs and loopholes that allow players to work their magic in virtual worlds. As long as the hack is the secret knowledge of only a few, it is unlikely that the world-builders will notice it – and even noticing it, they rarely choose to fix it. When a hack is adopted by legions of script kiddies, however, the good wizards of the world notice and develop and deploy countermeasures. The magic dies from overuse.

## The Moral Significance of a Ludic Conception of Dating

So we have seen two points of contact between dating and virtual worlds, inspired by Huizinga's work on play. First, we have seen that the script and activities of dating are infused by the play-spirit, just as virtual world culture is. Second, we have seen that the associations of spoilsports formed around virtual worlds and around the dating culture bear a remarkable similarity.

This leads us toward a ludic conception of dating, toward the idea that whenever one analyzes the philosophy or ethics of dating, the role of play in dating should be kept in view. One immediate consequence of this is that we must accept that dating is *always* ontologically risky. The uncertainty we experience meeting someone in *Second Life* is the same type of uncertainty that we experience meeting someone at a bookstore café.

Unfortunately, Huizinga's account of the morality of play seems to contradict this idea that dating has both ludic and ethical components. He says, "Play lies outside the antithesis of wisdom and folly, and equally outside those of truth and falsehood, good and evil. . . . It has no moral function."[21] This is not as big a problem as it first seems. Even if play serves no moral *function*, it is still the case that *how you play the game* is morally significant. We have seen two types of transgression against play. The first is "cheating," which means breaking the rules, but still according due respect to the magic circle and the play-world it contains. The second is "spoiling," which means acting in a way that destroys or subverts the play-spirit.

Viewed this way, we can conclude that Ric Hoogestraat was indeed cheating on his wife. Even if we were unaware that he eventually left Sue and married Janet in real life, we would still conclude that the arguments defending Ric are based on an incorrect assessment of the ontological status of virtual worlds. His dates with Tenaj were real dates and his virtual infidelity was real infidelity.

This analysis also sheds light on the phrase "Don't hate the player, hate the game,"[22] used by pickup artists to disclaim responsibility for their actions. Throughout his book, Strauss portrays the pickup artist as being, in some sense, morally neutral. For example, he makes a point of never lying to the women he picks up. He might claim that he is not transgressing (at least directly) against *episteme*. But even if he does not lie, we can still indict him for transgressions against *ludus*. One of his most powerful techniques is to insult or ignore his target and focus on her friend instead. This leads the target to think that she is not herself a player in the game, that she is only an observer. But when he acts this way he is acting as a spoilsport of dating and deserves moral censure.

According to Diogenes Laertius (in his *Lives of the Philosophers*), Aristotle was once asked what he had gained from philosophy, and he said, "That I do without being commanded what others do from fear of the laws." In my case, my ontological understanding of *Second Life* has made me shy away from private chats or dances with my *Second Life* friends, unless my wife is also present. What happens in the virtual world may not be *serious*, but it *is* very real.

# NOTES

1   Alexandra Alter, "Is This Man Cheating on His Wife?" *Wall Street Journal*, August 10, 2007, available online at www.online.wsj.com/public/article/ SB118670164592393622.html.

2   Michael Heim, *The Metaphysics of Virtual Reality* (New York: Oxford University Press, 1993), pp. 83–108.

3   Julian Dibbell, "A Rape in Cyberspace," *The Village Voice*, December 23, 1993, available online at www.juliandibbell.com/texts/bungle_vv.html.

4   Claude Vickery, "Strangers in Paradise." The Fifth Estate, January 28, 2009, available online at www.cbc.ca/fifth/2008-2009/strangers_in_paradise/video. html.

5   See, for example, Robert D. Hof, "My Virtual Life," *BusinessWeek: Online Magazine*, May 1, 2006, at www.businessweek.com/magazine/content/06_18/ b3982001.htm?chan=search.

6   See, for example, Katie Salen and Eric Zimmerman, *Rules of Play: Game Design Fundamentals* (Cambridge, MA: MIT Press, 2003), pp. 298–490.

7   Johan Huizinga, *Homo Ludens* (Boston: Beacon Press, 1950). Note that Amazon.com and several authors give the copyright date as 1971. The book was actually written in 1938, according to the author's foreword.

8   Ibid., p. 13.

9   Ibid., p. 132.

10  Roger Caillois, *Man, Play, and Games*, trans. Meyer Barash (Champaigne: University of Illinois Press, 2001), p. 5. The original edition is copyrighted 1958.

11  Huizinga, *Homo Ludens*, pp. 19–20.

12  Kathleen A Bogle, *Hooking Up: Sex, Dating, and Relationships on Campus* (New York: New York University Press, 2008).

13  Tom Boellstorff, *Coming of Age in Second Life: An Anthropologist Explores the Virtually Human* (Princeton: Princeton University Press, 2008), p. 166.

14  Ibid., p. 156.

15  Ibid.

16  Huizinga, *Homo Ludens*, pp. 11–12.

17  Julian Dibbell, "Mutilated Furries, Flying Phalluses: Put the Blame on Griefers, the Sociopaths of the Virtual World," *Wired*, January 18, 2008, available online at www.wired.com/gaming/virtualworlds/magazine/16-02/ mf_goons?currentPage=all.

18  Neil Strauss, *The Game: Penetrating the Secret Society of Pickup Artists*, 1st edn. (New York: William Morrow, 2005).

19  Ibid., p. 301.

20  Ibid., p. 397.

21  Huizinga, *Homo Ludens*, p. 6.

22  Strauss, *The Game*, p. 1.

CHAPTER 14

# HOW TO BE YOURSELF IN AN ONLINE WORLD

 My wife Karin and I "met" on the Internet (the quotation marks are deliberate) sometime around January 30, 2004. At any rate, I saw her profile on Match.com and responded to it on that day. The initial electronic message I sent her was entitled simply "Wow." I do not know whether she read my email precisely on the 30th, and she no longer remembers either, but she responded the very next day with an encouraging, positive message of her own. We met (this time no quotation marks) in person a couple of weeks later for dinner at a restaurant of her choosing, whereupon I very quickly became smitten with her. Within a year of meeting each other, she and I had moved into a house together. Within two years of that, we had married. This is not such an unusual order of events, I think, for the complex life of a 30-something couple in the early twenty-first century. We now (August 2009) have a baby daughter and enjoy spending time together as a family with my son from my first marriage.

As my personal story would suggest, I very much believe in the power of the Internet as a dating tool and a springboard for long-term romantic relationships. I have chosen to use my own personal experience (with Karin's consent) as a point of departure for this exploration because there is an obvious sense in which I know it better than anything else I might read or theorize about. I do not mean to issue universal prescriptions about specific ways to engage in Internet dating, for there are many ways constructively to use the Internet as a social tool. Rather, I shall try to show that Internet dating – at least Internet dating that eventually gives way to non-virtual, face-to-face meeting – does raise philosophical issues related to self-definition and authenticity in a significant and distinctive way.

## "Meeting" on the Internet

Whenever I am asked how Karin and I met, I always respond, "We met online." This is the shorthand way of describing how we became aware of each other, though in a strict sense it isn't true. Prior to the Internet age, people typically did not consider themselves to have *met* if they had only written each other letters or spoken on the telephone. I would argue that this is still true. It would have seemed, and continues to seem, appropriate for those who previously only sent each other messages or spoke on the phone to say "It's nice finally to *meet* you!" upon shaking hands in person. Likewise, it seems natural to say about those with whom I only ever exchanged emails or text messages but never encountered face to face that, though we corresponded, we never actually *met*. There is a difference between "meeting" online – henceforth, *virtual* meeting – and meeting in person. It is a difference in the phenomenology of the encounter (the "what it feels like") of which anyone who has exchanged emails or text messages with anyone, whether for business, pleasure, or romance, is aware.

These remarks are not intended to diminish the potential letters traditionally have had, and that emails, chats, blog postings, Facebook entries, and Twitter tweets now have, to express meaning and affect the recipients. Novels and poems, too, can express and elicit powerful emotions; treatises and manifestos can evoke deep thought or spark political revolutions. But, as Joseph Butler remarked, everything is what it is, and not another thing.[1] Communication, even profoundly meaningful communication, is not the same as meeting. And, as we all know, meetings (especially oft-dreaded business meetings) are not necessarily experiences laden with deep significance.

At least two features that distinguish the common virtual meeting from meeting in person are the temporal vagueness and fragmentariness of the former. The fact that I can locate when Karin became aware of my first message to her only within a frame of about 24 hours means that our virtual meeting was temporally smeared out in a way that real life meetings, such as our subsequent meeting at the restaurant, are not. Temporal vagueness is not a necessary feature of virtual meeting, since two people could become aware of each other via real time chats or teleconference. Virtual meetings, however, are not only often temporally vague; they also involve a kind of fragmentation of the experienced "other" that meetings in person do not.

The existentialist philosopher Martin Buber makes the point in *I and Thou* that encountering the other person as a "Thou" (or, less archaically, as a "You") involves more than being aware of a set of qualities (hair color, speaking style, moral goodness) constituting various pieces or aspects of the person.[2] In virtual meetings, and even in meetings that occur only by phone, the other is experienced only in parts or aspects. A voice on the phone is an aspect of oneself, but it does not convey body language or facial expression. Text on a computer screen, Blackberry, or iPhone is a trace of a person. Even videoconferencing involves a visual representation of the person who is not otherwise immediately (physically) accessible. Aspects, traces, and representations of persons may be very attractive and intriguing, but as such they are not quite the same as a person wholly present. At the extreme, such partial presentations can even be misleading, as in the 2006 case of teenager Megan Meier, a victim of cyber-bullying, who was reported to have committed suicide partly because of her distress over an Internet relationship gone sour with a teenage boy on the MySpace social networking site. It turned out that the boy's MySpace profile was the creation of the mother of one of Megan's friends, with whom Megan had had a falling out, who was using the profile as a way to torment Megan.[3]

Perhaps there will come a time when virtual meeting so approximates face-to-face encounters that the two come to be phenomenologically indistinguishable. We can imagine interactive holograms that flawlessly duplicate a physically distant person's appearance and movement. We can also imagine (and philosophers like to imagine) interactive "experience machines." Such hypothetical machines, like the machines in the *Matrix* movies, would realistically simulate different kinds of experiences – including meeting, dating, and having sex with others – even though all the while each participant "would be floating in a tank, with electrodes attached to [his or her] brain."[4] Such science fiction scenarios hold the promise (or threat) of undermining the distinction between virtually meeting and interacting with someone and meeting/dating that person face to face. For the time being, however, there is a marked phenomenological divide between the two.

# From Virtual to Real World Meeting

I initially contacted Karin because her profile on Match.com had intrigued me more than any other I had seen in many months. It appeared near the top of a gallery of profiles ranked by the percent of "match" with my own search desiderata. Karin's profile was listed as more than a 90 percent match for my own. Moreover, her profile photo showed her to be a very attractive, petite, Asian woman. In her profile narrative and emails she identified herself as Japanese and as having grown up in Tokyo. She came across as creative, witty, and light-heartedly sarcastic: she described herself as an "actor/performer" and mentioned her passion for writing and starring in one-woman stage shows. She wrote of moving from Japan to New York, which she came to love, in her twenties in order to pursue a degree in educational theatre. She dismissed tiresome "Asian fetish guys" who obsessively desire a woman for her ethnicity rather than her individuality. (She was also turned off by those who thoughtlessly confused Japan with China, Hong Kong, or Taiwan.)

As usual, I did not know quite what to expect from a first meeting, and the usual uncertainties were heightened by the potential cultural differences between us. I was a first-generation American myself, however (in fact, born in Argentina and reared in a bilingual household), so foreignness was hardly a problematic issue for me in itself. In any case, here was a person who, if her picture and self-description were to be believed, was clearly not only physically attractive but also had a creative spark and not a little sauciness. Unsure whether I had the charm, looks, or overall interestingness to be appealing to her, I had responded with a message that I hoped would sound very complimentary (but not fawning) and that would unambiguously but politely indicate my interest. Somewhat to my surprise, she took the bait, hinting at the possibility of "coffee with this crazy Japanese" at some point in the not-too-distant future if, I presumed, I passed some further tests.

Two weeks later, after several emails and a few telephone conversations, we met at a Japanese restaurant (an authentic one – a branch of a chain headquartered in Tokyo). We had a most enjoyable dinner. It was my first real foray into the world of sushi and Japanese cuisine, as I had previously only had what I came to discover are Americanized (or in some cases Chinese, Korean, or Vietnamese) variants. As things turned out, the spirited and adventurous Japanese woman of the profile was impeccably polite and considerate in person, yet also easygoing and funny. She encouraged me in my fumbling attempts to use chopsticks and seemed wholly unconcerned about my *naïveté* regarding Japanese cuisine and culture. She insisted, not in words but by her body language, on controlling the pot of tea that our server kept refilling. Karin kept the pot close on her side of the table, and, when my cup would get low, she poured more tea in before I had even noticed. She gave me a taste of her acting talent as well, as she told me about her adventures and misadventures, interspersing descriptions with impromptu impersonations of featured characters. Although Karin normally spoke with a distinct but easily understandable Japanese accent, she could somehow drop the accent and adopt an American one while doing one of her impersonations. At the end of the evening, when I walked her to her car, I was uncertain quite how to say goodbye – whether to shake hands like Americans, bow like Japanese, or even hug – and I mumbled something about not knowing the "cultural expectations." She surprised me by going for the hug, joking that she needed to perform an "upper body inspection." I drove home that evening more intrigued than ever by, and already taken with, this most unusual woman. We have often fondly spoken about that first date – her pouring me tea, the hug in the parking lot, and other tender moments. It has become part of the lore of our life as a couple.

Is there anything of significance in these events, in the unremarkable flow from profile viewing to email exchange, to phone conversation, and finally to face-to-face meeting? I mean not just personal significance for Karin and me, but significance of a kind that can be generalized. I believe there is. One might remark on the way that the Internet served as an effective vehicle for two people with rather high communicative skills to lay the groundwork for a genuine meeting and possible relationship down the road. Certainly in Karin's case, her personality shone through and gave me a foretaste of what she would be like when we met face to face. Indeed, some have argued that the current state of Internet technology favors those with high-level communication skills. Rufus Griscom notes, "At this point in their short history, online personals are long on wit and charm, the breeding ground for a reinvigorated epistolary tradition. For now, the literate have the run of the place."[5] If Griscom is correct, then the Internet dating success of effective communicators has at least sociological significance. I would argue that it has philosophical significance as well.

Philosophers from Plato to Derrida have theorized about the roles of different modes of communication in the constitution of human subjectivity and human relationships. For Plato, speech between real time interlocutors was the primary, undistorted form of communication. In his *Phaedrus*, he famously has Socrates make the case of speech over writing in terms of the inability of written words to interpret and defend themselves. The written word, unlike the spoken word, suffers from a kind of rigid vulnerability:

> I cannot help feeling . . . that writing is unfortunately like painting; for the creations of the painter have the attitude of life, and yet if you ask them a question they preserve a solemn silence. . . . And when [speeches] have been once written down they are tumbled about anywhere among those who may or may not understand them, and know not to whom they should reply, to whom not: and, if they are maltreated or abused, they have no parent to protect them; and they cannot protect or defend themselves.[6]

The Platonic prioritization of speech over writing remained largely unnoticed (or at least unquestioned) until Jacques Derrida, the founder of deconstruction, called it to the attention of philosophers and literary theorists in his *Of Grammatology*.[7] Fortunately, we do not need to enter into the confounding obscurities of Derrida's deconstructive play to appreciate his challenge to the Platonic view. However we make sense of or utilize the self-undermining literary strategies of deconstruction, at least one basic point seems central to understanding the approach – that, as Derrida puts it, "There is nothing outside the text."[8] In other words, all of reality, regardless of whether it is what we conventionally regard as "text," is like text in the sense of consisting of signs subject to interpretation. From the deconstructive perspective (if indeed it is anything integrated enough to be considered a perspective), there is no escape from the textual. Deconstruction readily applies to the Internet context as well, where it seems to blur the boundary between the virtual and the real, making even the non-virtual into the virtual. The Internet context invites us to paraphrase Derrida as claiming that there is nothing outside the hypertext.

Still, even if Derridean deconstruction succeeded in demolishing the foundation for a metaphysical distinction between virtual and real, there would remain a stubbornly persistent phenomenological distinction, which was discussed in the previous section. Granted, truths can emerge through text in philosophical discourse and academic studies, and, despite Platonic irony (Plato *wrote* his dialogues, after all), it has done so for millennia. But dating is a different kind of case, much more intimate, even if there is no "chemistry" and even if things don't "pan out" between the dating partners.

Rather than Derrida, the existentialists are more helpful as guides to making philosophical sense of the interpersonal encounter, and Buber's poetical philosophy seems especially relevant when applied to the transition from online to face-to-face interaction. In contrast to the mediated experience of the Internet, "the relation to the *Thou* is direct." Moreover, despite the fact that we can be prepared for the encounter with the other via an online profile, "no system of ideas, no foreknowledge, and no fancy intervene between *I* and *Thou*."[9] Once we meet in person, whatever preconceptions we may have had of each other recede into theoretical space, and, in contrast to the fragmentary character of the traces we read of each other online, we encounter each other and speak to each other "only with the whole being."[10]

Perhaps this Buberian take on the shift to face-to-face encounter seems too profound and pretentious for the quick and casual encounters – unmemorable and almost disposable encounters – that surely most first meetings are. The response to this dismissal, however, to which I am sympathetic, is that in most of our interactions with others, whether in the context of dating or other activities of daily life, we fail to relate to them as a "Thou" (or "You") in Buber's sense. Rather, we interact with the other as an object or instrument, as if she or he were an "It." So the existential response to the dismissal is to turn it back around and to observe that in fact most of the time, in most of our interactions with others, we fall into inauthenticity. Buber famously wrote that "All real living is meeting,"[11] a statement that has been quoted many times, often in the context of issues and problems that Buber probably did not anticipate. Since Buber died long before the Internet revolution, my use of his insight likewise applies it to a context other than those with which he was familiar. And yet it seems appropriate, especially for those cases in which we retrospectively project great personal significance onto that initial, face-to-face encounter. In such cases, "real living" is indeed meeting. It does not matter that, most of the time, even when we are not just lounging in front of the computer screen in our pajamas at home, we keep failing to "really live."

## Dating, Objectification, and Self-Definition

Perhaps the common failure to meet others in an "I-Thou" encounter is just part of the cost of doing business in a busy, overpopulated, and high-pressure world. And, Buber's utopianism notwithstanding, perhaps that is not such a bad thing. It is difficult to imagine what a world in which we were always immersed in the "I-Thou" would look like or how it could function. It remains hard to imagine even if we restrict ourselves to the activity of dating, given all the competitive pressures and anxieties it produces. There is something odd about relating to someone as a "Thou" when you are trying to determine whether you find the person sexually appealing or whether the person earns enough or has a sufficiently advanced educational background. Yet these are precisely the sorts of things that many people consider when they date others, especially if they are interested in a long-term relationship, much as they consider price, mileage, and color when purchasing a car. We do need to make such decisions, since dating, like negotiating over a vehicle, involves a significantly high potential investment (regardless of whether those involved admit this to themselves).

I could have begun this essay in the traditional style of a philosopher, noting all sorts of classificatory facts about dating, including online dating. If I had, I would probably have started by calling attention to the variety of motives and intentions with which people engage in dating behavior. As we all know, some pursue dating and/or online dating as a means to establishing long-term romantic relationships or marriage. Others pursue them merely as a means to short-term liaisons. The same person may shift intentions over time or even at the same time with different dating partners or prospective partners. These variations are common to both traditional face-to-face dating and Internet dating. The very variability of human intentions, which gives us the freedom to pursue meaningful relations with others, can be an impediment to them, as one person's intentions are often incompatible with another's.

In the case of Internet dating, the fluidity and ease of contact with other people – people who are at least at first essentially anonymous – highlights two related features of dating that pose philosophically interesting challenges to authentic interpersonal "I-Thou" relationships. These are the facts that dating exists as a means of exchange in a market and that it encourages participants to experiment with themselves. Both, of course, appear in traditional forms of dating as well, but the Internet brings them to greater prominence. I address the first of these challenges here and develop the second in the last section of the essay.

Consider that, whatever else it may be, dating exists as a form of exchange and is governed by principles of supply and demand. Just *what* is being exchanged for *what* varies. It could be sex for sex, or sex for some other benefits, whether emotional, pecuniary, or some combination of these. Soulmates search each other out in the hope of exchanging their commitments to each other. Some of these exchanges may be noble and some may be base, but our human condition seems to require them as the means for realizing even the loftiest interpersonal ambitions. Insofar as it operates under these constraints, the realm of dating thus operates as a market, and the arrival of the Internet calls attention to its status as such. Consider Griscom's insightful description:

> Most of us who have found our soulmates relied on the randomness of the bar scene or the party circuit or life in general. This serendipity is cultur-ally important – we have a collective investment in the idea that love is a chance event, and often it is. But serendipity is the hallmark of inefficient markets, and the marketplace of love, like it or not, is becoming more efficient.[12]

The serendipity of love is important, among other things, because it affords us the illusion of uniqueness. If our love relationships are seren-dipitous, then they are spontaneous and therefore (improbably) break free of the conditions that otherwise deterministically condition our lives. They are special and meaningful as islands of blissful freedom in a sea of mundane, mechanically ordered events.

There is surely self-deception here, and findings in evolutionary psy-chology increasingly render implausible the self-flattering proposition that love is unfixed and spontaneous. None of us wishes to be a mere cog in a biologically deterministic system, shorn of unique individuality. Rather than supposing that love is and ought to be pure chance at its core, however, a reasoned approach would integrate our view of love with what we know about the constraints of biology and market by denying that our personal love lives are entirely reducible to systemic factors. Each of us plays a part in the impersonal love market, but it does not fol-low from this that our love lives are *nothing more than* the result of the play of forces of supply and demand.

Most of us are repelled when we consider the world of dating as a mar-ket because doing so seems to threaten all of its participants with objec-tification. Each individual, with his or her gifts and powers, is simply an exchangeable object that may be traded for another of equal value. At the extreme there is the specter of commodification, where, at least within a certain portion of a market, goods are distributed without any qualitative differentiation. Were the commodification of the "love supply" to become a reality, it wouldn't matter with whom one was paired as long as one had someone or other to "love."

All of this is in stark contrast to the moral ideal of human community championed by most Western philosophers since at least the rise of modernity. Immanuel Kant, one of the most influential advocates of this broadly democratic tradition, which emphasizes the fundamental and irreplaceable worth of individuals, famously calls attention to the difference between price and dignity. In describing a morally ideal community of persons, which he calls a "kingdom of ends," Kant wrote, "everything has either *price* or a *dignity*. Whatever has a price can be replaced by something else as its equivalent; on the other hand, whatever is above all price, and therefore admits of no equivalent, has a dignity."[13] Kant insists on the dignity of individuals and the impossibility of "replacing" one with another, even though, in the end, all human beings possess the same absolute worth.

Commodification across the board would threaten Kantian dignity, but fortunately it does not seem possible, given the variability of human preferences. On the other hand, bare objectification, which does admit qualitative differences, seems not only possible but actual, and the Internet as a dating tool makes it salient. We obscure the objectifying nature of the love market when we engage in dating in ways that admit at least the possibility that our purpose is not sex, marriage, or other forms of short- or long-term commitment. Taking part in the bar or party circuit allows the cover of seeking a drink or simply socializing. But the Internet, and especially online personals, has a no-nonsense quality that tends to strip away the pretenses. For those who are very busy or who feel especially uncomfortable with ambiguities, the clarity of purpose afforded by the Internet is a blessing, even though it makes romance (with its apparent spontaneity) even more difficult to achieve.

None of this is to say that the Internet is irredeemable or that the love market is evil. The market, even with its objectifying, depersonalizing tendencies, is the real world means to potentially transcendent, life-transforming ends. It would therefore be irrational to wish to defeat or destroy the system that makes these worthwhile ends possible. Rather, the challenge is to harness the power of the system, making use of it to pursue one's purposes, while creating a zone of autonomy for oneself and one's dating partners.

One way to do this in the Internet context, although it is probably not the only approach, is through thoughtful and consistent self-definition. Articulating who one is in speech or writing, which requires reflecting about oneself, leveling with oneself, and penetrating through self-deception, ultimately means knowing oneself. "Know thyself" was the classical injunction, carved on the ancient temple of Apollo at Delphi, that inspired Socrates and other philosophers to pursue a life of inquiry into the fundamental values that make life worth living. In connection with dating and its potential to give rise to intimate, long-term, transformational relationships, it means being knowledgeably honest with one's prospective partners, being forthright about one's values and purposes. At the most basic, literal level, this involves truth in advertising – for example, posting an Internet profile that includes truthful information about oneself, posting a photograph (if one chooses to post one) that accurately represents one's current appearance, and the like. Beyond that, however, authentic self-definition means living consistently and relating to others as the person one has claimed oneself to be.

When I met Karin, I recognized her as the person she had claimed herself to be in her profile, her emails, and our phone conversations. I hope that she too recognized me as the person I had claimed myself to be as the weeks, months, and years of our relationship progressed. (I hope she continues to do so most of the time, when, I trust, I am on good behavior.) But in the era of the Internet there is no dearth of stories of those who fail the test of authentic self-definition – not only those who fail to live up to their idealized visions of themselves, but also, more notoriously, of those whose inauthenticity falls below morally acceptable standards. In the last section of this essay, I turn to consider the nature of this challenge.


## Dating and Authenticity

Internet daters have the capacity to shift from one mode of interaction to another and, even more than in face-to-face dating, to take on different roles and personae. Online dating thus intensifies the tendency that dating in itself already has to invite participants to experiment with the ways they present themselves to others and thereby define themselves for themselves. Experimentation with one's mode of presentation and self-definition can be associated with varying degrees of authenticity and inauthenticity. At the extreme of inauthenticity we have blatant dishonesty: there is the person who knowingly misrepresents him or herself, for example, by lying about income, age, and/or appearance on an Internet profile, or the person who invents a profile for a person who simply does not exist. But there are gradations of inauthenticity, including the kind ordinarily described as "self-deception," akin to what existentialist Jean-Paul Sartre calls "bad faith" (*mauvaise foi*). Online dating, with its invitation to experiment with self-definition, makes avoidance of inauthenticity difficult, but not impossible.

If Buber points us to the transformational, even ecstatic, possibilities of human relatedness, Sartre is the philosopher to turn to for elaborate descriptions of human interaction in its inauthentic forms. For Sartre, the bad faith of the inauthentic person involves a refusal to acknowledge the implications of his key existentialist dictum – that in the case of human beings, "existence precedes essence."[14] Sartre's point is that human beings are fundamentally unlike inanimate tools such as knives, whose essence as cutting instruments is determined in advance by a proper function. The purpose of a knife is to cut, and something is a better or worse knife insofar as it succeeds or fails to achieve this purpose. Humans are unlike other sentient beings as well, because we have the cognitive awareness of our own freedom from such essential definition.

To live authentically involves (somehow) living in light of the knowledge that we exist as beings who find ourselves in the world, inheritors of a history (including our own personal history), but who are not fixed or determined by that history and are therefore free, within the inherited circumstances, to make of ourselves what we will. In Sartre's terms, this means that the twin features of "facticity" and "transcendence" characterize a human being.[15] Facticity involves those traits that humans find themselves saddled with and which make them more like objects or other sorts of organisms – their physical dimensions and abilities, need for nourishment, sexual desire. Transcendence involves the human ability to project beyond what is factically given, to envision ways of living that take facticity into account as I make choices for my future. As Guignon and Pereboom, interpreters of Sartre, put it, "nothing in our facticity can be thought of as absolutely fixed and determined, for our facticity always presents itself to us as already endowed with a meaning that is constituted by the projects we freely choose."[16]

In Sartrean terms, we fall into bad faith (inauthenticity) when we deny either our facticity or our capacity for transcendence. The person who denies facticity fails to admit that circumstances exist that place obstacles in his or her path. Such people will be prone to deceive others because they deceive – or at least attempt to deceive – themselves. Perhaps this is what is at work in some of the more familiar types of deception that occur in the world of Internet dating: the man who lists his height on his profile as 5 ft. 10 in. when he is really 5 ft. 6 in., the woman who lists her age as 35 when she is really 45, the person who includes a 15-year-old photograph on the profile in the hope that viewers will be attracted to a younger person. Such deceptions indicate a desire, perhaps born of desperation, to flee from or deny factual aspects of one's being, one's facticity. On the other hand, those who deny transcendence seek to make excuses for their current state by appealing to their factical circumstances. A recent tour of Match.com profiles of both sexes revealed many photographs of people who seemed willfully unkempt, people who with some thought and effort could have presented a much more attractive appearance. Could this to be a sign of bad faith, a desire to flee from transcendence and embrace facticity, to make excuses for oneself based on the limits one has inherited? Although it would be unlikely that all such cases could be explained this way, the Sartrean analysis probably applies to more than a few.

Consider by contrast the case of a small, physically under-endowed man discussed by Guignon and Pereboom.[17] We can imagine him living authentically by admitting to himself that his small frame and short stature pose a challenge for him in a "heightist" society, including the increased challenge of finding a suitable dating partner on the Internet. He may be troubled by the challenge and frustrated by the superficial judgments of society, but, if he understands his circumstance merely as part of his facticity, he will not view it as a damning stamp on his being. Part of his authentic approach will mean not being embittered by rejection, some of which may indeed be based on his size. Rather, he will do what he can, for example, through diet and exercise, to develop his physical frame to the extent that is possible, making the most of what he has. Nor will he necessarily dismiss even those who reject him as stupid or superficial, since, as an authentic person, he will recognize preferences within himself that are idiosyncratic and rationally indefensible. He will therefore have forbearance towards others even as he seeks to improve himself in his own eyes.

Avoiding the pitfalls of bad faith in the context of Internet dating is challenging, and I do not profess expertise in how to tread the minefield. Beyond advocating self-exploration, self-definition, and openness towards the other, it is difficult, in a general, philosophical vein to offer more. (I do not in any way mean to disparage self-help literature, which really amounts to a different genre.) Nor is Sartre especially helpful, not so much because he pre-dates the Internet, but rather because his existential analyses are primarily aimed at elucidation, not moral edification. Inauthenticity seems an ever-present risk, especially in the Internet age, with all of the opportunities it presents us for deceit, thoughtlessness, and banality. What do we make of all the Internet profiles that state favorite pastimes as "moonlit walks on the beach," apart from the fact that they are so trite as to make it difficult to begin getting to know the people who post them? What do we make of the Internet "players" who present different personae to different dating partners, falsely assuring each that they are "the One," apart from the fact that by cheating others like this they forfeit the ability to relate to others in truly meaningful ways?

The Internet provides those who seek to meet others a rich opportunity to make contact with people, to meet them face to face in real relationships that build upon the suggestive virtual meetings made possible by today's technology. As I have argued, virtual meetings are not a substitute for the real, and they do not by themselves constitute the kinds of fulfilling relationships so many people seek. The Internet also highlights and intensifies problematic features of dating that more traditional forms of the practice might obscure. In the end, however, the Internet can give rise to real meetings between people who might well otherwise never have met at all. It therefore has the potential for great – even life-transforming – good, as some of us have been fortunate to learn from our own experience.


## NOTES

1   Joseph Butler, *Five Sermons*, section 39, quoted in G. E. Moore, *Principia Ethica* (Cambridge: Cambridge University Press, 1903), title page.
2   Martin Buber, *I and Thou*, trans. Ronald Gregor Smith (London: Continuum, 2004), p. 15.
3   The Associated Press, "Key events in the Megan Meier case," *USA Today*, May 15, 2008, available online at www.usatoday.com/tech/ products/2008-05-15-1838288037_x.htm (accessed August 21, 2009).
4   Robert Nozick, *Anarchy, State, and Utopia* (New York: Basic Books, 1974), p. 42.
5   Rufus Griscom, "Why Are Online Personals So Hot?" *Wired*, 2002, at www.wired.com/wired/archive/10.11/ view.html?pg=2 (accessed August 1, 2009).
6   Plato, *Phaedrus*, trans. Benjamin Jowett, Project Gutenberg E-book, 2008; available online at www.gutenberg.org/files/ 1636/ 1636.txt (accessed August 13, 2009).
7   Jacques Derrida, *Of Grammatology*, trans. Gayatri Chakravorty Spivak (Baltimore: Johns Hopkins University Press, 1997), p. 6 ff.

8  Ibid., p. 158.
9  Buber, *I and Thou*, p. 17.
10  Ibid.
11  Ibid.
12  Griscom, "Why Are Online Personals So Hot?"
13  Immanuel Kant, *Groundwork for the Metaphysics of Morals*, trans. Lewis White Beck (Indianapolis: Bobbs-Merrill, 1959), p. 53.
14  Jean-Paul Sartre, "The Humanism of Existentialism," in Charles Guignon and Derk Pereboom (eds.) *Existentialism: Basic Writings*, 2nd edn. (Indianapolis: Hackett, 2001), p. 292.
15  Jean-Paul Sartre, *Being and Nothingness*, trans. Hazel E. Barnes (New York: Simon and Schuster, 1956), p. 98.
16  Charles Guignon and Derk Pereboom (eds.) *Existentialism: Basic Writings*, 2nd edn. (Indianapolis: Hackett, 2001), p. 258.
17  Ibid., pp. 257, 265.

# PART V

# FROM DATE TO MATE

"Natural" Selection?

CHAPTER 15

# EVOLUTIONARY PSYCHOLOGY AND SEDUCTION STRATEGIES
## Should Science Teach Men How to Attract Women?

 Let's say you are an average looking man having trouble finding someone. Like many other guys, you have fears and anxieties when it comes to being close to a potential significant other. You don't feel good looking enough, smart enough, or interesting enough, and end up not even trying to talk to the women with whom you can see yourself. In a way, this is natural: you won't try to spend any time seducing such women because you are evolutionarily designed to adapt to your level of mate value, that is your value as a potential mate. If you are an average looking man with an average intelligence, you will probably not end up with the supermodel you saw yesterday coming out of the Gucci store, from which, by the way, you fear you might be rejected because of your bad looks, as you were from that nightclub the other night. Needless to say, you never find in nature a supermodel with an insecure, average looking man like you.

Now, what if we told you that, with the right kind of practice, the right kind of mental attitude, and some nice clothes, you will not only be able to seduce more women, you will have the ability to seduce the women you want? Would you be interested in engaging in such a program? Based on studies on women's mating preferences and strategies, we can now predict what kind of features you may need to display, and what kind of behaviors you may need to engage in, in order to raise your mate value and attract the women whom everyone finds unanimously attractive (if you don't, it may well be wishful thinking and self-deception based on your lower mate value). To get to that point, you will, however, need to deliberately (and, often, very painfully) use a large number of strategies (yes, on women) that have been designed by a couple of empirically informed seduction coaches. In the process leading to a better you as a mate, you may find yourself deceiving, manipulating, and, especially at the beginning, bothering women in order to gain enough empirical knowledge about what works and what doesn't.

Now you may feel uneasy (especially if you actually are a woman). Besides cases in which you may find yourself engaging in multiple short-term relationships without telling the women in question that you are, you may find it problematic to artificially create situations in which, instead of merely getting to know someone, you're practicing on her the latest routines you have been working on for the past few weeks. Kant would not be happy hearing this: you should never use someone as a means to an end; human beings should be ends in themselves!

In this essay we discuss some of the ethical issues that are raised by this sort of program. Our goal is to show you that, whether you are a man or a woman, whether you are average or gorgeous, you should after all not reject it, for it is an extension of what already exists: in dating, at least some deception, lies, and manipulation are there in the first place.


## Sexual Selection, Women's Preferences, and Mating Intelligence

Natural selection is the theory that tells us that, in order for a species to survive, it must be adapted to its environment, and that the most adapted organisms are the most likely to pass on their genes to their offspring. If you have a long neck in a land of high trees, you will have an advantage over those who cannot get that high to eat their favorite food. This feature will be passed on to your children, who in turn will have an advantage over others. If you are put in an environment without high trees, you may, by contrast, have a disadvantage over smaller organisms that can reach food more easily, and your children will inherit this unfortunate feature. Within a few generations your species might go instinct.

HICHEM NAAR AND ALBERTO MASALA

Why? Because nature prefers those who are well adapted (or rather, adapted enough) to their environment. Eventually, random mutations may occur that would make some organisms of the species a little more fit than their peers (by having a shorter neck, for instance), giving them more chance to pass on their genes. Natural selection is therefore the product of the interaction between the genes of organisms and the environment(s) in which they find themselves.

Many things can be explained by appeal to natural selection. Indeed, it is hard to imagine how a long neck in certain animals could be explained without appealing to any survival advantage to the species in question. If you have a certain feature that is shared by all of the organisms of your species, the story goes, it is very likely that it evolved because it confers an evolutionary advantage, that is, an advantage in your ability to survive in the environment you are in.

Could this sort of reasoning apply to all the natural features of a species? If a feature that was selected must have had some evolutionary advantage (at least in the past), there must therefore always be an evolutionary story that must account for it. In other words, if a natural feature of (say) ours is said to have been selected, we must find the survival advantage that permitted our ancestors to survive in their environment. There are many things, however, that do not seem to be directly related to a putative survival advantage. Take language, for instance. We evolved a faculty that enables us to utter a virtually infinite number of sentences and to convey an infinite number of ideas. We can even in principle utter sentences of infinite length ("I know that you know that he knows that I know that . . ."). Along with several other characteristics, the productivity of language is a puzzle to the evolutionary theorist. If language has evolved only because it conferred a survival advantage on us, why do we have so many words and so many ways of expressing things? Why don't we just have a few sentences that would be sufficient for conveying information about the environment? Language, it seems, has not evolved solely as a survival advantage.[1]

Another popular example of hard-to-imagine-a-survival-advantage cases is the peacock's tail. Having such a magnificent tail does not confer on the peacock any obvious survival advantage. A tail cannot grasp food; it cannot be used as a defense device; and it can more easily be seen by predators. The peacock's tail does not seem to make much evolutionary sense if we base evolution on the idea of the "survival of the fittest." Evolution is stingy about what it selects; it won't keep a beautiful tail for no reason. Even Darwin was puzzled by this fact. In a letter to Asa Gray (April 3, 1860), he wrote: "The sight of a feather in a peacock's tail, whenever I gaze at it, makes me sick!"

It is mainly in his *Descent of Man and Selection in Relation to Sex*[2] that Darwin gave us a plausible answer to this striking problem: if some organisms have evolved useless features from the perspective of natural selection, it is probably because they are useful from the perspective of another kind of selection. This kind of selection, called *sexual selection*, is selection based on the other sex's mating preferences. If the females of a species prefer shiny plumages to darker ones, and if this feature has some degree of heritability, it will have a higher chance of being selected. Consequently, if an organism is able to pass on its genes in spite of a superfluous-looking feature (e.g., an ornamental tail), this means that this feature confers a mating advantage to its owner, even if it can in principle be a handicap from a survival-advantage perspective.[3]

Since it is impossible to directly check if the genes of others are good ones, evolution has endowed us with the capacity to infer from outside information the mate value (that is, the quality of the genes) of members of the opposite sex. Roughly, men's primary focus is on women's level of physical attractiveness, while women's primary focus is on men's social status.[4] Of course, many other factors play a role in people's mate choice. The point here is that there is a basic sex difference in what is prioritized in mating. Men have a propensity to require a minimal level of physical beauty, while women have a propensity to require a minimal level of social status. No wonder now that, in *Beauty and the Beast*, the female is the beauty and the male the beast. The reason why men focus on women's attractiveness (and, more generally, signs of youth) is the relatively short period of fertility in women as opposed to men: women should (and do) care less about a man's age than men care about a woman's age. Of course, physical attractiveness is an important factor for women (especially in short-term mating), but as long as a baseline has been reached (you are average looking, remember), other traits are preferred. Among them, creativity, intelligence (general and emotional), social power, eloquence, assertiveness, confidence, personal wellbeing are all examples of qualities that you should want if you would like to be seen as a great potential partner (or, if you are a woman, that you would want to see in a potential partner). In other words, if you want to be seen as having a high mate value, you need to raise it by becoming the kind of person women are attracted to; you need to acquire what has been called a "mating intelligence."[5]

## The Seduction Community: Human Excellence
## and Empowering Social Art in a Post-Scarcity Era

In scientific circles the Darwinian emphasis on sexual selection has been severely attacked. Only in the second half of the twentieth century have evolutionary psychologists come to again recognize Darwin's major role in the explanation of humans' sexual preferences. This implied a radical change in the status of the discipline: departing from a technical and boring inquiry into the survival and death of our ancestors, evolutionary psychology has become highly "sexualized" and popularized by the media since the beginning of the 1990s. Indeed, the new science of evolutionary mating psychology has since then been very popular in great part because it appears extremely politically incorrect to the general audience: a woman cheating on her boyfriend with that sexy and muscular pool man at the right time of ovulation, just to increase the chance of having access to better genes for her children (the strategy is unconscious, of course) doesn't fit very well with the stereotypes of romance found in Hollywood movies.

Around the same time, the Internet allowed people with minority interests to connect systematically online in order to discuss and share their passions. These two trends explain the birth of what was called the "Secret Underground Internet Seduction Community" (SUISC). People around the world started to read the new popular science books on seduction and discuss tips and strategies online, their main goal being to improve their love life.[6]

At this point, something quite remarkable happened. One could have predicted that the SUISC would be composed of desperate men searching for the easiest and fastest way to find at least a decent girlfriend. On the contrary, the community endorsed an ideology that objectively deserves to be considered ambitious and philosophically sophisticated, whether one accepts it or not. This ideology is, in fact, a blend of (1) an Aristotelian conception of happiness as human excellence, with the evolutionary flavor that most contemporary naturalist philosophers and scientists are fond of, and (2) contemporary thinking on a post-scarcity era, argued to be dominated by art and creativity.[7]

According to the members of the SUISC, seduction should be seen not only as a form of human excellence in the social domain, which contributes to developing a well-rounded personality, but also as a sublime form of art. These bold claims deserve to be analyzed: they strike us as surprising, since they could not stand in starker contrast to the negative stereotype of seducers as mean womanizers.

Let's begin with excellence. Aristotle thought that happiness is not to be found in pleasure or in material possessions, but in the exercise of virtue, that is, excellence in the most fundamental domains that characterize human life.[8] Whatever the culture and society, human beings have to cope with dangers, manage complex relationships, and try to decide what is the right compromise between individual and collective wellbeing in difficult situations. This could be done either in a decent or acceptable way, or in a virtuous and excellent way, by being courageous, just, generous, and so on. According to Aristotle, virtues are not only for the good of the community, they are above all crucial for individual fulfillment: the exercise of human excellence in the most fundamental domains is the key to individual happiness.

These thoughts are largely confirmed by the contemporary psychology that studies the level of satisfaction of people. The exercise of excellence in general is associated with levels of gratification far greater than those associated with material pleasure.[9] This is why people spend long hours on the activities they are extremely good at. But the exercise of excellence in some fundamental domains is even more gratifying than the exercise of excellence in technical domains. This is the reason why, at a certain point in their lives, people may feel the need to use their skills to help others or serve some higher cause. This choice puts their excellence at the service of some fundamental social function. Virtue is an excellence in the core skills of the art of living. The fact that virtue is extremely gratifying for the individual makes sense evolutionarily: if you are virtuous, you are an excellent and successful human being, capable of spreading your genes reliably, and evolution rewards you.

Is seduction a virtue? At first, to answer "yes" doesn't sound plausible, but evolutionary psychology may help us here, too. First, it must be clear that here we are talking about an excellent level of seduction: being a well-rounded seducer who is able to seduce virtually any kind of woman in any kind of context; it is not about finding specific tricks to get a specific kind of girls at art galleries. Now, in order to be reliably attractive, you need to have social intelligence, emotional intelligence, leadership, a sense of humor, and many others features, namely skills that have been highly beneficial in the small groups of people in which our ancestors found themselves. These skills are still beneficial today, but, since our society is highly specialized, one can have a great career (e.g., as a computer programmer) and still afford to have very weak social skills. In

HICHEM NAAR AND ALBERTO MASALA

small groups of hunter-gatherers (the most common social organization in the history of humankind), specialization is, by contrast, more the exception than the rule. As a result, social intelligence in gaining leadership and alliances was, for our ancestors, the most important kind of intelligence. There were no successful nerds back in the days.

Since, according to this evolutionary interpretation of Aristotle's theory of happiness (implicitly endorsed by the SUISC), the most fulfilling skills are those that were fundamental in the evolutionary environment that determined our psychology, the exercise of the social skills possessed by a well-rounded seducer will be extremely gratifying and qualify as virtue. If this hypothesis is true, you are going to be happy and fulfilled by being an extremely sociable person, as opposed to a nerdy programmer or investment analyst dedicating her whole life to her job. In this scenario, the emphasis our society puts on developing analytical intelligence, while prescribing a simplified social life (family with a few children and just a few friends), could limit people's wellbeing, given that excellent social skills are not encouraged by the social environment. Overall, the main goal of the SUISC is to achieve human excellence and live life to its fullest; sexual relationships are just a part of this scenario.

Striving to become a happy and fulfilled seducer as well as an extremely sociable person, however, is just one part of the philosophical background of the SUISC. Nothing about the program of the SUISC would make sense if life and social interactions were not conceived as a playful field of creativity and artistic expression. Human societies have lived most of their history in a condition that fostered a mentality of scarcity: scarcity of everything that is valuable, such as food, tools, alliances, partners, friends, care, love, affection, and whatnot. As affluent Western societies solve the scarcity problems along several dimensions (food and tools, for example), social interactions and relationships are still strongly marked by the mentality of scarcity. The social world is dominated by fear of loneliness and rejection: losing friends, support, and partners. Even the merriest party is governed by fear: fear of approaching that cute girl, fear that someone may "steal" our girlfriend, etc.

According to the philosophical outlook of the SUISC, there is no more reason to retain a mentality of scarcity in the context of social interactions than in the context of food or tools. We live in a world of 7 billion people, in which there is as much social variety and stimulation as one could ever desire. When human beings achieve freedom from fear, they enter the endless domain of art, playfulness, and creativity. As a result, the story goes, social interactions should be considered as a form of art and life itself should be seen as a huge game field.

The most widespread metaphor is that social interactions are a particular kind of videogame. In a videogame, you are not afraid of dying because you can start again and have endless opportunities. For the members of the SUISC, the same is true for social interactions: in a world of 7 billion people, the number of possible interactions is virtually endless, and a good way to get the social skills one wants is to engage in as many interactions as one can. Survival, danger, and death are not the issue here (unless you hit on a gangster's wife). For this reason, the SUISC members think of themselves as practicing a form of social art, breaking the chains of social fear, approaching any woman or any group, everywhere, and providing them with a positive experience. In their self-understanding, by approaching women, they are spreading an empowering message of freedom from fear, an exploration of human potential and creativity. But nothing about this would be possible without a plausible scientific account of mating psychology and mating intelligence.

## Is It Wrong to Try to Raise Your Mating Intelligence?

Even though you may agree in principle with the idea of raising your mating intelligence by means of a specific training, you may feel uneasy about the nature of this training. A beginner can expect several things to happen to him. He will first need to force himself to approach women and use discursive devices (traditional "pick-up lines," for instance) in a systematic way in order to internalize a number of routines that will subsequently be used in a more natural way. The point of such a systematic repetition is both to get rid of the fear of rejection and judgment any beginner might have, and to sound progressively more spontaneous and sincere with time. By being rejected a number of times you not only come to feel less anxious when you realize that your fear was irrational (you don't die when you are rejected by a couple of women), but you are also able to relate to, and have confidence in, what you are saying as if it was an integral part of yourself. Overall, you will become the kind of man many women see themselves with. The uneasiness that you have regarding this program doesn't come from uneasiness with the results of the process, but rather from the process itself: if you have to lie, manipulate, and deceive to a certain extent (even if not systematically) in order to be the kind of person you want to be (a stable, confident, and honest person, say), does it not make the whole project ethically problematic?

We would like to give a negative answer to this question along two main lines. First, we are going to show in what sense such an enterprise is a good thing. Second, we will try to show that the question of knowing in what sense it is wrong makes very little sense.

## Is Raising Your Mate Value a Good Thing?

It is quite easy to answer this question. Of course, displaying a higher mate value is a good thing for anyone. Who would refuse to gain some extra points of attractiveness? Virtually nobody. Nevertheless, remember, it is not a higher mate value *per se* that seems problematic, but the process leading to such a state of affairs. Still, it may be relevant to look at what good consequences such an enterprise might have before making any judgment about it.[10]

First, as we have showed, at the individual level, raising our mate value would be a source of happiness along several dimensions. If you are better as a mate, you will attract more people, which is fulfilling in itself. Less trivially, mating intelligence has been shown to be somewhat correlated with both higher social intelligence and emotional intelligence.[11] Raising your mating intelligence might therefore make you not only a more emotionally stable person, but also a better social actor. By raising your mating intelligence you will have more chances to become not only a good companion, but also a good friend, a good family member, and even a good father. And if problems occur at some point (people around you will not be as virtuous as you, and, of course, virtue is a lifelong process, not something that you reach), you will have enough know-how to adjust to the situation.

Second, at the collective level, an improvement in the male population's mating intelligence would be a good thing, for it would prevent certain bad events and would create less conflict between the sexes largely due to a lack of understanding regarding what the other sex wants. Those with higher mating intelligence, correlated as it is with a higher social and emotional intelligence, will be less likely to commit awful acts such as rape and obsessive stalking. And knowing about the preferences of women as well as their mating patterns will significantly reduce the conflicts that are based on a misunderstanding of the mating psychology of women. A man with high mating intelligence will, for instance, not feel the urge to blindly blame a woman for rejecting him; he will make hypotheses about what went wrong in the interaction, and if he realizes that he didn't adjust well to the other person, he will take responsibility for it. In short, a man with a high mating intelligence is (ideally) a man who has the right attitude in most situations in which he finds himself.

## A Deflationist Solution to the Problem

In philosophy we call "deflationist" any solution that tries to dismiss the problem dealt with. In other words, such a solution aims at showing that there is actually something problematic about the problem itself, and that it should after all not be taken seriously. Our aim in this section is to provide such a solution regarding our original problem.

The uneasiness we felt earlier seems justified. Displaying a higher mate value is desirable for most of us. But the way of getting to that state may not be as appealing as more classical self-development methods. Meditation, for instance, has been shown to enhance social skills by reducing social anxiety.[12] So why go to clubs in order to practice on complete strangers? Why not use alternative methods that have been shown to be effective? The answer, hinted at earlier, lies in a particular conception of mating excellence according to which a man with a high mate value should (ideally) be able to attract any woman in any kind of context. The excellence lies in the potential of attracting anyone, not in the actuality thereof. A man with such a high mate value might want to build a family, for instance. There is no incompatibility between having a high mate value and desiring a lifelong monogamous loving relationship. In any case, if your goal is to have multiple short-term relationships and not tell your girlfriends that you are, then it is your choice. If you find it ethically problematic it is perhaps because it is, but that form of behavior should not be considered as a necessary part of the enterprise we have been talking about. This enterprise is morally neutral; it doesn't tell you what you should want out of it and it doesn't tell you what you should not want. Everything depends on you, your attitude, and your behaviors. Perhaps, therefore, it is certain men's *attitudes* toward women that need to be judged, not the project of raising their mate value. You can try to raise your mate value by going to bars and clubs, and still have high ethical standards about what you can do and what you cannot.

This answer may not satisfy, for there is still the problem that manipulation and deception are part of the process, independently of your attitude toward it. To this objection, we may answer that if this manipulation and deception are ethically problematic in this project, then they are problematic for dating (and relationships) in general. Women use makeup, fashion, and surgery to conceal physical imperfections; men try to look tough and dominant, even if they don't feel like they are. Some women might deliberately lie about their age (by lowering it) in order to display their fertility. And some men might lie about how many girlfriends they have had in the past to induce in others a perception of high mate value. In everyday interactions in which mating is a potential outcome, we normally engage, mainly unconsciously, in deceptive behavior and use strategies in order to attract members of the opposite sex.[13]

You may object that such behaviors and strategies, though legitimately called deceptive, cannot be subject to any kind of ethical consideration, for, contrary to the kind of strategies we have talked about in this essay, they are based on motives that are located below the conscious level and therefore we cannot have any control over them. Granted, such behaviors and strategies are sometimes based on unconscious motives. It still makes sense to wonder, however, what would be right and what would be wrong about them when they *are* based on consciously accessible motives. Indeed, what makes lying about the number of girlfriends you've had morally worse than dressing well, if both strategies are based on the conscious desire to raise your mate value? What are the criteria for determining that a given strategy is wrong, as opposed to another one? As long as we do not have such a way to demarcate between cases of consciously deceptive behavior, we should not reject our project to raise men's mate value by means of a systematic application of designed strategies.

One last reason why we should reject for now the ethical question raised at the outset of this essay and stop feeling uneasy about the whole project, is that this project is not problematic from an evolutionary point of view. Both men and women spontaneously adopt strategies in order to attract members of the opposite sex, strategies aiming at signaling the "goodness" of their genes. Men display ambition and intelligence; women first display their physical beauty. (Of course, we are caricaturing a little bit here.) If a strategy doesn't work, it means that the opposite sex doesn't take it to be the right way to attract them. Evolution is neutral about the wrongness of seduction strategies (nasty-looking strategies are already going on). If they work, they will be selected, i.e., individuals using them will be preferred for mating to individuals who do not use them. That is all that matters, from an evolutionary perspective. Committing yourself to a better understanding of mating psychology, theoretically and practically, therefore gives you an advantage over many individuals who lack enough mating intelligence to produce reliable intuitions about the other sex's expectations and desires. More importantly, succeeding in such a project (i.e., increasing your mating intelligence) tells us something about yourself: it tells us that you are strong enough, smart enough, creative enough, and ambitious enough to go through such a painful and difficult process; in short, it tells us that you have enough mate value to desire to become a great person, and to realize this desire.

## Conclusion: What About Women?

A possibility that has not been raised in this essay, and that we deem very important, is that women may also need to enhance their mating intelligence. According to a popular and oversimplified understanding of the relative sex roles in the evolutionary history of our species, it would be natural for men to chase women but unnatural for women to chase men. But if you think for a second about the phenomenon of groupies, you suddenly realize that, under certain conditions, women very naturally chase high-value men!

It is not the case that women don't have active seduction strategies in their repertoire; it is just that passive seduction makes sense strategically most of the time. Since the social skills women like in men are the very same skills that actually allow men to seduce women, why not just wait? If he doesn't manage to seduce me, he just doesn't have the skills I am searching for in a man. Unsurprisingly, this strategy fails as soon as one wants to attract very high-value men, who have no reason to seduce you because they have so many options. For this reason, historical female seducers like Cleopatra have been well known for the energy they invest in seducing high-value men. As a result, ambitious women need to increase their mating intelligence as much as men do; otherwise, they may need to settle for non-optimal partners.

Women may also need to increase their repertoire of passive seduction strategies. The same way men make a lot of mistakes in active seduction, women often make mistakes in the signals they implicitly give to the other sex. For example, their look or attitude could signal openness to short-term mating, while what they really want is in fact to find a boyfriend.

HICHEM NAAR AND ALBERTO MASALA

As a second example, here is a good dating tip for female readers: don't take to the extreme your passivity, for example by letting a promising conversation with a guy be interrupted by silly things such as a phone call or a friend who wants to go to the bathroom. Too often, you will not recover after the interruption. And you may tell yourself that, if it doesn't happen, it wasn't meant to be – a perfect recipe to stay single forever! Playing correctly a passive role can be difficult at times.

Overall, a scientific understanding of human mating psychology could hugely benefit social interactions and relationships: men should better understand the mating psychology of women, and women should better understand the mating psychology of men. Indeed, it is equally important to reduce the lack of understanding on each side. Centuries ago, we used to base our understanding of the physical world on myth and tradition; contemporary science gives us a superior account of the way the natural world really works. A similar revolution is possible in the domain of human interactions.

## NOTES

1   Geoffrey Miller, *The Mating Mind: How Sexual Choice Shaped the Evolution of Human Nature* (New York: Doubleday, 2000).
2   Charles Darwin, *The Descent of Man and Selection in Relation to Sex* (London: Murray, 1871).
3   Hence Zahavi's "handicap principle" according to which, if an organism can afford a survival disadvantage (by having a handicap but still surviving), its genes must be good, and therefore it must have a high mate value. See Amos Zahavi, "Mate Selection: A Selection for a Handicap," *Journal of Theoretical Biology* 53: 205–14.
4   David Buss, "Sex Differences in Human Mate Preferences: Evolutionary Hypotheses Tested in 37 Cultures," *Behavioral and Brain Sciences* 12 (1989): 1–49.
5   Glenn Geher and colleagues have defined "mating intelligence" as "the total set of psychological capacities for sexual courtship, competition, and rivalry; for relationship-formation, commitment, coordination, and termination; for flirtation, foreplay, and copulation; for mate-search, mate-choice, mate-guarding, and mate-switching; and for many other behavioral capacities that bring mainly reproductive (rather than survival) payoffs" (p. 10). See Glenn Geher, Geoffrey Miller, and Jeremy Murphy, "Mating Intelligence: Toward an Evolutionary Informed Construct," in Glenn Geher and Geoffrey Miller (eds.) *Mating Intelligence: Sex, Relationships, and the Mind's Reproductive System* (New York: Lawrence Erlbaum Associates), pp. 3–34.

6   The best and funniest introduction to the history of the community is the bestseller *The Game* by Neil Strauss (New York: Harper Collins, 2005). This book is representative of the indirect approach to seduction (hiding your intention and approaching with an excuse, for example asking a female opinion on something) popularized by Mystery (the first seduction coach to give live classes in clubs), while today the direct approach is much more popular. A good example of direct strategies can be found in Mehow, Get the Girl (online at www.mehowgetthegirl.com).

7   Members of the seduction community are rarely aware of the history and philosophical sophistication of the positions they defend, and they certainly don't cite Aristotle directly. The term "post-scarcity" describes a hypothetical form of economy or society in which any kind of resource is so easily available that it is practically free. The scenario is seriously studied by economists, futurologists, philosophers, and science fiction writers. Human life is thought to be influenced by resource scarcity to such an extent that a post-scarcity era would coincide with a completely new existential condition, usually associated with the free expression of creativity and art.

8   Aristotle, *Nichomachean Ethics*, trans. J. A. K. Thompson, revd. H. Tredennick (London: Penguin, 1976).

9   Mihaly Csikszentmihalyi, *Flow: The Psychology of Optimal Experience* (New York: Harper Collins, 1990).

10  In moral philosophy such a methodology or point of view, focusing on consequences of actions, is called "consequentialism."

11  Geher, Miller, and Murphy, "Mating Intelligence."

12  Barbara Fredrickson, *Positivity* (New York: Crown Publishing, 2009).

13  Maureen O'Sullivan, "Deception and Self-Deception as Strategies in Short- and Long-Term Mating," in Glenn Geher and Geoffrey Miller (eds.) *Mating Intelligence: Sex, Relationships, and the Mind's Reproductive System* (New York: Lawrence Erlbaum Associates, 2008), pp. 135–57.

CHAPTER 16

# MATING, DATING, AND MATHEMATICS

## It's All in the Game

Why do people stay together in monogamous relationships? Love? Fear? Habit? Ethics? Integrity? Desperation?

In this essay I will consider a rather surprising answer that comes from mathematics. It turns out that cooperative behavior, such as mutually faithful marriages, can be given a firm basis in a mathematical theory known as *game theory*. I will suggest that faithfulness in relationships is fully accounted for by narrow self-interest in the appropriate game theory setting. This is a surprising answer because faithful behavior is usually thought to involve love, ethics, and caring about the wellbeing of your partner. It seems that the game theory account of faithfulness has no need for such romantic notions. I will consider the philosophical upshot of the game theoretic answer and see if it really does deliver what is required. Does the game theoretic answer miss what is important about faithful relationships or does it help us get to the heart of the matter? Before we start looking at lasting, faithful relationships, though, let's get a feel for how mathematics might be employed to help in matters of the heart. Let's first consider how mathematics might shed light on dating to find a suitable partner.

# A Lover's Question

Consider the question of how many people you should date before you commit to a more permanent relationship such as marriage. Marrying the first person you date is, as a general strategy, a bad idea. After all, there's very likely to be someone better out there, but by marrying too early you're cutting off such opportunities. But at the other extreme, always leaving your options open by endlessly dating and continually looking for someone better is not a good strategy either. It would seem that somewhere between marrying your first high school crush and dating forever lies the ideal strategy. Finding this ideal strategy is an optimization problem and, believe it or not, is particularly amenable to mathematical treatment. In fact, if we add a couple of constraints to the problem, we have the classic mathematical problem known as the *secretary problem*.

The mathematical version of the problem is presented as one of finding the best secretary (which is just a thin disguise for finding the best mate) by interviewing (i.e., dating) a number of applicants. In the standard formulation, you have a finite and known number of applicants and you must interview these $n$ candidates sequentially. Most importantly, you must decide whether to accept or reject each applicant immediately after interviewing him or her; you cannot call back a previously interviewed applicant. This makes little sense in the job search context, but is very natural in the dating context: typically, boyfriends and girlfriends do not take kindly to being passed over for someone else and are not usually open to the possibility of a recall. The question, then, is how many of the $n$ possible candidates should you interview before making an appointment? Or in the dating version of the problem, the question is how many people should you date before you marry?

It can be shown mathematically that the optimal strategy, for a large applicant pool (i.e., when $n$ is large) is to pass over the first $n/e$ (where $e$ is the transcendental number from elementary calculus – the base of the natural logarithm, approximately 2.718) applicants and accept the next applicant who's better than all those previously seen. This gives a probability of finding the best secretary (mate) at $n/e$ or approximately 0.37. For example, suppose that there are 100 eligible partners in your village, tribe, or social network; this strategy advises you to sample the population by dating the first 37, then choose the first after that who's better than all who came before. Of course, you might be unlucky in a number of ways. For example, the perfect mate might be in the first 37 and get passed over during the sampling phase. In this case, you continue dating the rest but find no one suitable and grow old alone, dreaming of what might have been. Another way you might be unlucky is if you have a run of really weak candidates in the first 37. If the next few are also weak but there's one who's better than the first 37, you commit to that one and find yourself in a sub-optimal marriage. But the mathematics shows that even though things can go wrong in these ways, the strategy outlined here is still the best you can do. The news gets worse though: even if you stringently follow this best strategy, you still only have a bit better than a one in three chance of finding your best mate.[1]

This problem and its mathematical treatment are instructive in a number of ways. Here I want to draw attention to the various idealizations and assumptions of this way of setting things up. Notice that we started with a more general problem of how many people you should date before you marry, but in the mathematical treatment we stipulate that the population of eligible partners is fixed and known. It's interesting that the size of this population does not change the strategy or your chances of finding your perfect partner – the strategy is as I just described and, so long as the population is large, the probability of success remains at 0.37. The size of the population just affects the number of people in the initial sample. Still, stipulating that the population is fixed is an idealization. Most pools of eligible partners are not fixed in this way – we meet new people, and others who were previously in relationships later become available, while others who were previously available enter new relationships and become unavailable. In reality, the population of eligible candidates is not fixed, but is open ended and in flux.

The mathematical treatment also assumes that the aim is to marry the best candidate. This, in turn, has two further assumptions. First, it assumes that it is in fact possible to rank candidates in the required way and that you will be able to arrive at this ranking via one date with each. We can have ties between candidates, but we are not permitted to have cases where we cannot compare candidates. The mathematical treatment also assumes that we're after the *best* candidate and anything less than this is a failure. For instance, if you have more modest goals and are only interested in finding someone who'll meet a minimum standard, you need to set things up in a completely different way – it then becomes a satisficing problem and is approached quite differently.

Another idealization of the mathematical treatment – and this is the one I am most interested in – is that finding a partner is assumed to be one sided. The treatment we're considering here assumes that it is an employers' market. It assumes, in effect, that when you decide that you want to date someone, he or she will agree, and that when you decide to enter a relationship with someone, again they will agree. This mathematical equivalent of wishful thinking makes the problem more tractable but is, as we all know, very unrealistic.

A natural way to get around this last idealization is to stop thinking about your candidate pool as a row of wallflowers at a debutants' ball, and instead think of your potential partners as active agents engaged in their own search for the perfect partner. The problem, thus construed, becomes much more dynamic and much more interesting. It becomes one of coordinating strategies. There is no use setting your sights on a partner who will not reciprocate. In order for everyone to find someone to reciprocate their interest, a certain amount of coordination between parties is required. This brings us to game theory.

## The Game of Love

Game theory is the study of decisions where one person's decision depends on the decisions of other people.[2] Think of games like chess or tennis, where your move is determined, at least in part, by what you think the other player's response will be. It is important to note that games do not have to be fun and are not, in general, mere diversions. The cold-war arms race can be construed as a "game" (in this technical sense of game) between military powers, each second-guessing what the other would do in response to their "moves." Indeed, the cold war was the stage for one of the original and most important applications of game theory. The basic idea of game theory is quite simple and should be very familiar: a number of players are making decisions, each of which depend on the decisions of the other players.

It's probably best to illustrate game theory via an example. Let's start with the *stag hunt*. This game originates in a story of cooperative hunting by the eighteenth-century political philosopher Jean-Jacques Rousseau.[3] In its simplest form, the game consists of two people setting out to hunt a stag. It will take the cooperation of both to succeed in the hunt, and the payoff for a successful stag hunt is a feast for all. But each hunter will be tempted by lesser prey: a hare, for example. If one of the hunters defects from the stag hunt and opportunistically hunts a passing hare, the defector will be rewarded, but the stag hunt will fail so the non-defector will not be rewarded. In decreasing order of preference, the rewards are: stag, hare, and nothing. So the cooperative outcome (both hunt stag) has the maximum payoff for each of the hunters, but it is unstable in light of the ever-present temptation for each hunter to defect and hunt hare instead. Indeed, hunting hare is the safer option. In the jargon of game theory, the cooperative solution of hunting stag is *Pareto optimal* (i.e., there is no outcome that is better for both hunters), while the mutual defect solution is *risk dominant* (in that it does not leave you empty-handed if your fellow hunter decides to defect and hunt hare) but it is not Pareto optimal. That is, the cooperative solution is best for both hunters and given that the other party cooperates in the stag hunt, then you should too. But if the other party defects and hunts hare, then so should you. Most importantly, both these outcomes are stable, since neither party will unilaterally change from cooperation to defection or from defection to cooperation (again, in the jargon of game theory, the mutual defect and cooperation solutions are *Nash equilibria*).[4] So, in particular, if you both play it safe and hunt hares, there seems no easy way to get to the mutually preferable cooperative solution of stag hunting. Cooperation seems both hard to achieve and somewhat fragile. This game is important because it is a good model of many forms of cooperative behavior.[5]

Consider another example, just to get a feel for game theory: the *prisoner's dilemma*. The scenario here is one where two suspects are questioned separately by the police and each suspect is invited to confess to a crime the two have jointly committed. There is not sufficient evidence for a conviction, so each suspect is offered the following deal: if one confesses, that suspect will go free while the other serves the maximum sentence; if they both confess, they will both serve something less than the maximum sentence; if neither confesses, they will both be charged with minor offenses and receive sentences less than any of those previously mentioned. In order of preference, then, each suspect would prefer (1) confess while the other does not confess, (2) neither confess (3) both confess, and (4) not confess while the other confesses. Put like this, it is clear what you should do: you should confess to the crime. Why? Because, irrespective of what the other suspect does, you will be better off if you confess. But here's the problem: if both suspects think this way, as surely they should, they will both end up with the second worst outcome (3). As a pair, their best outcome is (2) – this is Pareto optimal, since neither can do better than this without the other doing worse – but the stable solution is (3) where both defect – this is the Nash equilibrium, since given that one confesses the other should too. Group rationality and individual rationality seem to come apart. Individual rationality recommends both confessing, even though this is worse for both parties than neither confessing. Again, we see that defection (this time from any prearranged agreement between the suspects to not confess) is rewarded and cooperation is fragile.[6]

What has hunting stags and police interrogations got to do with dating – crude metaphors aside? First, these two games demonstrate how important it is to consider the decisions of others when making your own decisions. What you do is determined, in part at least, by what the other players in the game do and vice versa. So, too, with relationships. In fact, the stag hunt is a very good model of cooperation in a relationship. Think of cooperatively hunting stag as staying faithful in a monogamous relationship. All going well, this holds great benefits for both parties. But there is always the temptation for one partner to opportunistically defect from the relationship to have an affair. This is the "hunting hare" option. If both partners do this, we have mutual defection where both parties defect from the relationship in favor of affairs. This game theoretic way of looking at things gives us a very useful framework for thinking about our original question of why people stay in monogamous relationships.

## Where Did Our Love Go?

We are now in a position to see one account of how monogamous relationships are able to persist. Sometimes it will simply be the lack of opportunity for outside affairs. After all, there's no problem seeing why people cooperate in hunting stags when there are no alternatives. The more interesting case is when there *are* other opportunities. According to the game theory account we are interested in here, an ongoing monogamous relationship is a kind of social contract and is akin to the agreement to mutually hunt stag. But what binds one to abiding by this contract when there are short-term unilateral gains for defecting? Indeed, it seems that game theory suggests defection as a reasonable course of action in such situations. If the chances of catching a stag (or seeing the benefits of a lasting monogamous relationship) are slim, defecting by opportunistically catching a hare (or having an affair) seems hard to avoid, perhaps even prudent. But we must remember that the games in question are not isolated one-off situations, and this is key.

While defection in the prisoner's dilemma or the stag hunt may be a reasonable course of action if the situation in question is not repeated, in cases where the game is played on a regular basis, there are much better long-term strategies. For instance, both players will see the folly of defecting in the first game, if they know that they will be repeatedly playing the same player. A better strategy is to cooperate at first and retaliate with a defection if the other player defects. Such so-called tit-for-tat strategies do very well in achieving cooperation. If both players are known to be playing this strategy, they are more inclined to cooperate indefinitely. There are other good strategies that encourage cooperation in these repeated games, but the tit-for-tat strategy illustrates the point. In short, cooperation is easier to secure when the games in question are repeated, and the reason is quite simple: the long-term rewards are maximized by cooperating, even though there is the temptation of a short-term reward for defection. It's the prospect of future games that ensures cooperation now. Robert Axelrod calls this "the shadow of the future"[7] hanging over the decision. This shadow changes the relevant rewards in a way that ensures cooperation.

We can make the cooperative outcome even more likely and more stable by sending out signals about our intentions to retaliate if we ever encounter a defector. In the stag hunt, we might make it very clear that defection by the other party will result in never cooperating with them again in a stag hunt. (Translated into the monogamous relationship version, this amounts to divorce or sleeping on the couch for the rest of your life.) We might even make such agreements binding by making the social contract in question public and inviting public scorn on defectors. All this amounts to a change in the payoffs for the game so that defection carries with it some serious costs; costs not present in the simple one-off presentation with which we started.

It is interesting to notice that this is pretty much what goes on in the relationship case. We have public weddings to announce to our friends and the world the new social contract in place (thus increasing the cost of a possible defection); we, as a society, frown on extramarital affairs (unless they are by mutual consent); and most important of all, we are aware of the long-term payoffs of a good, secure, long-term, monogamous relationship (if, indeed, that is what is wanted).

Now it seems we have the makings of an explanation of such relationships in terms of self-interest. While cooperation might look as though it has to do with love, respect, ethics, loyalty, integrity, and the like, the game theory story is that it's all just narrow self-interest. It's not narrow in the sense of being shortsighted, but in the sense that there's no need to consider the interests of others, except in so far as they impact on oneself. As David Hume puts it: "I learn to do service to another, without bearing him any real kindness; because I foresee that he will return my service, in expectation of another of the same kind."[8] In particular, there seems to be no place for love (and acting out of love) in the account outlined here.


## Love is Strange

If all I've said so far is right, it looks as though we can explain faithful relationships in terms of narrow self-interest. It's a case of "this is good for me, who cares about you." According to the game theory story, a faithful relationship is just a particular form of social cooperation. And all that is needed to keep the cooperation in place is mutual self-interest. It has nothing to do with right or wrong, or caring for your partner. It's all in the game and the focus on payoffs to the individual – or at least, payoffs to the individual plus the shadow of the future. We might still frown upon non-cooperation, but not for the reasons usually assumed. We, as a society, frown on defectors because that's also part of the game and it's an important part of what is required to keep cooperation alive in the society at large.

You might be skeptical of all this. You might think that people fall in love and enter a relationship, not because they can get something out of it but . . . well, why? If you're not getting something out of it, surely you're doing it wrong! Okay, perhaps you get something out of it, but you stay committed through the hard times, through the arguments, through your partner's bad moods, not *purely* because it's good for you; you stick with a partner because he or she needs you and you're a good person, right? It might help if that's what you believe, but one take-home message from the account I'm offering here is that there's no need for anything outside the game. We don't need to entertain anything other than self-interest as a motivation for monogamous relationships. It may well be that it's useful to believe in such things as loyalty, goodness, and perhaps even altruism, but all that might be just useful fictions – a kind of make-believe that's important, perhaps even indispensable, but make-believe all the same.

MARK COLYVAN

Let's look at these issues in terms of ethics. The game theory account not only leaves no room for love and romance, it also seems to leave ethics out of the picture. You might think that staying faithful is *ethically right* and engaging in extramarital affairs is *unethical*. In so far as game theory says nothing about ethics, it would seem that it cannot be the whole story. But we can take this same game theoretic approach to ethics. Ethics can be thought of as a series of cooperation problems. Thus construed, ethics is arguably explicable in the same terms.[9] The idea is that ethical behavior is just stable, mutually beneficial behavior that is the solution to typical coordination problems (basically ethics is just a matter of "don't hurt me and I won't hurt you"), and societies that have robust solutions to such coordination problems do better than those that don't have such solutions. As in the relationship case, it might be beneficial to engage in the pretense that some actions really are right and some really are wrong, but again such pretense will be just a further part of the game. This new twist about ethics either makes your concerns about the dating and relationships case a lot worse or a lot better, depending on your point of view. On the one hand, this broader game theoretic story about ethics allows that there is room for ethics in dating and relationships. But the ethics in question is just more game theory.

The picture of relationships I'm sketching here might seem rather different from the one we find in old love songs and elsewhere. I think the difference, though, is more one of emphasis. Think of the picture offered here as a new take on those old love songs rather than a different kind of song altogether. All the usual ingredients are here, but in an unfamiliar form. We have fidelity, but it's there as a vehicle for serving self-interest; ethical considerations are also there, but they too are not what they first seem. I suggested that all the romance and ethics might be merely a kind of make-believe, but perhaps that's overstating the case. The pretense may run very deep and it plausibly has a biological basis. If this is right, the game theory picture can be seen as offering insight into the true nature of romantic relationships. Love, for instance, is seen as a commitment to cooperate on a personal level with someone, and it licenses socially acceptable forms of retribution if defection occurs. Perhaps this conception of love doesn't sound terribly romantic and is unlikely to find its way into love songs, but to my ears, this is precisely what all the songs are about – you just need to listen to them the right way. Love is less about the meeting of souls and more about the coordination of mating strategies. If this makes love sound strange, then so be it: love is strange.

## NOTES

1 For more on the secretary problem, see Thomas S. Ferguson, "Who Solved the Secretary Problem?" *Statistical Science* 4 (1989): 282–96; for the many fascinating connections between mathematics and relationships, see Clio Cresswell, *Mathematics and Sex* (Sydney: Allen and Unwin, 2003).

2 For classic treatments of game theory, see John von Neumann and Oskar Morgenstern, *Theory of Games and Economic Behavior*, 2nd edn. (Princeton: Princeton University Press, 1947); and R. Duncan Luce and Howard Raiffa, *Games and Decisions: Introduction and Critical Survey* (New York: John Wiley, 1957).

3 Jean-Jacques Rousseau, *A Discourse on Inequality*, trans. M. Cranston (New York: Penguin, 1984).

4 Named after John Nash, the subject of the Sylvia Nasar book *A Beautiful Mind* (New York: Simon and Schuster, 1998) and the Ron Howard movie of the same name based on the Nasar book.

5 See Brian Skyrms, *The Stag Hunt and the Evolution of the Social Contract* (Cambridge: Cambridge University Press, 2004). This is an excellent treatment of the stag hunt and its significance for social cooperation.

6 See William Poundstone, *Prisoner's Dilemma* (New York: Doubleday, 1992). This is a very accessible introduction to the prisoner's dilemma and game theory. It outlines the origins of game theory in the RAND cooperation during the cold war (with a frightening application to the nuclear arms race).

7 Robert Axelrod, *The Evolution of Cooperation* (New York: Basic Books, 1984).

8 David Hume, *A Treatise of Human Nature*, ed. L. A. Selby-Bigge (Oxford: Clarendon Press, 1949), p. 521.

9 Richard Joyce, *The Evolution of Morality* (Cambridge, MA: MIT Press, 2006).

CHAPTER 17

# WHY LESS MAY BE MORE

## Dating and the City

In one of those ironic circles that often enclose our lives, dating often leads to marriage, and marriage, about half the time, leads to divorce, which in turns leads to . . . more dating. So when I found myself newly single, new to the bright lights of the Big City, and new again to dating, I did what any self-respecting woman would do: I went shopping – for sexy new lingerie, of course. Where? To Macy's. Not just any Macy's, but *the* Macy's, the original megastore, host of the Macy's Thanksgiving Day Parade, on 34th St. in Manhattan. After several wrong turns and I don't know how many escalator rides, I found myself in the midst of the equivalent of two football fields filled with women's lingerie. At first, I was overwhelmed with delight, but soon I was just plain overwhelmed; nevertheless, I took a deep breath and began browsing the nearest rack. About halfway through it, I abandoned the search and reversed my trip. Not two blocks from my apartment, I passed a small shop with some pretty frills in the window and stepped in. Twenty minutes later, I left with exactly what I had envisioned in my mind's eye when I left home hours before. Why didn't I go to the local shop first? Because I didn't think it would have a large enough selection from which to choose. I thought a dizzying array of choice would make me happy, but it only made me dizzy. Can there be such a thing as *too much choice*?

This essay will argue that choice overload can inhibit, if not paralyze, and that too much choice often – at least for a time – prevents any choice at all. These days, we shop even for people, as the proliferation of consumer goods in the past decade or so subliminally extends itself into the human dimension. For those in situations where the number of choices seems almost limitless – an urban center, say, or a reasonably large college campus – decisions become ever more difficult, if not impossible. For that matter, even those on remote desert islands with a computer can go to Match.com, type in parameters, and if the geographical range is wide enough, *thousands* of potential "perfect" matches will light up the screen. And for those looking to maximize their choice, to find the best, most perfect date, decisions, i.e., "commitment," must inevitably be postponed. And postponed. And postponed. Because when the number of options seems infinite, a more perfect, as yet unknown prospect may still present him/herself, so why "settle"? Is it at all surprising then, as recent articles have noted, that dating itself is becoming a thing of the past, replaced by "hook-ups," "friends with benefits" and casual, no-strings-attached encounters?

I wrote the above paragraph, including the word "maximize," prior to reading Barry Schwartz's recent book, *The Paradox of Choice: Why More Is Less*.[1] After reading his study, I better understand my selection of this word in its context and the relationship between it and the overall bias in the framing of my argument: almost twenty years in an urban center, where the "market" for everything – including dates – seems virtually limitless, have turned me into what Schwartz characterizes as a "maximizer." Maximizers, according to Schwartz, "accept and seek only the best."[2] But before we all jump up and affirm our maximizer tendencies, especially when seeking a date or a mate, we should also note that Schwartz charts an alternative path, that of approaching choice as a "satisficer," i.e., one who is able "to settle for something that is good enough and not worry about the possibility that there might be something better."[3] The psychological studies informing Schwartz's argument support what many daters would be loath to admit, but also what most of us at least intuitively, if not empirically, understand: satisficers are generally happier than maximizers. Just as child psychologist D. W. Winnicott's research demonstrates that a "good enough" mother is exactly that – a mother, though far from perfect, "good enough" to provide the kind of maternal infant care necessary to the psychological wellbeing of the future adult – "good enough" choices, including those of dates and mates, often lead us to more felicitous psychological paths: to more satisfaction, optimism, and happiness, and significantly, less depression than experienced by maximizers. But it should be noted that maximizing correlates with, rather than causes, unhappiness.[4] That is to say, though maximizers experience more clinical depression and describe themselves as "unhappy" much more often than satisficers, maximizing is not the *cause* of their unhappiness; maximizing and unhappiness, unlike most maximizers, just seem to hold hands. And it should also be stressed that the same individual can maximize in some areas of life choice and satisfice in others.[5] The crux of the matter is, no matter to what extent a person may satisfice when committing to a condo, a car, or a kitten, the explosion of choice in the dating arena correlates with both increased maximizing and less and less satisfaction in interpersonal relationships. Also, importantly, like me, Schwartz believes it possible that "a wide array of options can *turn people into maximizers*":[6] "If this is true, then the proliferation of options not only makes people who are maximizers miserable, but it may also make people who are satisficers into maximizers."[7] My own experience, and observing that of friends, tells me this insight is, perhaps unfortunately, true. As Carrie Bradshaw, while staring at the blank screen of her laptop at the beginning of every episode of *Sex and the City*, might frame the question: Is there any hope for those of us willing to accept only "the absolute best"? Put another way, once a maximizer, always a maximizer?

A closer look at the television loves and lives of Carrie, Miranda, Charlotte, and Samantha may lead us to some tentative answers to the above questions. Note well that the series (1998–2004) begins just as the economy of New York City takes off like a rocket bound for the outer limits of economic space since called the Second Gilded Age. And significantly, the city itself is portrayed almost as a "character" in this series, like a giant cruise ship replete with candy-colored lights, glamorous "openings," endless parties, luxury shops, squadrons of cabs, gallons of pink cosmopolitans, and beautiful people.[8] As such, the show represents a particular kind of maximizing. Though it is true that – as my mother used to say – one woman's meat is another woman's poison, so is it entirely possible that a beautiful, gym-fit, Vogue woman's idea of maximizing may be falling head-over-heels in love with a short, average looking, tweed-clad nebbish of a philosophy professor with an appalling salary, while the bartender pouring drinks thinks only a liberally inked and pierced rock musician will do. Of course, in the right environment, each of these women probably would maximize by relentlessly searching for the "absolute best" nebbish or rock musician. But this series sells instead a pervasive and widespread dating/mating fantasy and, I would argue, one that most daters buy into at one point or another in their dating lives, particularly when there appears to be a large pool from which to choose.[9] For the conceit, perhaps the premise of the series presents Carrie and her friends, with the possible exception of Samantha, as maximizers in a quite limited sense, all seeking dates that will lead to mates with that certain *je ne sais quoi* or perhaps *sine qua non* that seems almost a prerequisite in densely populated settings, especially those marked by wealth: What characteristics might this person have to make him/her an *enviable* choice? Rich? Exceptionally good looking? A degree of "celebrity" in some sexy arena – the arts, entertainment, media, finance, sports? A "big man on campus"? An "It" girl? It would seem that in the kind of maximizing endorsed and enhanced by the choice-proliferating setting of this series, the most important quality in an object of desire is that the person *be* an object of desire, and not just for me. Two words to the wise, however, come due: *caveat emptor*.

To enlarge my point, let us begin with a review of the dating life of Charlotte York, the most conventionally social-register and marriage-minded of the quartet, with her lady-like glamour and penchant for "proper" behavior (she often blanches at the others' graphic descriptions of their sexual encounters), eternally preoccupied with china and silver patterns, the "right" apartment, the prospect of wedded and stay-at-home-mother bliss with the perfect provider – handsome, old-money wealthy, Upper East Side to the core. She kisses many frogs while seeking her prince, and yet, eventually, her prince does materialize in the form of Dr. Trey MacDougal. He embodies everything Charlotte's kind of maximizer hopes to find. They date, and marry, but the marriage quickly becomes an unmitigated disaster. In addition to being a bit of a tippler, his aptly named mother, Bunny, is a harridan, who sees Charlotte (whose own upper-middle class credentials seem solid enough) as at best a parvenu, at worst a slutty social climber. The company she keeps certainly doesn't help her image in her mother-in-law's eyes, and neither does her roll in the bushes with the family tennis pro, which happens because . . . Trey is mostly impotent. At first, his impotence is blamed on Charlotte's rigorous schedule to overcome infertility; it soon becomes apparent that Bunny probably was not a "good enough" mother. Be that as it may, Charlotte's dream becomes a nightmare; the two divorce. She's left her art gallery job to be the sort of "perfect" full-time wife and mother she envisioned, but her mother-in-law is hell-bent on seeing Charlotte out in the street, penniless. She retains the gorgeous apartment they shared only because Trey for once intervenes and overrules Mummy at the last possible moment.

Harry Goldenblatt (Yiddish, "gold leaf"; German, "golden plateau"), Charlotte's divorce lawyer, on the other hand, nice-enough looking but not handsome, bald, Jewish working class, and totally lacking in social graces, in short (literally) the very antithesis of Charlotte's ideal match, possesses one important quality Trey couldn't muster: he is hot for Charlotte and he can deliver on his passion. At first, Charlotte enjoys Harry mainly as an antidote to Trey; Trey's impotence of course leads her to question her own desirability. With Harry, there is no doubt. He offers, shall we say, hard evidence of her desirability whenever he comes into contact with her. Though he is far from the "maximum" mate Charlotte envisioned, even to the point of at times needing "schooling" in the social graces with Charlotte as his tutor, as she gradually becomes aware of Harry's more admirable traits beyond the erotic, he wins her over. They marry and begin the adoption proceedings Trey could not pursue with any enthusiasm.

Miranda Hobbes' story follows a somewhat similar trajectory, though her dating life is less unambiguously aimed at marriage than is Charlotte's. As the series winds down, after many, many he's-just-not-that-into-you dates with men who at first seem "perfect," she finally finds her maximum date-to-mate, Dr. Robert Leeds. No wonder he leads: he's tall; he's handsome; he's smooth; he's a bigwig in the sports industry; he's very well off; and he loves Miranda. She is just about to concede her inability to really love anyone and settle in with this vision of male perfection, when second thoughts about another man with whom she has relationship history, Steve Brady, the father of her son, begin to haunt her. Miranda is Main Line Philadelphia; Steve is Queens, complete with accent. Miranda is a white-shoe lawyer chasing a partnership; Steve is a bartender. Miranda has purchased her own fabulous Upper West Side classic six; Steve rents. Class imbalance wrecked havoc on their relationship, true, but another rupture tore them apart as Steve senses – correctly – that he is so much "less" than Miranda's dream date. And Miranda, still following her *Sex and the City* maximizer assumptions, is unwilling or unable to offer him much in the way of reassurance; so enter Robert and exit Steve, despite the powerful connection of their child, conceived in the wake of what Miranda calls a "mercy fuck" date after Steve is diagnosed and treated for testicular cancer. Nevertheless, it doesn't take long for Miranda to get ambushed by the strength of her own repressed feelings after seeing Steve with another woman, and soon after, as Brady's parents jointly carry his first birthday cake from the top of the washing machine to the table, she blurts out the words she thought she could never say to anyone, let alone Steve: "I love you." With Brady as a witness they are soon married and tackling life's problems together in Brooklyn.

It's not without irony that Carrie Bradshaw, who much more than Charlotte and somewhat more than Miranda sees the potential of life as a perpetually single big-City career woman, early on literally bumps into her ideal date who just happens to carry a maximizer like Carrie's ideal name: Mr. Big. Big is so rich he does not have to work at all. He has a car and driver. Like Trey MacDougal, he is old-money WASP and he has a formidable mother on whom he dotes. Like Robert Leeds, he is suave and self-assured, radiating oodles of charm. He has fame; his name is so well known throughout the City that he always and only is referred to as "Big" – to protect his identity from the prying ears of eavesdroppers. By this quartet's maximizing standards, Big potentially is the biggest "catch" of all, especially since it is suggested that Carrie's social class background is not so illustrious as Charlotte's or Miranda's. Although Big always enjoys Carrie's company – her intelligence and wit closely match and complement his own – and though she demonstrates again and again that she understands him and loves him for himself, and though the sex is great, Big can't "commit" because Carrie and Big are compatible in yet another important respect: Big, too, is caught up in the maximizing of the moment. In the case of Carrie and Big, many of their relationship hiatuses (during which Carrie again ascribes to zeitgeist maximization, but let's face it, Big is a tough act to follow) happen because Big can't "settle" for Carrie when all he has and is would seem to indicate he could do "better." And do "better" he does: wife number 2, Natasha. She is young; she is ethereally beautiful and very poised; she more accurately mirrors his social milieu; and she is absolutely vapid. Not surprisingly, Big almost immediately begins to cheat on his new wife – with Carrie, of course.

Up from the ashes of what becomes for her a humiliating affair with her former lover, the indomitable Carrie manages a personal best once again, this time outdoing herself by maximizing even maximization. She begins to date Aleksandr Petrovsky, a world-famous artist. He's quite a bit older than she, but in most other respects he is Carrie's type of maximizer's dream in that he is an enviable date, a very big fish in the largest possible pond. He's bigger than Big! And she is miserable. Titanically self-absorbed, Petrovsky alternately ignores and patronizes Carrie. There is no rapport between them, none of the clever repartee shared with Big. And she has to overcome the "yuck factor" which comes with dating an older man. Nevertheless, Carrie agrees to marry him. Fortunately, at the eleventh hour, while once again left forgotten by Petrovsky, this time in her Paris hotel room, she is "rescued" by the newly free Big, regretting his choice to "pass" on Carrie.

And what of Samantha? Samantha's dating teleology never included marriage; on the contrary, her stated goal is to "fuck like a man." Samantha's idea of maximizing, unlike that of her friends, centers around quantity rather than "quality." For her, that philosophy includes dating only for the purpose of having lots and lots of great sex with whomever she chooses, no strings attached. No attachments attached. Since she is not looking for a mate, her choice of partners departs from the dominant paradigm of the others: her lovers need not be rich, handsome, or famous; so long as he is good in bed, the guy who works at the gym is a "great date." She recoils when any of her lovers begins to show signs of wanting a more permanent arrangement and moves on in no uncertain terms. That is, until she meets Mr. Right. Richard Wright, like Samantha, is a sexual predator, and following a *Sex and the City* maximizer's train of thought, he has every "right" to be. He is tall, handsome, rich, suave, and ruthless. He also possesses the literal manifestation of Samantha's kind of maximizing, an usually "*big . . . pink . . . penis*" she adores. Equally taken with one another, the two soon attempt monogamy – at Samantha's urging! – but Richard, in this respect at least, falls short. Confronted with evidence of his infidelity on a regular basis, Samantha nearly becomes unhinged, until she is preoccupied with a worry much more heart stopping: breast cancer.

When Richard proves impossible to tame, Samantha returns to her old style of dating, and one of her first new conquests is Smith Jerrod, her waiter in an haute-vegan restaurant. Young and cute, and more importantly, athletically libidinous, Smith restores Samantha's faith in herself and her serial sex philosophy of dating. Smith, however, sweetly refuses to limit their liaison to "just sex," an attitude Samantha finds vaguely endearing in the short term but unacceptable in the long. To reward him – and get rid of him – Samantha supports his ambitions as an actor; soon, thanks to her PR savvy, Smith's career soars, culminating in the celebrity triumph of seeing his handsome face magnified many times over on a billboard high above Times Square. Samantha engineers the arc of Smith's career not to make him into a *Sex and the City* maximizer's prize, but rather as a sort of "thank you" for his puppy-like devotion after the rigors of Richard's faithlessness. Once she has "made" him, she fully intends to send him on his way, surrounded by adoring fans, *sans* the first-time-ever jealousy suffered over Richard. But illness twice forces

Samantha to rethink her dating strategy as a correlate to the sudden prominence of her own long-repressed vulnerability: first she breaks an ankle in a fall; then cancer strikes. And Smith just won't go away. He insists she hold on to him for support as she limps along on her cast. He shaves his head in solidarity when Samantha defiantly preempts the inevitable consequences of chemotherapy. For the first time, Samantha falls in love, and yet Samantha remains Samantha: she pushes the outside of the envelope for one more rendezvous with Richard's endowment. When she emerges from the elevator, however, Smith stands there waiting for her, no judgments. Samantha finally appreciates what Smith offers.

At the end of the series, happily married Charlotte and Harry await the arrival of their adopted daughter from China; softened Miranda trades her extreme autonomy for a web of affiliation woven with her husband, housekeeper (Magda, almost a second mother), son, and Alzheimer's-stricken mother-in-law in brownstone Brooklyn; newly monogamous Samantha settles in with Smith; and Carrie begins her trip "home" to New York and her closest friends with Big, who finally has a name: John. From the perspective of choice, the resolution of each of these story lines represents a surprising and profound development: all the main series maximizers – Carrie, Big, Charlotte, Miranda, and Samantha – have morphed into satisficers, to their benefit. What happened? September 11, 2001 is what. The change in mood in the series after this event is palpable. The cruise ship may not have capsized, but the lights dimmed; the endless party finally broke up, the deck littered with debris. A sobered city pushed the kind of maximizing privileged by this series into the shadows, and the series itself, following suit, became much more meditative. "Needs" suddenly became much more paramount than "wants." As the Rolling Stones' song, a potential satisficer's anthem if ever there were one, would have it, "You can't always get what you want, but if you try sometimes, you just might find, you get what you need."[10] The proverbial 180° turn in the characters' choice mode is likely at least partially unconscious among the *Sex and the City* maximizers, but palpable nonetheless. Volte-face they do – to embrace those who meet their most salient emotional needs. In other words, the change in mood in the series helps to support the notion that our choice modes enjoy some flexibility: previously, the series seemed to validate the thought that a proliferation of glittering choice has the potential, at the very least, to turn satisficers into maximizers, but from this point forward the series substantiates instead the idea that life lessons learned and personal situations endured often transform maximizers into satisficers. To put it another way, if one were to look at the entire series as one long episode, the answers to the questions I suggested Carrie hypothetically pose at its beginning would at its conclusion be "yes" and "no."

From the standpoint of the inveterate *Sex and the City*-type maximizer who chooses to cling to the handsome-rich-famous triad, however, this turn of events could signal the disappointment one would expect to accompany any compromise. Yet that conclusion most likely proves false. To return to Barry Schwartz's study once again:

> To a maximizer, satisficers appear to be willing to settle for mediocrity, but that is not the case. A satisficer may be just as discriminating as a maximizer. The difference between the two types is that the satisficer is content with the merely excellent as opposed to the absolute best.[11]

Remember – and this too is sometimes a paradox – each and every maximizer in *Sex and the City* does, despite the odds, manage to maximize his or her way, and yet each is dreadfully unhappy once the maximum is real(ized). To their respective and prospective partners, Trey MacDougal, Robert Leeds, Aleksandr Petrovsky, Richard Wright and, let us not forget, the ethereal Natasha, all represent the actualization of a dream, the achievement of a "personal best" in dating and/or mating, at least in theory. But in praxis, the dreams quickly turn into nightmares. Perhaps what Schwartz calls "the tyranny of overwhelming choices" blinds them to the "merely excellent" while they myopically pursue what they imagine as the "absolute best."[12] What is certain is that Charlotte, Miranda, Carrie, Big, and Samantha all improbably do manage to win the grand prize, a relationship with someone at the very pinnacle of choice when a plethora of choices is available to them, a mirror who reflects that required *je ne sais quoi* or *sine qua non* back to themselves and simultaneously projects the same outward toward the crowd: a mate who by his or her attachment alone appears to elevate the maximizer, and perhaps even more important, display the maximizer for what s/he is, i.e., someone with what it takes to maximize. Isn't that, after all, the true psychological goal of maximizers? For something resolutely narcissistic – in the clinical rather than colloquial sense – inheres in maximization. Like the probably not-good-enough mother overly invested in shaping her child into a vision of extreme talent and beauty as a means to the end of most accurately portraying her own narcissistic ideal, each of these characters is stymied by choice in that they are distracted, however unconsciously, by the *image of themselves* their choice will project to the larger group, even to the largest group, consisting mostly of strangers. But images even – maybe most especially – of ourselves are chimerical. Attempts to flesh out chimera can only result in disappointment if not outright failure, since as Plato tried to teach us, there is never much to be gained in trying to make real the ideal. Though each of the main characters of *Sex and the City* appears to succeed in making his or her ideal real, each wisely comes to see such a victory as Pyrrhic. Not one of them feels more satisfied, more optimistic, more happy during the time they spend with their ostensibly "absolute best" choice; in fact, for most of the duration each is wracked by a sense of sadness, worthlessness, insecurity, and/or emptiness, if not out-and-out depression. Here, too, another paradox:

> When Nobel Prize-winning economist and psychologist Herbert Simon initially introduced the idea of "satisficing" in the 1950s, he suggested that when all costs . . . about all options are factored in, satisficing *is*, in fact, the maximizing strategy. In other words, the best people can do, all things considered, is to satisfice.[13]

This paradox, too, holds. For in satisficing, each of these characters maximizes.

How so? To Big's Natasha, for example, Carrie's outrageous outfits and forthright good humor are anathema; poised and proper, in love with her own beauty, she is cold as ice, a Potemkin village of a woman, a mannequin on Big's arm. It is simply impossible to relate to such a person, and not surprisingly, Big misses the deep connection between his and Carrie's spirited spontaneous wordplay, their shared silliness and sense of whimsy. Carrie experiences much the same loss with her "find" Petrovsky. In her case, the language deficit is even more pronounced, since Petrovsky's English often prevents him from understanding Carrrie's New York humor at all. Trey MacDougal, though well meaning, is far too damaged a man to communicate fully with Charlotte; his whole life has been one of appearance rather than substance, and his relationship with Charlotte again traces that well-established pattern. Harry Goldenblatt, on the other hand, really listens to Charlotte and tries his best to accommodate her needs in a partner. Charlotte, in a poignant demonstration of reciprocity, converts to Judaism to meet Harry's generosity. There is nothing particularly amiss with Robert Leeds, he just lacks the chain of relationships to which Steve Brady is yoked and to which rugged and cynical individualist Miranda sorely needs link herself. And Richard Wright is simply all wrong for Samantha, especially when her illness requires a partner with empathy and stick-to-itiveness, both of which Smith, despite his relative youth, readily demonstrates.

In satisficing, in "settling" for the "merely excellent," each of these characters in fact maximizes, opting for a true relationship, one of love and communication, one marked by genuine, reciprocal accommodation, and attempted, at least, understanding. As each of these characters begins to realize, looks, in the sense of what the partner looks like as a reflection of themselves to the outside world, are much less important than the inner and private truth of the partnership. A man such as Big need not necessarily demonstrate his "big-ness" – his wealth, power, looks, desirability – by displaying those qualities in his partner; they inhere in him and that is sufficient. Similarly, a woman of Miranda's intelligence need not announce it by her choice of super-smart mate; that she has made partner in an extremely competitive legal environment is proof enough. Though not touched upon in this essay, one suspects that the main attraction of Berger (another of Carrie's disastrous inter-Big relationships) is that he is a "serious" writer and reflects Carrie back to herself as such; yet the success of Carrie's own book and column provide substantial proof of her talent. It takes Charlotte a while, but she eventually does understand that she need not land the "ideal" husband to be an excellent wife and mother; she just is because she works to be. Finally, could any man other than Richard Wright reflect the emotional impenetrability of Samantha's unique "no holds barred" ethos of dating? Probably not, but then she no longer needs that mask; cancer frees her to it throw away, along with her wig. And Smith helps her dispense with both. Once all of these inveterate TV daters understand that maximizing just means more looking at the expense of actually seeing, they chuck the panoramic long-shot and hone in on the close-up.

Works wonders.

## NOTES

1   Barry Schwartz, *The Paradox of Choice: Why More Is Less* (New York: Harper Collins, 2004).
2   Ibid., p. 77.
3   Ibid., p. 78.
4   Ibid., p. 86.
5   Ibid., p. 78.
6   Ibid., p. 96, my emphasis.
7   Ibid.

8   Surely, under the veneer of all this gloss lies the almost invisible work-a-day world inhabited by most New York women, those who take the subway to cater the opening or party, sell the Hermès scarves, drive the cabs, pour the cosmos, cut and color the hair. But those women are not the focus of this series.

9   The more general ramifications of this phenomenon are echoed in the words of Peter D. Kramer in his recent introduction to Erich Fromm's *The Art of Loving* (New York: Harper Perennial, 2006), p. x: "If the culture rewards narcissism, how shall we transcend ourselves? If the culture is alienating, how shall we find what we long for: intimacy, passion, attunement, what Fromm calls 'reunion by love'? With the passage of time, these questions have become more pressing. The commercial taints the personal, openly. Successful men seek trophy wives. Almost half of marriages end in divorce, in part because of the temptation to 'trade up' – as if each individual had a fixed worth, some calculable integration of youth, beauty, cleverness, status, and (especially) wealth. Often as not, these rearrangements result in marriages that feel empty."

10   This train of thought reminds me of the opening scenes of the 1983 Lawrence Kasdan film, *The Big Chill*. The film begins with a funeral director dressing the body of a young man who has apparently committed suicide. When his friends gather in a South Carolina church for his memorial service, Glenn Close flexes her fingers at the organ, takes a deep breath, and then begins to play this very song as a "processional." The memory of the lyrics that should accompany the tune bring a rueful smirk to the faces of his friends in their pews, since of all of them, Alex was the most gifted. The message seems to be that had their friend Alex learned to satisfice, he may not have been moved to take his own life. Ironically, "Alex" was to be Kevin Costner's breakthrough film role, but all but the faceless scenes of him as a corpse were cut.

11   Schwartz, *The Paradox of Choice*, p. 78.

12   Ibid., p. 79.

13   Ibid.

# NOTES ON CONTRIBUTORS

**ANNE BARNHILL** is a Greenwall Postdoctoral Fellow in Bioethics at Johns Hopkins University. After completing her PhD in philosophy at New York University, she was a Faculty Fellow at the Safra Center for Ethics at Harvard University before coming to Johns Hopkins. Her philosophical work is focused on normative ethics, practical ethics, and feminist philosophy, and her dissertation, "Beyond Consent," was on the place of consent in ethics. She considers herself something of an expert on sex.

**BO BRINKMAN** is an assistant professor in the Department of Computer Science and Software Engineering at Miami University in Oxford, Ohio. He studies both computer algorithms and the ethical implications of computing. His work has appeared in the *Journal of the ACM*, and he has received paper awards at the Annual Meeting of the Association for Practical and Professional Ethics and at the ACM Symposium on Foundations of Computer Science. He refuses to slow-dance with female friends in Second Life.

**CHRISTOPHER BROWN** is an assistant professor of philosophy at the National University of Singapore. He works in ethical theory and his research focuses on Kant's moral philosophy, accounts of human virtue, and our duties toward non-human animals. Chris was born in England, spent (endured) his early adolescence in Germany, moved to Florida, where he fiercely resisted growing up, graduated high school, and eventually completed an MA in mathematics, before being lured onto the path to wisdom at the University of Arizona. With PhD in hand, he landed his job in Singapore, where he loves life more than ever, teaches some of the most inspiring students in the world, and doesn't mind waiting for the perfect match.

**MARLENE CLARK** is an associate professor in the Division of Interdisciplinary Arts and Sciences at the City College of New York, City University of New York. Her research interests include the sexual allure, and consequent empowerment, of Shakespeare's "cougars," as well as interdisciplinary writing pedagogy. Her textbook on the latter topic, *Juxtapositions: Ideas for College Writers*, is in its third edition. After completing a PhD in English, she missed philosophy and so is now again a student in the MA program in philosophy and the arts at Stony Brook University. Her current project explores connections between object relations, color theory, body parts, and Willem de Kooning's six numbered *Woman* paintings.

**ANDREW I. COHEN** is an associate professor of philosophy at Georgia State University, where he also directs the Jean Beer Blumenfeld Center for Ethics. His research focuses on ethics and practical ethics. He has published on themes in rights theory, friendship, Hobbesian political theory, and contractarianism. He is co-editor (with Christopher Heath Wellman) of *Contemporary Debates in Applied Ethics* (Blackwell, 2005), and his work has appeared in many journals. He usually treats his wife as an end in herself.

**MARK COLYVAN** is a professor of philosophy at the University of Sydney and the Director of the Sydney Centre for the Foundations of Science. He is also a chief investigator in the Australian Centre of Excellence for Risk Analysis and a core researcher in the Commonwealth Environment Research Facility: Applied Environmental Decision Analysis. His research focuses mostly on the philosophy of mathematics, logic, decision theory, and ecology. His books include *The Indispensability of Mathematics* (2001) and *Ecological Orbits: How Planets Move and Populations Grow* (with Lev Ginzburg, 2004). He believes in a mathematical approach to pretty-much everything.

**TINASHE DUNE** is a higher degree research student and a postgraduate teaching fellow in the faculty of health sciences at the University of Sydney, Australia. After being awarded a BA in psychology from Carleton University, Tinashe moved to Australia to pursue graduate studies in sexual health. She is presently researching a doctoral thesis, which is focused on how sexual expectations in Western societies impact on individuals who are sexually marginalized. A synthesis of her undergraduate honors thesis, which discusses the basis for her present work, can be found in *Sexuality and Disability* 27, 2 (2009). As this is her first book chapter, she aspires to "get around" in the world of sex and academia.

PATRICIA HALLEN graduated with a degree in philosophy from Purdue University Calumet in Hammond, Indiana, in December 2009. Her primary interests are in social philosophy and areas of applied ethics, including topics in the philosophy of sex, love, and relationships.

RICHARD PAUL HAMILTON is Senior Lecturer in philosophy and ethics at the University of Notre Dame Australia in Fremantle, WA, where he is primarily responsible for teaching surly and unresponsive medical students. He received his PhD in philosophy from Birkbeck College, University of London. His thesis was a sustained analysis of love as a complex social and biological phenomenon. His previous publications have been on philosophy of biology and philosophy of law. When not cruising the bars of Fremantle, he likes to brew his own beer while thinking about the relationship between biology and society and is currently working on a defense of Aristotelian virtue ethics in the light of contemporary biology. He enjoys a complicated ongoing relationship with his cats, Sophie and Serendipity, who are constant sources of insight into the human condition.

JOSHUA S. HETER is a graduate student in philosophy at St. Louis University. His research interests include epistemology, metaphysics, and the philosophy of mind. His favorite date activities include going out for sushi, long walks on the beach, and speculating about the ontological status of date activities.

CARRIE S. JENKINS is an associate professor and reader in philosophy at the University of Nottingham. She is interested in epistemology, metaphysics, and the philosophy of logic, language, and mathematics. Her book *Grounding Concepts* was published in 2008. Carrie enjoys philosophizing about flirting and, from time to time, conducts impromptu empirical research on the subject.

EMILY LANGAN is an assistant professor in the Department of Communication at Wheaton College. She teaches and has published in the areas of communication theory, friendship, and non-verbal communication, but is most keenly interested in interpersonal relationships, oftentimes more as observer than practitioner. At first glance, a single woman may seem an odd choice to write an essay on male flirting. But, then again, who better to write about it than one who's been perplexed by the phenomenon? Perhaps knowledge comes through study after all.

ALBERTO MASALA holds a temporary teaching position in the Department of Philosophy at University Paris-Sorbonne. Before receiving his PhD from Paris-Sorbonne, he studied also at the University Ca' Foscari of Venice and at Columbia University of New York (visiting student). His main focus is the interdisciplinary study of virtue and human flourishing, connecting ancient wisdom with contemporary empirical evidence from personality psychology, psychology of expert performance, and cognitive science. He is interested in human enhancement, in general, including the enhancement of mating skills.

KRISTIE MILLER is a research fellow in philosophy at the University of Sydney, Australia. She works primarily in metaphysics, particularly in the philosophy of time, worrying about issues such as personal identity, the persistence of objects over time, the nature of space-time, the possibility of time travel, and the laws of nature. Her book *Issues in Theoretical Diversity: Persistence, Composition and Time* was published in 2006, and she has written numerous journal articles on related topics.

HICHEM NAAR is a doctoral candidate in philosophy at the University of Manchester. Before that, he received a BA in philosophy and sociology from the Université Lille III, an MA in philosophy of science from the Université Paris-Sorbonne, and an MS in cognitive science from the Jean Nicod Institute, Paris. His current focus (besides trying desperately to raise his mate value) includes the cognitive foundation of morality, the nature of emotion, and the psychology at the basis of global social changes.

KYLA REID is a PhD student in philosophy at the University of Sydney, Australia. Her current research for her doctoral thesis concentrates on the importance of indigenous justice claims for political theory. Specifically, she is interested in how indigenous claims to autonomy raise important questions about the legitimacy of the modern settler state.

Despite being a borderline anarchist, Kyla still enjoys a dinner and a movie (especially if she pays half).

**JOHN ROWAN** is professor of philosophy and Chair of the philosophy program at Purdue University Calumet in Hammond, Indiana. His teaching and research interests focus on areas in ethical theory, applied ethics, and political/social philosophy. He is the author of *Conflicts of Rights* (1999) and numerous articles in many journals.

**JENNIFER A. SAMP** is an associate professor and graduate coordinator in the Department of Speech and Communication at the University of Georgia. Her research focuses on how romantic "dating" partners think and talk about difficult situations and behaviors that often contribute to relationship disharmony and conflict. Her work has appeared in many journals. Consequently, none of her relationships demonstrate any conflict whatsoever. She notes that Professor Cohen may disagree with this claim.

**JOSHUA WOLF SHENK** is a correspondent for Slate.com, a contributor to *The Atlantic, Harper's,* and other magazines, and is the author of *Lincoln's Melancholy: How Depression Challenged a President and Fueled His Greatness.* Shenk's work has been featured on National Public Radio, PBS, and the History Channel, and he has consulted for the Library of Congress, HBO, and the Austen Riggs Center. You can see his work at www.shenk.net.

**DAN SILBER** received a PhD in philosophy from Vanderbilt University and has pursued research and teaching interests primarily in the areas of ethics and the theory of knowledge. For most of his career he has taught philosophy at Florida Southern College in Lakeland, Florida, where he now also serves as an associate provost. He initially met his wife online, then for dinner for their first face-to-face date, at which he promptly found himself struck by Cupid's arrow. His personal good fortune and the testimony of others have convinced him of the positive potential of Internet dating.

**ANDREW TERJESEN** is currently a visiting assistant professor of philosophy at Rhodes College in Memphis, TN. He has taught previously at Washington and Lee University, Austin College and Duke University. Andrew's main interests are in the areas of ethics and the philosophy of mind, which he has explored in essays for Wiley-Blackwell's Pop Culture and Philosophy series, including *The Family Guy and Philosophy*, *X-men and Philosophy*, *Heroes and Philosophy*, and *Twilight and Philosophy* (which he co-wrote with his more talented wife). His "serious" work has been focused on issues in business ethics, which, despite his lack of experience (see his chapter in this volume), he thinks is a lot like dating: with the bluffing, the seducing, and the inevitable "walk of shame."

DAVID W. TIEN earned his PhD from the University of Michigan. He specializes in Chinese philosophy and religion, as well as the comparative philosophy of religion, comparative ethics, and philosophical psychology. He is currently assistant professor in the Department of Philosophy at the National University of Singapore.

MARY BETH YOUNT received a BA in theology from the University of St. Thomas and an MA in theology at St. Mary's University, and is currently finishing her doctoral degree at Duquesne University. Her academic interests include ethics, economics, and church ministry; and she is currently editing a two-volume series on the political, religious, and economic legacy of Bernard Lonergan.